The Distortion of Nature's Image

SUNY series in New Political Science
———————
Bradley J. Macdonald, editor

The Distortion of Nature's Image
Reification and the Ecological Crisis

DAMIAN GERBER

Cover: iStock by Getty Images

Published by State University of New York Press, Albany

© 2019 State University of New York

All rights reserved

No part of this book may be used or reproduced in any manner whatsoever without written permission. No part of this book may be stored in a retrieval system or transmitted in any form or by any means including electronic, electrostatic, magnetic tape, mechanical, photocopying, recording, or otherwise without the prior permission in writing of the publisher.

For information, contact State University of New York Press, Albany, NY www.sunypress.edu

Library of Congress Cataloging-in-Publication Data

Names: Gerber, Damian, 1988– author.
Title: The distortion of nature's image : reification and the ecological crisis / Damian Gerber.
Description: Albany : State University of New York Press, 2019. | Series: SUNY series in new political science | Includes bibliographical references and index.
Identifiers: LCCN 2018021866 | ISBN 9781438473550 (hardcover) |
  ISBN 9781438473543 (pbk.) | ISBN 9781438473567 (ebook) Subjects: LCSH: Global environmental change—Social aspects. | Human ecology.
  | Nature—Effect of human beings on. | Social ecology. | Capitalism—Environmental aspects.
Classification: LCC GE149 .G465 2019 | DDC 304.2/8—dc23
LC record available at https://lccn.loc.gov/2018021866

10 9 8 7 6 5 4 3 2 1

For Alexandra,
the one who opened my eyes to all the hope and beauty
in a biosphere worth preserving

Contents

Preface	ix
Acknowledgments	xvii
Introduction	1
Ecology and Critical Theory	1
On Some Limitations of Contemporary Nature Ontologies	4
Reification and the Historical Context of Nature Philosophy	8
The Dialectic of the Nature-Concept	14
The Concept of Dialectical Naturalism	16
Chapter One	
Anti-Naturalism, the Bourgeois Enlightenment, and the Modern Origins of a Dialectical Naturalism	25
The Becoming of Nature	25
Epistemology and the Bourgeois Image of Nature	27
The Kantian "Block" and the Distancing of Reason from Nature	30
An Alternative Perspective on Kant: Schiller's *Aesthetic Letters*	35
Fichte's Nature-Concept as the Non-Ego	38
"The Struggle of Spirit with Itself"	42
Hegel's Critique of the Concept of Natural Law	45
The Representation of Nature as Reification	49
Hegel's Doctrine of the Notion	55
The Anti-Naturalism of "Spirit" and the Limits of Hegel's Idealism	63
Feuerbachian Interlude	67

Chapter Two
Nature in Marx and Anarchism 71
    Marx and the Historicization of Nature 71
    The Younger Marx's Naturalism 73
    The Concept of Nature in Marx's Middle Period and the
        Ethical Dimension of Marx's Anti-Naturalism 77
    Beyond the Limits of Marx's Nineteenth Century 84
    Post-Proudhonian Anarchism and the Persistence of
        Mythopoeic Naturalism 87
    Nature Against Itself: The Contradictions of Bakunin's
        "Natural Human Society" 89
    The Ambiguities of Kropotkin's Concept of "Anarchist
        Morality" 96
    Digression: On the Historical Scars of Nature Philosophy 105
    The Self-Contradictory Historicism of Kropotkin's
        "Mutual Aid" Thesis 107
    Naturalism as Politics 110
    The Determinate Negation of Kropotkin's Theory of Society 115
    The Necessity of a Dialectical Naturalism 117

Chapter Three
Recovering a Dialectical Naturalism 119
    The Basis of a Dialectical Naturalism 119
    Precursory Models of Dialectical Naturalism 120
    Bloch's Notion of "Technological Contact" 129
    Murray Bookchin's Social Ecology 132
    The Nature-Concept and the Anthropology of Hierarchy 149
    Toward a Communalist Image of Nature 174

Epilogue 179

Appendix
Theses on Communalism 183

Notes 189

Bibliography 213

Index 221

Preface

This book attempts to explore, in the context of a critical history of Western nature philosophy, how the organization of our global market society, its institutions, and prevailing ideas are reflected in prevailing concepts of nature. It is concerned primarily with a critical examination of the "nature" that prevailed and remained influential throughout the liberal enlightenment tradition, through to three of the most extant avenues of radical philosophy (Marx, anarchism, and social ecology) and their images of nature, which have offered us the means to think in innovative ways about the increasingly tenuous relationship between human social organization and the ecology of the planet on whose surface we live. The American radical philosopher Murray Bookchin (1921–2006) is one of the chief contributors to the theory of social ecology, and, accordingly, a good part of this book concentrates on Bookchin's attempt to construct a philosophy of dialectical naturalism. A dialectical naturalism, it is contended herein, is a way of looking critically at humanity's relationship to nature that resists reified thinking and expands our consciousness about new configurations of human-ecology relationships.[1]

Before we turn to an outline of the book, it would be helpful to briefly explain the book's relationship to some predominant trends in the contemporary environmental movement, and what it hopes to contribute to studies of Bookchin and social ecology, and environmental thought more generally.

The study of social ecology, and in particular the thought of Murray Bookchin, is an emerging field of influence in radical political ecology, and it is within the broader tradition of Bookchin studies that this work is situated.[2] A backdrop to this tradition, as explored elsewhere, often appears to be a tacit acceptance of certain flashpoints between divergent movements in Western political ecology, in particular the debate between deep ecology and social ecology, between Neo-Marxist ecologists and social ecologists, the distinction between reformist and revolutionary political theory and, as an outgrowth of this, the Bookchin-Eckersley debate of the 1990s, often perceived as a clash between liberal environmentalist and more radical social ecology perspectives.[3] It is not the intention of this book to recapitulate all of the parameters of these debates, not least because in many respects they have become outmoded and aspects of them may be of dubious relevance to contemporary ecology movements. The introduction that follows this preface looks to some of the most pertinent contemporary scholarship in political ecology and concisely examines its relationship to the analysis of reified thinking and dialectical naturalism that follows. However, three recurring themes of this work are worth mentioning in brief here, for they are of great significance to the possibility of rethinking the contribution of social ecology to ecology movements. These are the relationship of Bookchin's thought to Marxism, the argument that social ecology can be regarded as a continuation of the radical tradition of critical theory (in the sense of Max Horkheimer's formative *Traditional and Critical Theory* essay) and the theoretical distinction between reformist and revolutionary perspectives, which often informs how ecology movements develop in practice.

As Bookchin's idea of a dialectical naturalism took an increasingly distinctive shape, it defined itself both as an outgrowth of, and against, varied elements of Marx's thought. Nonetheless, this book seeks to illustrate that it is not so much in antithesis to Marx's thought itself, but in antithesis to certain trends in the subsequent development of *Marxism* (sometimes referred to by Bookchin, rather too vaguely, as "Neo-Marxism"), that the most vociferous aspects of the Bookchin critique can be understood to be directed.[4] It is well beyond the subject matter of this book to delve into the voluminous debates that define this critique, and at any rate, these are addressed to some degree elsewhere.[5] However, it would be useful to note here an important difference in the relationship between Bookchin's thought and Marx, and the development of what is nowadays called Eco-Marxism. The renowned Marxist political geographer Castree, in a survey of the contribution of Marxist thought to political geography, emphasizes the influence of Neil Smith in particular, whose work *Uneven Development*, published in 1984, postulated that nature itself is "produced" not "given."[6] For Castree, it is above all Smith's "insistence that there is no nature intelligible outside contingent social discourses, relations and practices" that has proven to be one of the most influential turning points in the development of contemporary Eco-Marxism.[7] While it is only implicit in this book, a valuable critique of this position could be made by illustrating how its undialectical attempt to absorb the concept of nature within the predominant mode of production (in Marx's terms) is actually more of a return to a pre-Hegelian, Fichtean metaphysics (a metaphysics detailed in the first chapter of this book), and that an alternative and more dialectical interpretation of Marx's concept of nature is left open: namely, that nature can be perceived as both what is given (and hence the "first nature" of eco-communities independent of human labor) and that which is, in turn, mediated and modified through the prevailing mode of production (that is, the "second nature" of market society). It is this alternative interpretation of Marx that is left open to Bookchin to develop in a decidedly ethical and aesthetic direction in the form of a philosophy of dialectical naturalism, and that he himself directs against the productivist trend characteristic of much contemporary Eco-Marxism.[8]

A more complex question arises from the development of Frankfurt School critical theory, given both its stated aims of preventing the members of society from falling victim to reified thought[9]—an underlying motivation that, as this book will demonstrate, is also at the core of social ecology's dialectical concept of nature—and the shared interest of several foundational members of the Frankfurt School in the notion of an ecological, rational society. The extent to which the Frankfurt School and social ecology align, in their attempted recovery of a dialectical naturalism from a common theoretical heritage in Marx, is apparent in one of Herbert Marcuse's pivotal essays on the ecology movements of the 1970s:

> Certainly, nature has always been an aspect (for a long time the only one) of labor. But it was also a dimension beyond labor, a symbol of beauty, of tranquility, of a non-repressive order. Thanks to these values, nature was the very negation of the market society, with its values of profit and utility.[10]

Hence, regardless of Bookchin's perhaps justified attempts to define his own anthropological research against Horkheimer and Adorno's interpolation of reason and domination in historical terms,[11] there is much more that could be written on the commonalities that bring together both critical theory's and social ecology's interest in the social significance of ecological movements against capitalism, not to mention the philosophical basis according to which both critically explore the concept of nature in light of its historical mediation. This is well beyond the scope of the present book. Nevertheless, this book does rely on several groundbreaking studies of the Frankfurt School in developing its account of the concept of nature in German Idealism and in Marx, and it is in this implicit form, at the very least, that the study of nature reification and the development of a dialectical naturalism can be seen to align.

The relationship between reformist and revolutionary thought has often been defined as a fractious one, including by Bookchin himself, who was at pains to characterize social ecology as an inherently revolutionary philosophy, as against attempts to "green" capitalism or accommodate ecological thinking within the ideological poverty of market society.[12] Yet while this book does not delve much into the subject matter of liberal environmentalism, other than its exploration of the Bookchin-Eckersley debate in chapter 3, nor does it simplistically or tacitly endorse any attempt to hypostatize the divide between revolutionary and reformist ecology movements. Rather, its aim is a little more expansive than this: the book attempts to portray social ecology's goal as the provoking of critical thinking in ecology movements, spurring thought toward the consideration of radical alternatives to market society. The form that such movements can take is, of course, deeply varied, from revolutionary Kurdish communalism to single-issue environmental campaigns in the communities of Western metropolises. Rather than dismissing liberal environmentalism outright, it may behoove us to see the border between liberal and more radical environmental theory as porous. This seems to be precisely what Marcuse was gesturing toward in his essay on ecology movements:

> The ecological movement is attacking the "living space" of capitalism, the expansion of the realm of profit, of waste production. However, the fight against pollution is easily co-opted. Today, there is hardly an ad which doesn't exhort you to "save the environment," to put an end to pollution and poisoning. Numerous commissions are created to control the guilty parties. To be sure, the ecological movement may serve very well to spruce up the environment, to make it pleasanter, less ugly, healthier, and hence, more tolerable. Obviously, this is a sort of co-optation, but it is also a progressive element because, in the course of this co-optation, a certain number

of needs and aspirations are beginning to be expressed within the very heart of capitalism and a change is taking place in people's behavior, experience, and attitudes towards their work. Economic and technical demands are transcended in a movement of revolt which challenges the very mode of production and model of consumption.[13]

It is in the challenging of reified thinking—which places ecological, ethical, and human needs on at least an equal footing with economic and technical ones—that, perhaps, liberal environmentalism and social ecology can find some fertile, common ground.

There are important differences between reformist and revolutionary traditions, and many noteworthy reasons for questioning the merits of a political ideology based on the notion of greening capitalism, or economizing nature according to the premises of market society. Yet what may seem to some liberal environmentalists so deeply unsatisfying about the revolutionary theoretical tradition, namely, its lack of a politics of the microcosm (that is, its barrenness of interest in how individual destinies, characterized by decisively ethical character structures, proceed to influence political and social changes) is simply a nonissue for reformistic liberal environmentalism: for what is perhaps a strength and weakness in equal measure of the liberal theoretical tradition is that it often places an emphasis upon the striking characterological differences between individuals, despite structural determinations of social life. Despite their ideological hijacking by the influences of market society, the political theories of pluralism and neopluralism capture the popular imagination by dint of their acknowledgment of the diversity of individual aims and the realities of the struggle to have these effectually represented under representative-democratic polities. Correspondingly, the participation of individuals in political change is perceived by liberal reformistic thought as, by and large, subject to a great variety of aims and motivations, and seemingly insignificant microcosmic efforts, such as petitions and single-issue protest movements, are not dismissed as ineffectual but regarded as harbingers of potentially valuable changes, not to mention the possibility of a ripple effect across the breadth of communal trends and lifestyles. One might even go so far as to perceive the differences between liberal environmentalist reformism and revolutionary social ecologism as, at heart, differences in a theory of ethics: while reformistic thought often appears concerned with the pursuit of individual virtue ethics or deontological principles (the precautionary principle would be but one example of this), a revolutionary social ecology so often seems to be founded on a far broader, consequentialist view of our collective failure to overcome capitalism and the increasingly severe ecological crises left in its wake.

It is, perhaps, as a result of this ontological divide about the nature and purpose of political action that reformist and revolutionary trends in ecological thought so often seem to be speaking at cross-purposes. Bookchin's social ecology, for example, is little interested in individual destiny, in the study of virtue, biography, or the subjective pursuit of the good life. Rather, Bookchin's purview is focused, for the most part, on the historical institutions and structures that have determined the collective destiny of societies and their prevailing images of the natural world, and the manifold ways in which social structure has made possible, or has inhibited, the collective pursuit of ethical ends. For social ecology, the very concept of virtue only has meaning as a structural concept; social ecology holds as ecologically valuable the prevailing ideas that have influenced a given society, not individual personalities and their competing motivations within the microcosmic viewpoint of subjective and familial life. Hence, while from the viewpoint of virtue ethics, ethical consumerism may attain real significance in the biography of an individual, for social ecology ethical consumerism could only be evaluated as a feeble and abortive attempt to transcend an ecologically harmful society, in the same way that for radical veganism a goal of structural change in the human diet is considered as that which has the highest inherent worth, rather than the mere attainment of dietary lifestyle choices for particular individuals. It may well be, on the other hand, that the vast complexity of our world and the destinies that are lived out upon its surface render liberal environmentalists far less interested in the shifting sands of future systemic changes; they may see as far more achievable and tangible down-to-earth concerns, such as saving a particular local forest or ecosystem from encroachment by developers, as opposed to the far-off and, for some, the unimaginable possibility of social revolution.

Yet even a very sympathetic account of Bookchin's theoretical efforts, of which this book is certainly one, cannot shy away from candidly acknowledging the persistence of his defensiveness about the revolutionary tradition and his sometimes-impatient disregard of reformistic trends and orientations as counterproductive at best and actively counterrevolutionary at worst. It is clear from Bookchin's own words that he had little time for attempts to accommodate ecological ethics within the ideological parameters of late capitalist society.

The interpretation of dialectical naturalism and social ecology offered in this book does not, for the reasons explored earlier, hypostatize an impassable divide between the reformistic and revolutionary trends in political ecology in the way that Bookchin, in his most polemical moments, perhaps sought to. Nor does it, however, seek to render the reasons for Bookchin's defense of the revolutionary tradition, much less his criticisms of the weaknesses of reformism, invalid. Rather, it centers upon validating Bookchin's concerns with the defects of the liberal-reformist tradition as being directed, above all else, at the vulnerability of liberal environmentalism to reified thinking. In other words, it seeks to show, by way of a journey through several key German liberal enlightenment thinkers, that the flaws of liberal thought and its image of nature manifest as a result of reification, and this can be seen to be carried through right into liberal environmentalist thought of the twenty-first century (although the latter is largely beyond the subject matter of this book).

What this book attempts to illustrate is of greatest worth in the liberal tradition in its application to ecological thought—particularly in illuminating this often neglected point in social ecology theory and Bookchin studies—is how human emancipation from unthinking nature is, paradoxically, to be regarded as a vital first step, in an anthropological sense, in humanity's coming to be an agent for rational and ethical change, and thus a manifestation, in the language of social ecology, of a *thinking* nature. Part of this thinking nature is the development of a critical-theoretical tradition capable of resisting the imprisonment of ecological thought within the ideological chains of market society—and, hence, the fertile grounds of a critique of the economic basis of liberalism. However, this book differs from the approach suggested by some followers of Bookchin, and perhaps at times by Bookchin himself, in its attempts to perceive the border between reformistic and revolutionary thought as a porous one, and social ecology itself as a form of critical theory whose aims can be regarded as provoking critical self-reflection in the environmental movement. The interpretation of social ecology developed herein is thus more open-ended than that of a political polemic; the goal of social ecology is advanced as a *pedagogical* one, namely, to encourage ecological students and activists of varied traditions to think critically about the ecological consequences of market society, and to think more deeply about the dialectical relationality between social institutions and the ecological impacts in building the sort of world that they are trying to create. One key component of this aim is to resist reified thinking practices.

This leads to a related aim of this book: to properly elucidate the often misunderstood relationship between Bookchin's thought and that of Marx. In short, the second chapter aims to illustrate how the theme of humanity's emancipation from an unthinking and purely instinctive first nature, and its acculturation of what both Marx and Bookchin praise as a thinking second nature, is a vital element of Marx's contribution to the tradition of dialectical philosophy, and later becomes a crucial foundation in the development of a dialectical naturalism. In an important sense, the dialectical tension discussed here is the struggle of radical political thought to overcome falling into its own reifications of the natural world, a problem that is shown to afflict, at times, both Marxist and anarchist thought in the development of these radical traditions. Nonetheless, the account of these traditions offered here should be regarded as one far more sympathetic to Marx than to anarchism, for it is Marx who can be seen to have seriously grappled with the *ethical* implications of the relationship between humanity and nature under capitalism (a theme that manifests particularly in his journalistic writings). The extent to which the novelty of Bookchin's thought brought about vital advances in our ability to imagine more harmonious and rational human-ecology relationships is explored in the final chapter, which examines his concept of dialectical naturalism in detail.

One final qualification on the text is necessary. The introduction alludes to Adorno's conception of a "negative dialectic" and compares it favorably to the historical development of a dialectical naturalism. Such an equivocation could only be completely justified through a separate volume in its own right. In lieu of this, my more modest intention was to emphasize to the parallels between a dialectical naturalism's critique of the reification of nature, which resides in the significance of the gap between the concept and the thing signified, and the procedure of Adorno's negative dialectic, which aims to uncover the nonconceptual, or that which falls outside the traditional conceptual schemas of the prevailing ideological hegemony.

Acknowledgments

I wish to thank my partner Alexandra for her unwavering support and devotion, without which this book could not have been seen through to fruition.

I want to also thank Dr. Shannon Brincat (University of the Sunshine Coast) and Dr. Martin Weber (University of Queensland) for their inimitable advice and useful constructive criticism in preparing the various drafts of this book.

Introduction

> The real social function of philosophy lies in its criticism of what is prevalent. That does not mean superficial fault-finding with individual ideas or conditions, as though a philosopher were a crank. Nor does it mean that the philosopher complains about this or that isolated condition and suggests remedies. The chief aim of such criticism is to prevent humankind from losing itself in those ideas and activities which the existing organization of society instills into its members.
>
> —Max Horkheimer, *Eclipse of Reason*

> The well-known is such because it is well-known, not known.
>
> —G. W. F. Hegel, *Phenomenology of Spirit*

Ecology and Critical Theory

At no other time in history has a more rational, ecological society appeared so close, and yet so far. Never before the twentieth century did our species face such catastrophes of a world-historical nature as those that the potentialities of technology, subsumed under the instrumental reason of capitalistic forces, have unleashed. And yet if the ethical goals of the Enlightenment were not merely cruel illusions, the dialectic of world history still contains complexes of contradictions that promise redemption from all of the worst social and ecological calamities the prevailing trajectory of globalized capitalism will inevitably unleash.

However, there is so much that passes for ecological thought in our time that remains erroneous, wayward, and poorly developed. The reverence for ecology in popular thought redolent of our era may arise out of well-intentioned aesthetic and ethical desires of individuals, but so often it is crippled by the prevailing ideologies of market society and its mass culture, dissolving into petitioning, individual lifestyle choices, or the acquisition of more ecologically friendly travel options or property. To think in terms of the social structures that will benefit the destiny of our world's biosphere seems to be what is both sorely lacking, and desperately needed in our present historical moment. This wish at once expresses that the unspeakable, and for many unthinkable, hope that capitalism's egoistic struggle for existence, which is anathema to the development of a genuinely compassionate worldview and the pursuit of ethical life, might be done away with and a sense of mutual aid between sentient beings restored to its rightful place. To impart humanity's relationship with the natural world with an ethical aspect, nothing less seems necessary than building a new type of society where all sentient life is revered within an overarching ethical framework, as opposed to a system of competition and domination where, as Rosa Luxemburg highlighted in her ethically charged work, the accumulation of capital takes precedence over life itself.[1]

Nevertheless, such a spirit of hope, whether it falls under the label of Marxism, social ecology, or whatever else, would meet with ruination were it to naively avail itself, in the manner of much faddish "popular philosophy," of the prevailing concepts of nature espoused by political and social elites and subsequently integrated into mass culture. Such concepts, taken up as if they were somehow free from ideology, would offer no more hope against catastrophe than the fervent prayers of the Abbasids of Baghdad as the Golden Horde of the Mongols descended upon them. Capitalism's ideological hegemony, which seems destined to terminate in the reduction of organic life into the inorganic death of the commodity-form, cannot foresee a means beyond a state of affairs in which the earth's biosphere is slowly destroyed in the pursuit of profits. What appears more natural than wilderness to many individuals nowadays is the "nature" of the profiteers and the monolithic industries that place their rude stamp on the skylines of our metropolises. It is for such reasons that the concept of nature ought to always be reproached, following the inclination of Marxian theory, with the suspicion of reified consciousness. Even the concept of "ecology" betrays something of this in its popular association with that of the system. A nature rendered into an "ecosystem" by its cover concept, mechanized into flowcharts of constituent parts, "inputs" and "outputs," already betrays its mediated character as the reflected image of the exchange society that in practice violates the ecological logic—such as symbiosis—of the earth's eco-communities and rives them into little more than an instrumental analytics.

To this end, prevailing trends in the ecology movement may eagerly market ready-made slogans and correctives like commodities; but what they usually do not provide, in the spirit of a Socrates, are worthwhile questions that will interrogate the claims of ideological hegemony and spur society into a consciousness of its own discontents. Why, we may ask, despite the activities of half a century of a popular, global, and well-publicized ecology movement, is our planet still dying? Why is its all but inevitable destruction not being halted by the protests and petitions of liberal mass movements, and why are phenomena like global pollution, ocean acidification, global warming, deforestation, and species extinction proceeding at an unprecedented rate? We are often accosted at our front doors or in the streets by well-meaning young people for this or that NGO; we are often told to "vote with our feet," to purchase green products or "eco-friendly" solutions, or to vote for an increasingly narrow alternative of pro-capitalist parliamentary parties. And yet the prevailing logic of the very society that has led to the crisis remains unquestioned, no less among the so-called Left as elsewhere.

For these reasons, a critical ecological theory would be characterized by a negative dialectic: a dialectic of suspicion directed against the conceptual formations that have arisen out of the ideological hegemony underpinning the ecological crisis. This study hopes to provide a foundation for such an undertaking. It seeks to examine to what extent prevailing concepts of nature in Western philosophy, formed out of the historical contradictions of bourgeois society, reify the very logic underlying the social ideologies responsible for the crisis, and thereby implicitly prevent the existing society from becoming fully conscious of its range of historical potentialities. Consequently, it also aims to draw out immanently, via a critique of the bourgeois nature concept, the vestige of the social mediations according to which "nature" has taken on a contradictory character. It seeks to reveal how, in some of the most decisive moments of philosophical history, nature has appeared contradictorily as both potentiality to be subsumed by human civilization and yet also as a repository for repressed social hopes and unconscious impulses. Both of these images of nature remain ultimately abortive and undeveloped between the Enlightenment and this present historical juncture; and yet both must still, in their most rational and ethical moments, become the basis of a determinate negation in which a new, more ecological society could emerge, sustained by a cohesive ethical framework. Such a determinate negation, although always aware of its own inadequacy as thought, can provide us with an intellectual foundation for coherent and revolutionary ecological movements—an intellectual foundation that Murray Bookchin chose to call a dialectical naturalism.

On Some Limitations of Contemporary Nature Ontologies

The global prevalence of the ecological crisis has generated a substantial renaissance in nature philosophy within contemporary Western scholarship. Having provided an outline of this book, the extent to which its interpretation of the dialectic and application to nature philosophy, in the form of dialectical naturalism, differs from several prominent traditions in contemporary nature philosophy should be clarified.

One of the most promising developments in contemporary Western nature philosophy has been charted by the French philosopher of science Bruno Latour, who—in two of his most recent books, *Politics of Nature* (2004) and *Reassembling the Social* (2005)—expansively examines the failures of political ecology and various movements of mainstream environmentalism in terms of a lack of truly democratic deliberation governing the prevailing relationships between nature and technology, coupled with a critical rethinking of the interplay between social structure and subjective agency in modern life. For Latour, the distinction between fact/value and human/nonhuman emerges as a product of modernist ideology and positivism (or scientism) and is not ontologically beyond question, or to be taken as a given in philosophical speculation.[2] It is against this background—which closely parallels the Frankfurt School's critique of positivism—that Latour develops the notion that "nature" is a concept better sublimated into that of the "collective," inclusive of human and nonhuman life and "technologies," which, potentially at least, can democratically determine an ethics and a means of interacting with environments beyond immediate localities, including the ecological foundations of the planet.[3] Latour goes further than this in *Reassembling the Social* by way of a radical rethinking of metaphysics as such, resolving into an *imago* of a metaphysical life that is subjectively formed, and conditions—with a rationality uniquely its own—a given individual's experience with the social world.[4] Its rich and dynamic interest in subjective agency gives philosophical form to many insights of contemporary depth psychology, and its attempt to reground ontology in the terrain of psychological uniqueness—in Schopenhauer's terms, the *principium individuationis*—has important implications for the critical interpretation of democracy and the interaction between ecology and collective governance, notwithstanding the ethical ambiguities of Latour's relativism.

Interestingly, the novelty of Latour's focus upon the interrelatedness of social and environmental problems complements Bookchin's own interest in revitalizing the life of democratic collectives and its accompanying critique of the prevailing ideas under which the concept of nature has been captured by bourgeois, positivistic thought within various strands of the environmental movement. Moreover, Latour's interest in the plurality of ontological claims, beliefs and statements that originate with individuals, and the forms according to which these condition actions and influence institutions, might be viewed as giving a much-needed psychological grounding for how we explore the possibilities of social change along the lines of more ecologically harmonious values. On the other hand, Latour's use of parliamentary metaphors and frequent reference to professional politicians in *Politics of Nature* suggests that he has not gone far enough in developing a truly critical account of democratic governance beyond the ideological confines of purely "representative" forms of democracy, wherein the ethical interests of actual communities are largely marginalized by political and economic elites. The political theory of communalism, as developed by Murray Bookchin, may therefore offer a compelling corrective that points toward the possibility of reconfiguring the relationship between ecology and human communities by way of revolutionary changes in social institutions.

A similar theoretical impasse arises in the recent work of William Connolly and Timothy Morton on political ecology. In Connolly's *Facing the Planetary*, for instance, a politics of "swarming" via interlinked political movements is advanced as a hypothesis for overcoming the dire ecological calamities unleashed by globalized late capitalism.[5] Yet despite an insightful critique of "sociocentrism" and a valuable attempt to theorize the natural world beyond humanity as self-organizing, Connolly's theory ultimately terminates with the well-trodden ground of encomiums toward general strikes and platformist, pluralist "swarms" of democratic movements, bereft of any more concrete blueprint as to how a more ecological society could emerge institutionally out of the dialectical contradictions of late capitalism. Morton, even more drastically, regresses to a constructivist view of society-nature relationships, reducing the ecological crisis to a problem of poetics,[6] or perhaps more starkly, seeking to render the earth's eco-communities into a "mesh" of living and nonliving things.[7]

The lack of a philosophical foundation that overcomes the problem of monism, redolent in late capitalism's blurring of technology and ecological degradation, stands out as a weakness in Morton's work, and the lack of a model for an ecological society, as distinct from merely ecological movements within the framework of formal, or "representative" democracy, remains an unresolved quandary for both.

This is not so for the radical theory of Guattari and Deleuze—particularly so in the contribution to social ecology advanced in the former's *The Three Ecologies*—who counterpose "dissident subjectivities" and autonomous, egalitarian direct-democratic formations to the growth of psychological infantilization and passivity generated by the mass media, as the basis of a broader ecological movement.[8] The far-sighted holism of Guattari's concept of the three ecological registers—that is, the environment, social relations, and human subjectivity[9]—and the need to articulate an ethical and political solution to their prevailing global degradation, furnishes a refreshingly *psychological* critique of the ecological crisis. In Guattari's words:

> Social ecology will have to work towards rebuilding human relations at every level of the socius . . . it is equally imperative to confront capitalism's effects in the domain of mental ecology in everyday life: individual, domestic, material, neighbourly, creative or one's personal ethics. Rather than looking for a stupefying and infantilizing consensus, it will be a question in the future of cultivating a dissensus and the singular production of existence.[10]

Yet while there is much that is valuable in Guattari's articulation of the three ecologies in terms of a prognosis of the ecological crisis, as for many other contemporary political ecologies, a more precise framework for the cultivation of such a "dissensus" remains evasive and difficult to operationalize into a concrete politics. Without an anchoring in the anthropological foundations of the ecological crisis—the prehistory of prevailing "mental ecologies," as it were—nor a theoretical structure that would acculturate the development of technology and an ethical system within a plausible institutional blueprint of direct democracy, we are left without a coherent theory of dialectical transition from an ecologically informed dissensus to the social production of an ecologically informed *ethics*.

This problem is attacked from a different angle in the work of political theorists such as Robyn Eckersley, who in her more recent scholarship has attempted to devise a plausible theoretical model for a "green" state.[11] What delimits the work of scholars like Eckersley from the more historical approach to ecology advanced by Western Marxism and Bookchin is the more critical orientation of the latter on the question of the ecological merits of prevailing power systems of capitalism and the nation-state and how these, arguably, function to prevent the achievement of a veritably ecological society. As will be later explored in this text, the very notion that an ecological society is possible under the prevailing norms of liberal internationalism is one that a dialectical naturalism would invariably answer in the negative. What is crucial in formulating this answer is the problem of reification and, in particular, how liberal or social-democratic theorists of ecology may fail to resist the conquest of nature conceptually, by the reifying forms of late capitalism.

Despite the increasingly popular interest in political ecology redolent of our times, then, what we are so often lacking is a *historical* understanding of how Western thought has reflected the dominant ideas that have covered over nature with their concepts and have blinded civilization to its more rational and ecological potentialities. Contemporary environmental movements could therefore gain much from a critical evaluation of historical nature philosophy. A critical theory of ecology would offer a compelling vantage point for assessing the merits of various political theories by examining the kind of nature depicted by the most influential of philosophers, derived from the epistemological foundation, quite basic to critical theory and social ecology alike, that nature and politics are inextricably linked. This is demonstrated by Murray Bookchin, quite uniquely, in his illustration of the anthropology of hierarchy and its conditioning of historical reifications of nature. The interrelatedness of nature and politics in this sense has many ramifications, especially for aesthetics. In a world that is increasingly denatured, in which many children grow up in harsh urban environments overstimulated by technology and awash in various forms of pollution, the kind of human-ecological relationships we ought to work toward building in our communities becomes a fundamentally political, ethical, and aesthetic question. In order to begin to find the answers, we must first ask the right sort of questions. And in particular, we must seek to comprehend how the prevailing conceptual understanding of what *is* nature is a product of a social history that is reflected in the most influential themes of Western philosophy. This interest is one that many disparate environmentalists and ecologists surely share.

Reification and the Historical Context of Nature Philosophy

What social forces and factors ossify a given image of nature into a pervasive, cultural reification? It would seem that, up until the Enlightenment, various concatenations of social domination simply lacked the technologies of mass media, propaganda, and industrial economies of scale to create a reifying mass culture. And yet, we are also struck by the contradictions and emancipatory impulses brooding under the surface of contemporary mass culture, along with the pervasiveness of certain cultural ideas of nature in times past, despite the absence of sophisticated technologies of dissemination. What appears difficult to deny is that concepts of nature are always closely wedded to prevailing ideological refrains, and these are bound up within a cultural dialectic. For instance, when the Hellenic democrats invoked reason, they indicated something more substantial, and with greater ethical content, than the imperialist honorifics of Sparta or the instrumental reason of Thucydides's rhetoric might suggest. They expressed not a blind faith in the masses as such, but a rational faith in the virtues of democratic deliberation and personal responsibility to the *polis*; precisely this was what Pericles often appealed to in his funeral oration. Yet on the other hand, he also appealed to the apparently reasonable self-interest of a community of slave-owning patriarchs to preserve their imperial spoils and to avoid retribution for all of the various evils, petty and mighty, of the Athenian Empire. Such was the "nature" of the democratic Athenian culture in Hellenic times.

The origins of Western nature philosophy in the thought of presocratics illustrates the extent to which nature has been permeated by a variety of such cultural-historical reifications.[12] Though marred by often unbridgeable differences, what the presocratics, and the Hellenes more generally shared was a belief that the *kosmos* could be understood as intelligible and rational—a point of view that not only signified a break with various forms of religious mysticism but signaled a point of departure from a mythopoeic worldview to a greater degree of enlightened secularism, as Gregory Vlastos has emphasized.[13] For many of the presocratics the notion that nature could be understood rationally was directly derived from the idea that the *polis* or political community had its own objective standards of rationality.

The life of Anaximander of Miletus (born 610 BCE) offers an illuminating example of this origin. Anaximander's historical period was approximately coterminous with Solon's reforms in Athens, which were a significant turning point in the Hellenic world toward direct democracy. Such substantive democracy, needless to say, must be distinguished from the fictive bourgeois myth of representative "democracy." The radical connotations of *deme* can be taken to signify the confederal and participatory meeting of the "tribes" or "councils" directly populated by citizens, a form of intricately democratic social administration all but lost to us today.[14] At any rate, what is most compelling about Anaximander is that his nature philosophy seems to reflect a social viewpoint that, unlike the historical duality analyzed later in this study, neither perceived nature as a lifeless "other" nor as a reified "oneness" into which civilization ought to be dissolved. Rather, "nature" could only be made sense of, quite literally, within the nexus of social rationality; this metabolism alone constitutes the "whole." Thus, he stressed that there was a sense of "natural" equality bound up within change; conflict and strife may constitute the appearance of change but equality, not merely justice, is held to be its true essence. The natural world for Anaximander is rendered intelligible through its inherent rationality, just as the Athenian political culture is rendered intelligible to its citizens through its grounding in universal education (*paideia*) and their direct participation in governance through its political institutions.[15]

By the time of Empedocles's birth (492 BCE), Athens had entered its democratic phase, and the public fervor that underlay the democratic emphasis on popular assemblies, councils, and communal associations had begun to spread not only throughout Attica but also even to Sicily and Southern Italy. The close relation between the Hellenic notions of justice, natural equality, freedom and spontaneity, and the "spirit" of the Athenian democratic age can be observed in the structure of Empedocles's physics and cosmology. Empedocles, influenced by Parmenides, was convinced that there was no coming to be and no perishing in the world: "all is one." But Empedocles was clearly dissatisfied with the colorless immediacy of this form of monism. This "higher understanding" of a "oneness" of all things, he observed, seems to contradict what our senses reveal to us about the order of the world, involving as it does so much death and destruction alongside birth and renewal.[16] Empedocles's solution was to suggest that while all the world is united into one totality of Being, it is comprised of four elements or "roots" that are governed by the cosmological forces of what he calls Love and Strife.[17] These elements, comprising earth, wind, fire, and water ("earth and the billowy sea and the damp air, Titan, and the ether . . .") are "bound" in a "circle," a totality of Being.[18] Periodically, Love and Strife take turns at ruling over the physical world, which Empedocles represents as a "sphere"; this is much like Anaximander's own cosmology, which emphasized justice and equality in the rotation of rule in the natural world. During the periods in which Love reigns, there is the greatest mixture and Strife is banished to the surface of the Sphere; when Strife reigns, there is the greatest amount of separation of the roots, and Love is banished to the surface. Although the present generation, according to Empedocles, may be one of great Strife and suffering,[19] the strict equality of the roots in the *kosmos* means that, as Vlastos says, "none would be stronger than any of the rest . . . even when Strife rules the world, equality is a sufficient preventive of 'injustice.' "[20]

One could thus observe that Empedocles's philosophy embodied philosophical reflection wedded to the forms of social totality that the Greek democrats of Attica, Southern Italy, and Sicily were beginning to objectify in a political form.[21] This form was intimately mirrored in the conceptual mediations that many Hellenic nature philosophers placed in between their social experience and the world of nature. Vlastos discerns in his detailed commentary:

> It is just this [democratic] political experience which furnished the pre-socratics with the conceptual pattern which they applied to the comprehension of nature as a rule of law, an autonomous, self-regulative system, whose orderly 'justice' was guaranteed by the assumed 'equality' of its components.[22]

This development, as a characteristic example of a reifying tendency, seems to have been founded upon a unifying view of a rational *kosmos* in which the ecology of nature became an increasingly significant allegory for the material relations of society. Just as the pantheon of the Greek gods, in Feuerbach's analysis, reflect the "naturalism" of the Hellenic worship of sensuality, Empedocles's system of nature expresses a powerful optimism about the justice of rotational political powers vested in the citizenry.

Vlastos has further surmised the relation between the social relations of the Hellenic *demos* and the nature philosophy of the presocratics in the following, striking rejoinder to Nietzsche's cult of the "aristocratic man":

> The adventurous reason of Ionian science charted [the] realm of magic, detached it from the personal control of supernatural beings, and integrated it into the domain of nature. All natural events, ordinary and extraordinary alike, were now united under a common law. The equality of the constituents of this new commonwealth of nature was of the essence of the transformation, for it meant the abolition of distinctions between two grades of being—divine and moral, lordly and subservient, noble and mean, of higher and lower honor. It was the ending of these distinctions that made nature autonomous and *therefore* completely and unexceptionally "just." Given a society of equals, it was assumed, justice was sure to follow, for none would have power to dominate the rest. This assumption, as we have seen, had a strictly physical sense. It was accepted not as political dogma but as a theorem in physical inquiry. It is, nonetheless, remarkable evidence of the confidence which the great age of Greek democracy possessed in the validity of the democratic idea—a confidence so robust that it survived translation into the first principles of cosmology and medical theory.[23]

In contrast, he goes on to note:

> It was Plato, the bitter critic of the Athenian democracy, who carried through the intellectual revolution (or, more strictly, counterrevolution) to a successful conclusion; and Aristotle followed . . . in their systems we find at last the explicit and thorough-going negation of Anaximander's equalitarian universe.[24]

Plato's and Aristotle's thought imposed a distinction between "rational thought" and "rational thing" to the extent that they ended up "not . . . rationalizing material nature but . . . degrading matter to the realm of the irrational, the fortuitous, and the disorderly."[25] It is highly noteworthy that it was upon a very similar "counterrevolutionary" edifice—one that conceived nature as disorderly, irrational, and capricious—that the revolutionary bourgeois enlightenment was to build its own philosophies of nature. Not for faith in the process of direct democratic deliberation, nor for love of the naturalism of the senses and the freedom of sexual desire, did the bourgeois enlightenment concern itself with the subject of nature. Rather, the repressive holding down of the proletarianized masses, the negative moral characterization of natural needs under the dominion of the patriarchal family and property, and the Dickensian oppression of the proletariat in line with the prerogatives of capital were to prove the most decisive in the intellectual character of the revolutionary bourgeoisie.[26]

Yet the instrumental reason that epitomizes the social logic of capitalism was hardly without historical antecedents. Under the tyranny of the post-Macedonian and late Roman empires, the man formerly of the *demos* had already become the "private man," the "alienated soul" in Hegel's parlance; so too, with few notable exceptions, would the man of philosophy schools gradually become a paid professional, in short a *sophist*, hiring out his intellectual faculties to the appeasement of political elites. While the democratic tendencies of the Hellenes seemed to promise a unification of society and nature through the self-determining notion of *reason*, and therefore also projected this "rational" content, such as equality and justice, onto the natural world, the spirit of tyranny that snuffed out the flame of the *demos*, beginning with the struggles of Alexander's autocratic successors, was mirrored in the changing appearance of nature philosophy as it took shape during the ascendancy of Rome. Beginning with stoicism during the late Roman Empire, such changes were echoed subsequently in monotheistic theology's notion of a "natural" hierarchy. The natural world and social world alike could no longer be perceived as free, spontaneous, or sensually uninhibited; both sexuality and nature were forced into the chains of a metaphysical hierarchy that mirrored the really existing chains of the feudal and ecclesiastical relations.

Such developments had their philosophical forebears in the psychological orientation of the middle and late Stoa. Late Stoic philosophy galvanized intellection into an alienated private spiritualism devoid of social substance, oriented around a mystical concept of *logos*, or "nature." What is most remarkable about this nature-concept of late Roman Stoicism is that it seems to become culturally entrenched at a moment when, not without similarities to late, "neoliberal" capitalism, the masses had become politically disenfranchised and demoralized beneath the decadence of imperial conspiracies and the spectacular *panem et circenses* that simultaneously dominated and trivialized public life. Within this context of privation and the dissolution of objective culture, as Boethius demonstrated immanently in his prison cell, "nature" becomes little more than a solipsistic phantom of subjective consolation against a decaying social nexus. In the philosophy of Epictetus, Seneca, and Marcus Aurelius, empirical reality even becomes secondary to a personalized, mythopoeic "oneness" with the *logos*, or substance of nature. Stoicism's twisted reverence for this mystical *logos* was perhaps illustrated most dramatically in the disdain that Seneca showed for life when he committed suicide on Nero's orders. Here, along with the origins of idealism and monotheistic sexual repression, also perhaps originates the negative characterization of nature that was to become a recurring feature of Western philosophy.

Under the oppression of such historical conditions, "nature" takes on a denuded ethical form divorced not only from the lived realm of society and human needs but, with no small sense of irony, from the concrete lifeways of broader ecologies. Hence, as the former social ecologist Janet Biehl has observed:

> In "adequating" themselves to the cosmos, [the Stoics] were guided by the principle of apathy, not activity, except in the inner recesses of their private lives, as the writings of Epictetus so clearly demonstrate. The individual in declining Roman society could no more make a difference in the cosmos—or in society, for that matter—than could ordinary Mesopotamians and Egyptians millennia earlier.[27]

Despite the global ecological crisis, does liberal environmentalism not confront a similar impasse to that which confronted the acolytes of Stoicism or Christianity in decaying Rome? According to Leo Löwenthal's appraisal in the late 1980s, the Western environmentalist movement remains dominated by a liberal viewpoint that does not seek to theorize a social structure beyond capitalism.[28]

Such reflections might serve to indicate what has been obscured in philosophy with the triumph of a global market society and the philistinism of its mass culture: the dialectical notion that all attempts to fuse ecology with politics must invariably point back to what Marx originally called the "metabolism" between nature and society. The latter, which the culture industry's productions have denuded in the realm of popular thought, prolongs its actual existence only in an atrophied form: in the neoliberal rationality of a pseudo-subjective consumer "choice." Late capitalist culture's much-asserted nexus of "choice" and its attendant "identity" politics, however, ironically divests the subject of the democratic dimension that once infused itself with public life, a life in which alone the essence of individuality was completed and attained. Against this, critical theory would maintain the viability of the thesis that just as true subjectivity cannot be realized through the liquidation of the subject into a totally administered mass culture, no more can nature be truly known by dissolving social relations into a mythopoeic "nature."

The Dialectic of the Nature-Concept

The first two chapters of this study concern themselves with a reconstruction of the ontologies underlying the nature-concepts of Kant, Fichte and Hegel, of Marx, and of two of the most canonical figures of anarchism: Mikhail Bakunin and Peter Kropotkin. The interest of the first chapter is to explore how a reified concept of nature emerges from German Idealism's conceptual splitting between universal and particular, subject and object, and private freedom and public unfreedom, whose origin, according to Herbert Marcuse, can be uncovered within the philosophy of Luther and Kant.[29] This theme is subsequently developed further through critical expositions on Fichte and Hegel, as well as something of a running digression on Feuerbach.

Though the first chapter does not depart beyond a critique of concept formation, it nevertheless canvases the material basis of the nature-concept that the capitalist mode of production ushered into culture in the form of both its instrumental reason and its psychological orientation. Most fundamental of all points of development is the observation that, by reducing nature to an unknowable otherness, market society distorts the very living substance of nature and transforms it into a more or less asocial, unmediated, and abstract otherness: the mere plastic determinateness of Fichte's non-Ego. Such reification still resonates in the contemporary ecology movement, particularly in many aspects of liberal environmentalism, the ideological descendant of the liberal movements of the nineteenth century. To the extent that the first chapter is relevant to contemporary politics, its critique is directed at the ideological similarities between the idealist nature-concept of the nineteenth century and the nature-concept redolent of the liberal ecology movement of the twenty-first century. It also takes care to illustrate, however, what moments in Hegel were not identical with the steady march of the bourgeois pathology of anti-naturalism, what moments were more congenial to the development of a dialectical naturalism that elsewhere remained obscure in his system.[30]

Capitalism's ruthless imposition of the exchange economy at the expense of social freedom and human needs was laid bare by Marx. And yet, in accordance with the presuppositions of historical materialism first worked out in *The German Ideology*, Marx's understanding of the society-nature relationship was often colored by a positive evaluation of the acculturation of nature into the industrial machinery of the capitalistic World-Spirit. This contradiction forms the subject of the second chapter, which illustrates how Marx's later writings retained a somewhat positivistic championing of the nature-concept of the bourgeois enlightenment. Here it is contended that the nature-concept of bourgeois political economy was in certain subtle ways fundamental to the viewpoint of the mature Marx as well, who abandoned his Feuerbachian concept of human-nature relations. This unreflective continuity with bourgeois thought is, notwithstanding, quite at odds with the younger Marx's impulses and with his dialectical theory of society more generally, which resists reification.

On the other hand, what remains one of the greatest undertakings of modern anarchism, a political philosophy strongly influenced by a romantic cultural tendency, was its attempted recovery of the possibilities of an ecological ethics. Anarchism departed dramatically from the bourgeois enlightenment in defending the allegedly "natural" basis of society, redolent in its notions of "natural law" and the "instincts" of "mutual aid" that were assumed to govern the ontological substance of natural being. By seeking values that are essentially communitarian and what Bookchin once called, drawing on Aristotle's *Politics*, "humanly scaled," the great virtue of anarchism was to advance a political principle that, opposed to "the state" or indeed to social "authority" as such, at once aimed to recover the "natural" dimension of society vanquished in the colonizing waves of statist civilization.

However, within its excessive zeal for natural law and individualism, anarchism tends to pass over into an empty valorization of the natural. Deriving its ethical precepts not from an immanent criticism of the particular rationality of the prevailing society on its own terms—and by extension its dialectic with the natural world—but rather, as it were, from a transcendent moralism presumed to originate in the immediacy of "natural" relationships, anarchism presupposes moral criteria that emanate from a universal instinctivism, or in Kropotkin's terms "sociability," rather than from *determinate* social relations, culture, or history as such. Precisely because of their allegedly "unnatural" character, the historical and social mediation of "nature" is at once abandoned and thought lapses into a fetish of natural authenticity. This appeal to the authority of "nature" is here criticized immanently, following Hegel's insight, as articulated by Adorno, that "immediacy always already contains something other than itself—subjectivity—without which it would not be 'given' at all, and by that token it is already not objectivity."[31] In an antagonistic totality characterized by mass manipulation, in which assertions of subjectivity must always be approached with suspicion, the championing of immediacy is a pathway to falsehood, not to truth. The appeal to nature in human fate could only be justified were it to also acknowledge the fateful power of that which is not identical with nature.

An immanent criticism of this mythopoeic naturalism is the subject of the latter half of the second chapter. It seeks to show how anarchism's professedly radical opposition to "authority," via the cover concept of natural law, ultimately comes to reinforce the asocial ideology of late capitalism. By reducing society's metabolism with nature into the form of a transcendent moralism, anarchism substitutes a passive imaginary of nature for the active reality of historical mediation. Hence, revolutionary organization, and the social and political determination of nature, cede their necessary assertiveness to a passive and irrational faith in the goodness of nature: through spontaneous revolutionism, we are assured, all will be put right in the end. In place of the divine, anarchism substitutes a worship of the daimonic, imbuing it with a mystified goodness, but the daimonic is not always on the side of the good. This is illustrated via a succinct critique of Bakunin and a more elaborate exposition on Kropotkin. I must caution the reader that this chapter does not seek to present a complete image of anarchism, nor does it seek to deny the differences between certain anarchist traditions, nor does it delve into the legacy of anarcho-syndicalism, for which the nature-concept was a more marginal phenomenon. It is concerned instead with illuminating an *ontological tendency* common to most forms of anarchism, demonstrating via the psychoanalytic concept of passivity the ultimately counterrevolutionary implications of its philosophy.

The Concept of Dialectical Naturalism

Here it seems necessary to clarify the concept of dialectic, including its formulation by Adorno in terms of a "negative dialectic" and by Bookchin in the guise of a "dialectical naturalism."

Dialectic is indistinguishable from the greatest innovation of Plato—to articulate philosophy in the form of speculative discussion or dialogue, in which questions and one-sided answers lead to inevitable reformulations and digressions. Rather than merely listing an aggregation of "commandments," "principles," or "propositions," as in contemporary analytic philosophy, Plato's personification of Socrates encourages his interlocutors to rethink and reformulate their unreflected conventions and beliefs by revealing their contradictions. In this spirit, he refers to himself in the *Theaetetus* as barren of original ideas, and as a "midwife" to their own wisdom.[32] This notion of the inherent nonidentity between conventional concepts and what they signify is so essential to the process of dialectic that it is preserved all the way up to the young Hegel, whom (particularly in his early essay *The System of Ethical Life*) repeatedly stresses the necessity of "re-cognizing" reality in the spirit of Socratic negativity. A few years later, Hegel expresses this fundamental idea in the following maxim: "What is well-known is well-known, not known."[33]

Hence it should be of little surprise that the logical process of dialectic is closely bound up with the historical concept of what critical theory refers to as *objective* reason. That is to say that by logically educing the rationality of a particular statement or premise, dialectical philosophy furnishes a speculative turn to mind that aims to divest it of traditional prejudices, superstitious nostrums, and parochialisms that do not hold up to the scrutiny of reason. In obliging a participant in dialogue to think out the subject matter immanently, rather than to obey the commandments of authority or unthinking tradition, the very process of dialectic is synchronous with the image of a freethinking and participatory social body that was revived with the radical sansculottes of the French Revolution. The French Revolution was especially redolent in aspects of Hegel's dialectic, a relation that Herbert Marcuse explicates:

> In Hegel's view, the decisive turn that history took with the French Revolution was that man came to rely on his mind and dared to submit the given reality to the standards of reason. Hegel expounds the new development through a contrast between an employment of reason and an uncritical compliance with the prevailing conditions of life. 'Nothing is reason that is not the result of thinking.' Man [sic] has set out to organize reality according to the demands of his free rational thinking instead of simply accommodating his

thoughts to the existing order and the prevailing values. Man is a thinking being. His reason enables him to recognize his own potentialities and those of his world. He is thus not at the mercy of the facts that surround him, but is capable of subjecting them to a higher standard, that of reason. If he follows its lead, he will arrive at certain conceptions that disclose reason to be antagonistic to the existing state of affairs. He may find that history is a constant struggle for freedom, that man's individuality requires that he possess property as the medium of his fulfillment, and that all men have an equal right to develop their human faculties. Actually, however, bondage and inequality prevail; most men have no liberty at all and are deprived of their last scrap of property. Consequently the 'unreasonable' reality has to be altered until it comes into conformity with reason.[34]

Dialectical philosophy's form and content thereby both presuppose and participate in one another. Dialectical philosophy gives emphasis to the ability of speculative thinking to follow out the rationality of the "what could be" or the "ought" to be, rather than the merely analytical "what is." Crucially, as Hegel would emphasize in the second volume of his *Science of Logic*, this "what could be" is not an abstract property. It refers to a concrete possibility within a particular logic of development.

Dialectical philosophy is also characterized by an emphasis on the "whole," a theme already present in many of Plato's dialogues. For Plato's Socrates, all of the failures of the interlocutors to correctly articulate the substance of justice, or of piety, knowledge, and so forth are all in some way or another failures pertaining to the "one-sidedness" of their conceptions. They are one-sided insofar as their way of thinking has reduced, by way of the concept, the fecundity of social reality into rigid propositions that are contradicted by other equally valid ones. It is therefore the motivic force of contradiction, according to dialectical philosophy, that is the spur of logical development; dialectic lives through and in the contradictions, not by superciliously effacing them. Only through such a procedure could philosophy do justice to historical experience. In Hegel's parlance this is reflected in the notion of "determinate negation," a negation that is in a certain sense progressive for our reason. This essentially "progressive" function of dialectical reason serves a reconstructive purpose in allowing us to reflect upon the unfolding ecological possibilities of history. It is simultaneously, however, where the dialectic threatens to become most reified through aligning itself with the hegemonic colonization of that history. The latter aligns with the most well-known interpretation of Hegel's infamous *Philosophy of Right*.

In Bookchin's terms, the merit of dialectical philosophy is that it "moves from the undifferentiated abstract to the highly differentiated concrete (while most commonsensical forms of thought move in the opposite direction)."[35] Dialectical thinking takes concepts, such as justice or freedom, developing their potentialities under the conditions of both a social and historical mediacy, rather than applying a conceptual abstraction to history *in toto*, as if it were somehow universally valid despite its obvious anachronism.[36] Where formalistic philosophers such as Hume, Kant, and Husserl seek to reduce the phenomenology of social life into the assumed primacy of propositional concepts, dialectical philosophy arrives at its truths via the tension between identity and nonidentity, mirrored in the contradiction between the subject's speculative thought and concrete, historical possibility. Hence, as Feuerbach aptly observes in his critique of Hegel, a true dialectic would be that which consists of a genuine dialogue between the two.[37]

This is the point at which Adorno's concept of a "negative" dialectic begins. In Adorno's formulation, following Kant's distinction between the *constitutum* and *constituens*, a negative dialectic acknowledges the limit of dialectic as "the index of the untruth of identity, of the vanishing of the conceptual into the concept."[38] In the same manner that Feuerbach criticized Hegel for remaining distant from a true dialogue between speculative thought and material reality, Adorno illuminates how dialectic has traditionally failed to follow out the logic of its own premises by lapsing into an absolute identity that dissolves all contradiction into itself.[39] He seeks to reveal how "identity and contradiction in thinking are welded to one another."[40] Thus, he states, "the totality of the contradiction is nothing other than the untruth of the total identification, as it is manifested in the latter."[41] This leads to his definitive statement:

> Philosophy has, at this historical moment, its true interest in what Hegel, in accordance with tradition, proclaimed his disinterest: in the non-conceptual, the individual and the particular; in what, ever since Plato, has been dismissed as transient and inconsequential and which Hegel stamped with the label of lazy existence. Its theme would be the qualities

which it has degraded to the merely contingent, to *quantité négligeable* [negligible quantity]. What is urgent for the concept is what it does not encompass, what its abstraction-mechanism eliminates, what is not already an exemplar of the concept.⁴²

The force of a negative dialectic, which aims to encompass that which resides outside the cover concept of nature, serves as a constant corrective to the reified concepts illuminated in the first two chapters of this study. The final chapter seeks to reconstruct the sensibility of a dialectical naturalism, by uncovering the residues of ecological and social possibility that reified consciousness passes over. Specifically, Bookchin's "dialectical naturalism"—although by no means consistent with Adorno's philosophy in Bookchin's own appraisal of it—yields a dialectic that is arguably "negative" in Adorno's sense. It aims at an elucidation of the social potentialities glossed over by the World-Spirit, and yet present to us still, in a time of global ecological crisis. To attempt such an elucidation is to try to name that which is not permitted to speak in the predominant nature-concept of our historical period. What a dialectical naturalism seeks to accomplish is to give voice to those nonconceptual remnants of past history—in Bookchin's parlance, the unrealized possibilities of history's "turning points"—that could have yielded radical alternatives and could productively inform any future struggles for a truly ecological society.

In reconstructing a dialectical naturalism and presenting its philosophical beginning-point as one of negative dialectic, the final chapter draws on three fragmentary models that preceded the development of Bookchin's theory. Out of these models it is Ernst Bloch above all who reveals the immanently utopian aspects of these nonconceptual residues. Bloch characterizes dialectical thinking in terms redolent of Bookchin's later image of "social ecology":

> Thinking means venturing beyond. But in such a way that what already exists is not kept under or skated over. Not in its deprivation, let alone in moving out of it. Not in the causes of deprivation, let alone in the first signs of the change which is ripening within it. That is why real venturing beyond never goes into the mere vacuum of an In-Front-of-Us, merely fanatically, merely visualizing abstractions. Instead, it grasps the New as something that is mediated in what exists and is in motion, although to be revealed the New demands the

> most extreme effort of will. Real venturing beyond knows and activates the tendency which is inherent in history and which proceeds dialectically. Primarily, everybody lives in the future, because they strive, past things only come later, and as yet genuine present is almost never there at all. The future dimension contains what is feared or what is hoped for; as regards human intention, that is, when it is not thwarted, it contains only what is hoped for. Function and content of hope are experienced continuously, and in times of rising societies they have been continuously activated and extended.[43]

This seems a particularly vital political rejoinder under neoliberal conditions, or late capitalism. We live in the midst of a recurrent cynicism of private retreat into technology and the decay of meaningful social interactions. We are surrounded by a seemingly obsessive focus on individual health, but popular culture is conspicuously quiet on the subjects of social and ecological health. All such tendencies, as an extension of the ideological hegemony, implicitly deny the hope that is pregnant in material and cultural potentialities of the present, particularly in the lives of those individuals who do not fit cleanly into prescribed social roles.

According to Marcuse:

> Dialectical thought invalidates the a priori opposition of value and fact by understanding all facts as stages of a single process—a process in which subject and object are so joined that truth can be determined only within the subject-object totality. All facts embody the knower as well as the doer; they continuously translate the past into the present. The objects thus "contain" subjectivity in their very structure.[44]

Following this formulation, we may observe that no nature-concept is distinct from distorting subjectivity, no image of nature separate from the particular determinations of valuing and classifying nature enclosed within the historic development of bourgeois society. No less may we presume to "know" nature outside of this contradictory process of representation than may we posit a political ontology oriented around allegedly natural values. Such is the basis for the immanent critique of the "ontological need" governing predominant nature-concepts, from which a dialectical naturalism proceeds.

The philosophy of "social ecology" takes for its point of departure the possibilities that unfold when this notion of dialectical naturalism is applied to humanity's historical relations to the natural world. Social ecology first emerged as a heterodox social philosophy, principally in the writings of Murray Bookchin (1921–2006), a lifelong dialectician and radical ecologist influenced variously by Marxism and anarchism. Influenced by Aristotle, the French materialists, Hegel, Marx, and later Neo-Marxists, social ecology has also advanced programs for political praxis that began with "post-scarcity" anarchism and concluded in a model of confederalist direct democracy. In the working out of these programs Bookchin attempted to unite a wealth of historical experience, from the Parisian communards to the Left Social Revolutionaries of Russia and the syndicalists of Spain.[45]

The promise of "nature" for a dialectical naturalism is that of a *developing* substance, not one that is merely static and unchanging. It is ultimately a *historical* promise that unites natural and social history for social ecology. Such hope is by its very definition inexorable from the efforts of human beings to venture beyond an antidemocratic, class, patriarchal, and ultimately anti-ecological society; but coherent thought must *precede* action, and this is where so much of the contemporary Left, with its mania for unthinking activism, may be subject to valuable criticism. Rather than falling into the mystique of nature worship or the glorification of spontaneous street theatricality, social ecology emphasizes a nuanced materialist outlook that seeks to ground the development of a new ethics and politics in a responsible intellectual study of the failures of the socialist revolutions of the past. Such would form the essential precondition for a real revolutionary movement capable of reversing the ecological cataclysm.

While avoiding the logical pitfalls of ascribing any intrinsic morality to nature or biology as such, social ecology nevertheless holds fast to a "participatory" view of evolution that sees, in the expanding potentialities of consciousness and human second nature, the possibility of arriving at an ethical relationship with nonhuman nature. This need not be interpreted, as some spurious commentary would have it,[46] as a "teleology"; in Bookchin's terms, such possibility would mean the actualization of a potentiality that is latent within natural history. In the midst of particular revolutionary contexts and historical turning points, social ecology elucidates how greatly varied social movements have been well placed to effectively "choose" the form of society they would create, only—in all significant moments of the modern period at least—to fall woefully short of their historical possibilities. In Bookchin's words:

> Dialectical naturalism asks which is truly real—the incomplete, aborted, irrational "what-is," or the most fully developed, rational "what-should-be." Reason, cast in the form of dialectical causality as well as dialectical logic, yields an unconventional understanding of reality. A process that follows its immanent self-development to its logical actuality is more properly "real" than a given "what-is" that is aborted or distorted and hence, in Hegelian terms, "untrue" to its possibilities. *Reason* has the obligation to explore the potentialities that are latent in any social development and educe its authentic actualization, its fulfilment and "truth" in a new and more rational social dispensation.[47]

This notion, taken from the substance of Aristotle's and Hegel's philosophy, is thus redolent with implications for nature philosophy and ecological ethics—two subjects intimately related to social development that both Hegel and Marx nonetheless left substantially unexplored.

CHAPTER ONE

Anti-Naturalism, the Bourgeois Enlightenment, and the Modern Origins of a Dialectical Naturalism

> One recognizes one's course by discovering the paths that stray from it.
> —Albert Camus, *Absurd Creation*

The Becoming of Nature

It is a dialectical irony of history that the relationship of nature to civilization can never be grasped in its immediacy without being understood through the mediations of authority and tradition. Ludwig Feuerbach's artless edification of sensual immediacy, criticized in the first of Marx's eleven *Theses on Feuerbach*, blinds itself to this irony, missing the insight that what presents itself as nature is arrived at through the reifications of a cultural history. The illusion of immediacy therefore conceals a danger: recognition of biological immediacy might seem unavoidable as soon as philosophy tries to articulate the relationship between humanity and nature, and yet it is evident that a liberated human culture would not satisfy itself within conditions of mere instinctivism. It may well be that what pass for instincts themselves bear so much of the character of historical mediation—in other words, the stamp of acculturated mimesis, of what the concept of instinct would like to think lies beyond instinct as such.

This mediacy of the immediate must be borne in mind in appraising the approach of much bourgeois enlightenment philosophy toward conceptualizing nature. The nonconformity of the revolutionary aspirations of the bourgeoisie with prevailing monarchical, scholastic, or feudal reifications of "nature" is undoubtedly a contributing factor to the anti-naturalism of early German Idealism.[1] In the postrevolutionary context of German

Idealism from Kant to Hegel, a time of upheaval in which the ascendant class could not confidently rely on the authority of tradition nor on an appeal to the moral shibboleths that governed the earlier feudal relations, prominent attempts were made to justify its social outlook by preexisting philosophical means. The concept of knowledge in Kant and Fichte, entwined within the categories of the earlier Cartesian metaphysics, still reveals something of this history. Knowledge appears as that which exerts its power and its domination over its object as a process of allegedly rational becoming, distanced from a nature rendered as accidental and capricious. Such categorizing schemes are prefigurative. Nature takes on a number of conceptual associations not contained to merely external nature, but to inner nature; nature comes to resemble something divided off from the realm of productive human activity, both socially and psychologically.

To treat such negative associations of nature concomitant with the bourgeois enlightenment as a process of allegedly rational becoming, therefore, is to unjustly raise them above the suspicion of being less innocent than the mere categorization of nature's in-and-for-itself that they would pretend to be. What follows is an attempt to explicate the ideological dimension of this dualistic categorization of nature, as manifest in Kant and Fichte. It is based upon the premise, owing something to the procedure of Adorno's *Negative Dialectics*, that philosophy, far from being immune from reification, is complicit in it through the means of conceptual identity. Such reification, which would expel nature to the category of a lifeless other to be determined by the instrumental forces of abstract labor, becomes itself a rationalization for the entrenched interests of the dominant class. It thereby denies to the subjugated social forces, and with them nature, the basis of an *ethical* mediation that would sweep away dominatory relationships and give birth to a society of true humanism and freedom, a society without the ecological and social burden of domination.

By removing nature from the very content and ground of ethical life, the dominant ideology of enlightened market society effaces the ecological basis of social relations and, as is already indicated in the ethical philosophy of Kant and Fichte, debases ethics into an act of merely subjective willing. Biological nature does not attain to subjecthood in its own right in Kantian and Fichtean ethics; nor is it, however, quite an object in its own right. Rather it appears as an externality, and in Fichte's case, as a completely dominated and subsumed other. Despite the time that has elapsed between then and now, this image of nature still prevails today, particularly in many of the unexamined assumptions of the environmental movement, which tend to treat nature as nothing more than an assemblage of "resources," as mere things to be "managed" from above. The legacy of this externalizing anti-naturalism is clearly inadequate in a time of ecological crisis, in terms of its social, psychological, and ecological implications.

Moreover, by engendering an anti-naturalist epistemology, the conceptual legacy of the bourgeois enlightenment endures as an obstacle to the task of adequately *knowing* nature outside of its reified concept. In construing nature specifically in terms of an epistemological dualism with subjectivity, the sense in which natural history is truly complementary in the unfolding of social history becomes unintelligible to us. Yet an intelligible account of social history's enduring mediation through conditions of nature is essential not only to an undistorted view of natural history, but moreover to radical social movements that would aspire to institutionalize an authentic ecological ethics. In other words, we must seek to understand the ecological context of history and of social revolution.

Epistemology and the Bourgeois Image of Nature

The anti-naturalism enmeshed within the bourgeois nature-concept might first be elucidated at the most abstract level: within the prefigurative categories of Kant's epistemology. A decisive feature of Kant's philosophy, and the transcendental idealism that followed in its wake, is the assumption of a universal nonidentity between subject and object, a nonidentity posited as the very condition of all experience. Notwithstanding Descartes, throughout much of the earlier rationalist philosophy, such as that of Spinoza, subject and object were typically seen as unified through their determinate character, to say nothing of their mutual identity in the theory of universal substance. Even Leibniz's monadology, often interpreted as a philosophy of subjectivism, nonetheless advanced a view of the subject as the objective essence of the cosmos—a notion resplendent in Leibniz's idea of the "pre-established harmony" and his image of the monad as the *mirror* of the universe.[2] What is historically significant in Kant's philosophy, by contrast, is that a metaphysics of reason is elaborated on a ground that, originating in the conditions of a given social history, forgets itself and closes itself off from the very actuality of social determination within the kernel of the noumenal.

Thus in Kant's philosophy, subject and object are inclined to appear under the aegis of an eternal and unchangeable opposition. The subject is discovered to be the ground of all reason and reality, and through this appellation (drawn from Hume's skepticism) a judgment is rendered on nature. Nature becomes the repository of all those qualities that Hume had turned over to ontology. It takes on the character of the capricious, the arbitrary, and in the last analysis, the Heraclitean flux that reason can only apprehend by negating its nonidentity and rendering it into the subject's *own* categories of a priori consciousness.

The sublimated, yet strangely utopian element of this conception is most strikingly articulated by Kant's later disciple Schopenhauer. In Schopenhauer's aesthetic idealism, subject and object are only ever united in the brain of the philosopher—in the subject's *representation*, and thereby in her or his perceptive ordering of the external world according to the principle of sufficient reason (in other words, the relations of a cognitively grounded causality). Kant's object, the "thing-in-itself," for Schopenhauer takes the form of the irrational "will-to-life," the fickleness of an ultimately incorrigible animality. This tension is only seemingly resolved in the state of aesthetic contemplation—the ordering of natural relations through the configurations of the intellect—and, more resolutely, through the absolute negation of nature qua the "will" in the state of nirvana. Thus, in the purely negative aesthetic state alone, consciousness reaches the heights of a positive image of utopia; the forms of music and art appear to it not so much as historical but rather as eternal Platonic Ideas, passing intellect through a stream of consciousness that in the totality of its movement gives intellect an abstract mastery over nature. This mastery, however, appears less as one of ideological domination and more as one of a tranquil contemplation, a utopian image that came into its own in the literary reflections of Proust. The utopian identity between this universality of distanced reflection and that of the cessation of nature's caprice is even expressed by Schopenhauer spatially, as the overlapping of conceptual spheres in the realm of the intellect. In rendering himself more universal through knowledge, the gentlemanly subject is supposed to partake of that element of the divine that according to Cicero appeared as a residue in the exercise of right reason. As echoed by Proust's narrator, it is precisely such a totality of reflection and documentation, symbolized through the metaphor of the picture gallery or museum, that constitutes the utopian accommodation of nature within the superstructure of bourgeois life.

The historical tension between subjective consciousness and all that is externalized from it is, however, never genuinely resolved in the bourgeois sphere of the picture gallery or the museum; for this regime of free leisure is founded on the denial of all that property of surplus labor to the many, which is the asserted right of the few. Something of the violence that this privilege entails finds its way into transcendental idealism's rejection of ontology. As the regime of private property erects the fence and closes the door so as to muffle the suffering of those without property, so too Kant and Schopenhauer distance themselves from the reality of nature. This distancing is an essential element of their conception of reason. It is only through the most dramatic distancing of reason from the "in-itselfness" of the world—the transformation of nature into merely aesthetic concepts or, what is more or less the same thing, in the total assimilation of it into the Ego in Fichte's philosophy—that transcendental idealism attains an identity between subject and object.

As a reflection of the vantage point of the enlightened bourgeoisie, this irresolvable tension cannot be properly comprehended without reference to its concealed, yet ultimately illusory, utopian promise. Ironically, the ideological hubris that taints Fichte's championing of the domination of nature for its own sake—which we will soon come to in more detail—articulates in estranged form a potentially rational integration of humanity within its conditions of natural becoming. Only by completely reshaping nature in accordance with its underlying potentialities for reason—in short, by replacing its capricious aspect with an order that is rationally determined by a community of reasoned beings—could humanity redeem the historical promise of nature. This utopian image is given its most explicit and perhaps most poetic treatment in Schiller's *Aesthetic Letters*, which were, as is well known, strongly influenced by Kant's aesthetics. But its origins perhaps lie further back still, in Gottfried Herder's theme of *analogy*, which his bitter opponent Kant felt obliged to add to his third *Critique*—in the aesthetic unity between nature, the "in-itself," and the ordered, inner world of reason.

Yet in Kant, Fichte and Schopenhauer (and perhaps even Schiller), this concealed utopian hope of enlightened, universalistic liberalism never attains a concrete form; it is only ever present as a kind of abstract aesthetic unity. This abstraction, by the limit of its very form, subtly denies the principle of hope within itself—the *concrete, socially integrated* harmony between productive human activity and nature. The realization of such hope would require precisely the cessation of class antagonisms that the Ur-bourgeois competition of private interests would never permit to take place. In the midst of such repression and its historical context, reverence for nature is relegated to the domain of aesthetics and its actual despoliation at the hands of an ethically unhindered labor power remains securely in place. Failing revolutionary mediation, this image of natural subsumption beneath labor has since degenerated into ideology. By way of a perennial appeal to this image, it has become all too easy for the political and economic elites of capitalist societies to portray the actually existing degradation of nature as a necessary process in the pursuit of vague absolutes such as "progress" or "liberty." Nonetheless, the assertion of an a priori antagonism between humanity and nature is an ideological archetype that nowadays seems very distant from utopia indeed. For it still bears the traces of the antagonistic society that subsumes human relationships beneath the predatory marketplace and reduces all creative human endeavors into the form of abstract labor.

Following in the wake of such allegorical impulses, it is unsurprising that Kant's transcendental idealism construes the living reality of the world in terms of an essence no less arbitrary than that of the nature it wishes to expel, namely, the "reason" of an isolated subject and its various cognitive categorizations. At its best, as Adorno has demonstrated in a series of lectures, Kant's philosophy finds the objective in the subjective, but even this is constrained into the purely cognitive categories of logic that make up the core of his epistemology.[3] It is this socially mediated "limit" that emerges in Kant's epistemic categories (in Horkheimer's and Adorno's phraseology, a "block" on consciousness), a limit that fuels the motor of an epistemological anti-naturalism. This can be observed more closely in Kant's characterization of the thing-in-itself.[4]

The Kantian "Block" and the Distancing of Reason from Nature

At the birth of the bourgeois enlightenment a wide social and historical rift opened, a rift that swallowed up all it could of the social relationships that preceded it. The colonial bayonets and guns of the emerging market order, however, effaced more than a diverse constellation of communitarian cultures. They effaced our very contact with the past, the utopian dreams and myths constitutive of feudalism and medieval communalism, the intricate lifeways of a "nature" subject to the mediating limits of scholastic philosophy, theology, and the prevailing power structure, as well as the natural terrors of famine and plague that still haunt our imaginations today. And yet, with the advanced development of industrial technology that capitalism promised, some form of ecological reconciliation, of an ordered nature made safe and hospitable for human beings, may have seemed possible in the ethical purview of liberal universalism. Such a possibility, however, would crucially rely on the authentic unity of a subject and object emancipated from social suffering, a suffering that the early political economists, in their naivete, often believed would be abolished merely by capitalism's technological revolutions. What was really required for achievement of this was not the preservation of a hierarchical class society as the fait accompli of technological innovation, but a revolution within the social structure itself that would reconcile it to its rational potentialities. In the words of the younger Adorno, such a possibility of reconciliation is grasped as a *concrete* utopia. "In its proper place, even epistemologically, the relationship of subject and object would lie in a peace achieved between human beings as well as between them and their Other. Peace is the state of differentiation without domination, with the differentiated participating in each other."[5]

Kant's epistemology was formulated at a time when the development of capitalist industry was only in its infancy and still may have seemed to presage such ethical possibilities. Nevertheless, it bears the early residues of a class vantage point, a vantage point that carries the historical split between object and subject—whether in the form of human/nature, master/slave, laborer/owner, or whatever else—at its core. Consistent with this, the separation of subject and object comes to occupy the role of the leitmotif in Kant's separation of the empirical world from the a priori. Ethical determinations take place within the domain of a walled-off and socially abstracted subjectivity; the abstraction of the "categorical imperative" is merely one example. The generally dualistic approach of Kant's philosophy tends to obscure the preformation and continuation of concepts such as ethics, aesthetics, reason, and so on, in realm of social determination; it fails to grasp the extent to which the so-called "imperatives" of reason are concretely formed within historical relations of social life.

Accordingly, one of the most characteristic aspects of Kant's ontology is what Hegel rephrased as the concept of "limit," a concept redolent in Kant's claim that the "thing-in-itself" is essentially unknowable. The mind knows only, according to Kant, the shadows of reality; it knows only the effect produced by the interactions between the external object and sense perception. Kantian epistemology takes as given that subject and object are clearly delineated and immediately present as two mutually exclusive realms. Consequently, for Kant the possibility of a *social* experience of the object (and thus of nature, both inner and outer) is riven into the form of the merely representational (synthetic *a priori*) knowledge of the subject. The *Critique of Pure Reason* is a system that sets out to prove the infallibility of such a conception, yet on grounds that presuppose the very epistemological chasm that they would attempt to prove. It thereby concludes that philosophy cannot penetrate into the actual content of its object but only engage with its residues as they manifest within the realm of subjective representation (*Vorstellung*). This is perhaps most directly stated in a passage of the *Critique of Pure Reason* from the solution of the cosmological dialectic:

> The faculty of sensuous intuition is properly a receptivity—a capacity of being affected in a certain manner by representations, the relation of which to each other is a pure intuition of space and time—the pure forms of sensibility. These representations, in so far as they are connected and determinable in this relation (in space and time) according to laws of the unity of experience, are called *objects*. The non-sensuous cause of these representations [the thing-in-itself] is completely unknown to us, and hence cannot be intuited as an object.[6]

This allegedly "cosmological" dualism—which resonates throughout all three of Kant's *Critiques*—registers a key moment of the bourgeois social psychology that was to achieve its most lasting culmination in the decades following the French Revolution. This was the implicit notion that human civilization—and by implication, human mind itself—had attained its constitutive identity sui generis, as a unique ontological phenomenon birthed out of an irrevocable antithesis with nature, indeed with bodily experience itself.[7] As has often been observed, this assertion may have been already present in Descartes's notion of an ontological separation between internal reason and external phenomena, that is, the *res cogito* and *res extensa*, a separation that is preserved intact through Kant's assertion that the "sensuous cause" of the things-in-themselves "are completely unknown to us."[8] Kant, however, gave such dualism a decisive turn in equating nature with an unknowable contingency—a reality external to reason. Hence how, even in the thought of the great "universalist" Kant, "reason" already begins to assume the shape of a disciplinary tool that symbolizes not merely the conquest of an externalized nature but also, and bound up within precisely that nature, the repression of the social discontents that are never far beneath the streets of the triumphal procession of world-historical "reason."

As Hegel later observes of this dualism, it opens up an abyss between subject and object in Kant's philosophy that is never really resolved:

> When Kant (in the *Critique of Pure Reason*, p. 83) comes to speak of the old and famous question "what is truth?" in connexion with logic, he begins by granting (as something trivial) the description of truth as the correspondence of knowledge with its object—a definition which is of great and even of the highest value. If this is recalled in connexion with the fundamental assertion of transcendental idealism, namely, that cognition by means of reason is not capable of apprehending the things-in-themselves, and that reality lies utterly outside the Notion, then it is clear immediately that such a reason, which cannot establish a correspondence between itself and its object (the things-in-themselves), is an untrue idea; and equally untrue are things-in-themselves which do not correspond with the Notion of reason, a Notion which does not correspond with reality, and a reality which does not correspond with the Notion.[9]

This crucial contradiction of the Kantian philosophy forms the centerpiece of what Adorno has termed the epistemological "block" in Kant's thought. Adorno remarks on the role of this "block" between different "realms" of knowledge in Kant's philosophy and its connection with Descartes's dualism:

> This Kantian block can be understood as a form of unmediated Cartesian dualism that is reflexive, that reflects upon itself. It is a dualism in which a great chasm yawns between inner and outer, a chasm that can never be bridged. This chasm is the chasm of the alienation of human beings from one another, and the alienation of human beings from the world of things. This alienation is in fact socially caused; it is created

by the universal exchange relation. Through the idea that our knowledge is blocked Kantian philosophy expresses . . . the idea that in this society marked by radical alienation, we are denied access to existing reality as if by a blank wall.[10]

Thus, the ontological reality of nature tends to recede into the static unknowability of the contingent, of the shadows beyond the cognitive forms of epistemology. What remains as the ground of reason and ethical life is little more than the ahistorical abstraction of a "subject" in which reality alone is preformed and completed. Adorno observes of this that "the abstraction characteristic of [Kant's] transcendental subject is nothing but the internalized and hypostatized form of man's domination of nature . . . com[ing] into being through the elimination of qualities, through the reduction of qualitative distinctions to quantitative forms."[11] Furthermore:

> As soon as it is fixed without mediation, the separation [of subject and object] becomes ideology, its normal form. Mind then arrogates to itself the status of being absolutely independent—which it is not: mind's claim to independence announces its claim to domination. Once radically separated from the object, subject reduces the object to itself; subject swallows object, forgetting how much it is object itself.[12]

Adorno touches here upon a quite crucial point. It is precisely in mind's illusory claim to independence that the domination and assimilation of nature into its own realm is signaled. In this epistemic gesture is contained the hubris of bourgeois society at large, which denies to nature the very possibility of an unfolding substance differentiated from the instrumental reason of a market relationship. Such a relationship renders its concrete qualities into mere quantities, its forests and mineral architecture into abstract "wealth," "resources" or "commodities," and its living biosphere into little more than dead matter to be shaped by a mechanistic science. This ideological anti-naturalism still resides with us today, whether in the empty talk of advertising and mass culture or in the crudely positivistic "paradigms" of well-meaning, yet naive ecological science and city planning catchphrases.

However, it also formed a necessary point of departure and a negative moment or side in the development of Hegel's philosophy—and, much later, Bookchin's social ecology. For Bookchin's dialectical naturalism, it is perhaps the most ideological aspect of Kant's philosophy—mind's claim to independence—that forms a crucial point of determinate negation in the struggle for an ecological society. Bookchin, indeed, laments that Kant

> . . . opened the way to an epistemological focus on *systems of knowledge* rather than a naturalistic focus on *systems of facts*. Facticity itself was absorbed within systems of knowledge, and the Greek *onta*, the "really existing things," were displaced by *episteme*, our "knowledge" of the now "unknowable" *onta*.[13]

Through this reification of a divide between knowledge and the in-itself came the loss of the ethical nuances that much pre-Kantian philosophy, as early as the presocratics, once infused into its naturalistic ontologies. "Lost in this development," Bookchin notes, "were the *onta* that alone constitute the underpinnings of nature philosophy, which now had to be distinguished from Kantian philosophies of the nature of knowing."[14] For Bookchin, Kant's philosophy is symbolic of the bourgeois enlightenment's ideological break with pre-enlightenment conceptions of nature, particularly the vibrant outgrowths of presocratic philosophy that emphasized an *ethical continuity* between natural history and the historical cultures of human consociation. Without endorsing the problematic reifications of this earlier naturalistic philosophy, we might observe that the ecological tragedy of the bourgeois enlightenment is reflected in Kant's divestiture of nature to the status of a mere externality, or an abstract aestheticism, rather than as a participatory agent in the social fabric of human community. This limitation would prepare the way for tendencies to come; for Kantian epistemology establishes the necessary precondition for an even more drastically anti-ecological metaphysics in the system of Fichte.

An Alternative Perspective on Kant: Schiller's *Aesthetic Letters*

For all of its failings, Kant's aesthetic theory educes another moment of reflection that is evocative of a complementarity, albeit only within the realm of art. Schiller's *Aesthetic Letters* developed this theme further. Their point of departure was not the earlier critiques of Kant but rather Kant's *Critique of Judgment*, a work that often seems to moderate the rivenness that was at the heart of his *Critique of Pure Reason* and *Critique of Practical Reason*. The work is unique in Kant's writings insofar as it exudes a Herderian sensitivity to the identity between the potentialities of reason and those of nature, and by implication those of subject and object; he often speaks of a "harmony" between the rational and good (realized in art) and the concept of the beautiful as it appears in the landscapes of the natural world:

> There is . . . something in our judgements upon nature which makes us attentive to its purposiveness for our Understanding—an endeavour to bring, where possible, its dissimilar laws under higher ones, though still always empirical—and thus, if successful, makes us feel pleasure in that harmony of these with our cognitive faculty, which harmony we regard as merely contingent.[15]

Kant's conceptualization of judgment, what is more, practically invokes Aristotle's social theory, which anchored the gregariousness of the human species in quasi-biological terms:

> Empirically the Beautiful interests us only in *society*. If we admit the impulse of society as natural to man [sic], and his fitness for it and propensity to it, i.e. *sociability*, as a requisite for man as a being destined for society, and so as a property belonging to *humanity*, we cannot escape from regarding taste as a faculty for judging everything in respect of which we can communicate our *feeling* to all other men, and so as a means of furthering that which every one's natural inclination desires.[16]

These humane sentiments, often overlooked by devotees of Kant's bourgeois politics, were to go on to influence Schiller. Schiller writes the following in one of his *Aesthetic Letters*:

> Nature begins with Man [sic] no better than with the rest of her works: she acts for him where he cannot yet act as a free intelligence for himself. But it is just this that constitutes his humanity, that he does not rest satisfied with what Nature has made of him, but possesses the capacity of retracing again, with his reason, the steps which she anticipated with him, of

remodelling the work of need into a work of his free choice, and of elevating physical into moral necessity.[17]

There is perhaps no other passage in the philosophy of the early nineteenth century that could so eloquently anticipate the logic of a dialectical naturalism than the preceding. The notion that humanity, rather than dissolving itself into an antediluvian "natural law" as Rousseau would have it or a realm of "pure" reason severed from the "unknowable" empirical world as the younger Kant might suggest, must rather "retrace" nature's determinations through its conscious reason, bringing it into an identity with ethical life; that humanity "remodels" the "work of need into a work of free choice"; and above all, that it elevates "physical into *moral* necessity," is just as much a formulation for a dialectical naturalism as for an aesthetic tract. This can be traced to the fact that Schiller, contrary to what has become of the ideology of Romanticism, identifies the very foundation of human identity in the measure of its capacity for conscious reason. In and through this reason, nature is rescued from its positivistic caricature of a vacillating matter and restored to a consciously ordered, purposive, creative, and ultimately playful substance.

There is a further dialectical nuance in Schiller's *Letters* that evokes this differentiated unity in terms that could have been highly favorable to the development of a dialectical naturalism as a countering principle to the anti-naturalist values of the bourgeois enlightenment. Schiller maintains that the work of "retracing" nature through reason remains within the rational equilibrium determined by nature: humanity's own self-development, its trajectory of becoming, is to transform what is unconscious and biological into that which is conscious and ethical. Schiller thus expands Kant's rather too abstract aesthetic theory into what might be termed a "social" theory, rich with historical implications. Rather than construing that enlightenment implies a "break" with nature—a typical bourgeois prejudice—Schiller's imagery articulates this process as one of rational becoming, a becoming implicit within the very unfolding of natural history:

> When . . . Reason introduces her moral unity into physical society, she must not injure the multiplicity of Nature. When Nature strives to maintain her multiplicity in the moral structure of society, there must be no rupture in its moral unity; the triumphant form rests equidistant from uniformity and confusion.[18]

> The character of the time must first . . . recover from its deep degradation; in one place it must cast off the blind force of Nature, and in another return to her simplicity, truth and fullness—a task for more than a single century.[19]

In this nuanced dialectical formulation, according to which humanity must both cast off the "blind force" of nature and yet return to its "simplicity," we get a prescient glimpse of Hegel's model of sublation (*Aufhebung*), or determinate negation. For what is implied here is nothing short of a dialectical transcendence of reality according to its most ethical potentialities: a simultaneous bringing into nature what is rational, and a bringing into reason what is natural. In this way, Schiller's reformulation of Kant's aesthetic theory presented a reconfiguration of the concept of nature that placed it firmly within a complementary continuum of human-nature relations. It is this continuum that forms the basis for a dialectical concept of nature, and ultimately a dialectical naturalism, through the rescuing of the substance banished to the realm of the contingent by bourgeois thought.

Fichte's Nature-Concept as the Non-Ego

Both Kant's and Schiller's aesthetic theory spoke to the most universal and humanistic moments of the historical transition from the struggles of the burgher class to the triumph of the bourgeois class. However this moment, lacking further social revolutions that could alone transform them into truly universal principles, could only terminate with the purely idealistic concept of freedom in the realm of art; its human realization was still lacking. It is within this context that a critical analysis of the nature-concept of Kant's most immediate and eminent successor Johann Fichte (1762–1814) may begin. For, following out in theory the egoistic morality of the factory owner that took root in practice, Fichte does away with the very notion of an objective world, still present in Kant in the form of the noumenal realm; consciousness becomes for him the sole ground of being. Fichte's basic dictum, as extrapolated in the *Science of Knowledge*, is that the Ego posits itself into an objective world and then, returning into itself after having absorbed the content of the non-Ego, becomes the total ground of reason, that is, the Absolute. Nature assumes the appearance of, in Horkheimer's words, "mere material, mere stuff to be dominated, without any other purpose than that of this very domination."²⁰ Gunther Zöller emphasizes the ontological basis of this appearance: "[Fichte] transforms Kant's theoretical idealism, which grounds empirical reality by recourse to the cognitive forms of the subject, into a practical, and ultimately ethical, idealism built on the basic law of rational willing."²¹ Accordingly, Fichte is interested in the nature-concept only insofar as it can be conceived in the form of the determinate: as the "*conditions* for the possibility of self-consciousness."²²

Yet this transformation of the Ego from the simple a priori to the Absolute, that is, from the mere judgment seat of truth (as it was for his predecessor Kant) to the ground of all reality through its rational willing, is by no means inconsistent with the general schema of Kantian idealism. In fact, it can be considered as but a further phase of logical development. Ludwig Feuerbach, in his *Principles of the Philosophy of the Future*, illustrates precisely how Fichte's conception of the Ego as Absolute is a "natural" derivation from Kant's underlying skepticism:

> The Kantian philosophy is the contradiction of *subject and object, essence and existence, thinking and being*. In it, essence falls into the sphere of the intellect and existence into that of the senses. *Existence without essence is mere appearance*—these are sensuous things; *essence without existence is mere thought*—these are entities of the intellect and noumena; they are thought of but they lack existence—at least for us—and objectivity; they are things in themselves, the *true* things; only they are not *real* things, and consequently not objects for the intellect, that is, they can neither be determined nor known by the intellect. But what a contradiction to separate the truth from reality and reality from the truth! If we therefore eliminate this contradiction, we have the philosophy of identity in which the *objects of the intellect*, that is, the *objects that are true because they are thought* are also the real objects, in which the essence and constitution of the *objects* of the intellect correspond to the essence and constitution of the intellect or of the subject, and where the subject is no longer limited and conditioned by something existing apart from it and contradicting its essence.²³

By abandoning the notion of a material reality grounded within a continuum of natural and social history, and by reducing the ground of reality into the abstract freedom of the "Ego" and its communion with other Egos, Fichte's epistemology thus expressed a contrary movement. On the one hand, conceived as freedom, reason, and the universal "estate" that prevails over the arbitrariness of first nature, the Ego becomes the ornamental *symbolism* of a humanity that is freed from first nature's limitations. Hence Fichte's frequent encomiums to collective labor. "An individual's estate," he observes, is "determined through the reciprocal interaction between him [sic] and society, a reciprocal interaction that has to be initiated by the individual."[24] And as a testament to the social reciprocity of labor, Fichte grasps the liberatory dimension of technological progress, although he casts it in a characteristically negative image:

> If humanity is to make any considerable advance, then it must waste as little time and power as possible on mechanical work; nature must become mild, matter must become pliant, everything must become such that, with only a little effort, it will grant human beings that which they need and the struggle against nature will no longer be such a pressing matter.[25]

Formally, this notion of mechanical labor and a universal social interest in minimizing it is a humanistic thread that runs through Fichte's formulation of the philosophy of history. Yet it is humanistic only in a very illusory sense: for the surplus of labor power is dissolved into the jurisprudence of bourgeois private property in Fichte's concept of "natural right," placing it firmly on a class basis.[26] The abstract freedom to labor, to dominate and transform nature, conceals the class that ultimately benefits from the imposition of the wage system; it also obscures, beneath this principle of the unlimited expansion of abstract labor, the violence committed against nature by unchecked technological domination. As the advocate of such bourgeois interest masquerading as universal interest, he is able to write:

> From the standpoint of moral judgement all estates have the same worth. Reason's end is furthered in each estate, beginning with that estate that wrests from the soil its fruits, which is a condition for the preservation of our species in the sensible world, through the scholar, who thinks of future ages and works for them, and including the legislator and the wise ruler, who establishes institutions that embody the thoughts of the researcher for the well-being of the most remote generations.[27]

Couched in such rosy imagery of vocational harmony and ever-increasing production, Fichte attempts to justify in distinctly *ethical* terms the Victorian mystique of the "struggle against nature," a struggle made to appear as the substance of the World-Spirit. It reflects the conviction that pristine nature is not adequate to humanity's historical possibilities but must be reworked in order for human potentialities to be realized.

On the other hand, Fichte's philosophy of history, precisely because of its strictly formal and abstract character, all too easily becomes complicit in the cultural perpetuation of bourgeois domination, of the principle of enlightenment as instrumental reason. Horkheimer's distillation of this ideological side of Fichte is inimitable:

> In Descartes' philosophy, the dualism of ego and nature is somewhat blunted by his traditional Catholicism. The later development of rationalism, and then of subjective idealism, tended increasingly to mediate the dualism by attempting to dissolve the concept of nature—and ultimately all the content of experience—in the ego, conceived of as transcendental. But the more radically this trend is developed, the greater the influence of the old, more naive, and for that reason less irreconcilable dualism of the Cartesian theory of substance in the ego's own domain. The most striking example of this is the extreme subjectivist-transcendental philosophy of Fichte. In his early doctrine, according to which the sole *raison d'être* of the world lies in affording a field of activity to the imperious transcendental self, the relationship between the ego and nature is one of tyranny. The entire universe becomes a tool of the ego, although the ego has no substance or meaning except in its own boundless activity. Modern ideology, though much closer to Fichte than is generally believed, has cut adrift from such metaphysical moorings, and the antagonism between an abstract ego as undisputed master and a nature stripped of inherent meaning is obscured by vague absolutes such as the ideas of progress, success, happiness, or experience.[28]

In stripping nature of inherent meaning, Fichte thereby redevelops the skepticism that was at the core of Kant's philosophy and deploys it to form what has since become the centrifugal dogma of the bourgeois philosophy of history: the transformation of the domination of nature from a merely temporal and spatial *means* to realize human potentialities, into an unquestionably rational and metaphysical *end in itself*. It is the affirmation of such an instrumental conception of nature that divests Fichte's philosophy of history of genuine dialectic and mystifies natural history's substance into the purely negative and dead "conditions" of social self-determination. This assimilation of natural history beneath a cover concept of "intersubjectivity" or "social construction" remains influential in the prominent Neo-Kantian and systems theory–derived philosophical approaches that are common today, such as that of Habermas. In this sense, Fichte's Ego principle endures as a categorical moment in bourgeois enlightenment epistemology that continues to pervade many conventional attempts to think nature.[29]

"The Struggle of Spirit with Itself"

This negative characterization of nature is closely connected to another ideological allegory in Fichte, namely, where the "struggle" of spirit with itself proclaims itself *as* history. On this basis does natural history's developing complexity and potential for ethical mediation once again pass over into the empty bourgeois dogma of the freedom of practical reason. For Fichte, the primacy of subjective, moral willing begets an antagonistic and conflict-ridden social ground, a "struggle" with other subjects for the recognition of this willing. "In the human species," he writes in one of his earlier essays, "spirit constantly develops by means of this struggle of one spirit with another. Thus the whole species becomes richer in spirit."[30] This notion of social history as a self-constitutive process of mutual recognition or misrecognition taken up by Fichte, Hegel, and more recently Honneth, asserts struggle as the very motor of society. But there is an ever-present danger that lurks in the philosophy of recognition: namely, that in positing the struggle for recognition as an abstract general law of social development, the cover concept gives precedence to the victors of the struggle and sweeps aside those vanquished forces that lie outside the concept, yielding to precisely the kind of identity thinking, or myths of constitutive intersubjectivity, that earlier critical theorists such as Adorno rigorously sought to avoid in their own work. To take but one concrete example from Fichte's philosophy: although his work *Characteristics of the Present Age* presents an account of the origins and development of class society, it does so in a way that carefully disguises the repressive pathos of domination that shapes the historical victors of the valorized "struggle."[31] Even more dubiously, through the presupposition that the World-Spirit's resolution of the struggle for recognition is inherently rational, it "naturalizes" that reality into an appearance of freedom rather than one rooted in psychological relationships of hierarchy, aggression, and renunciation of earthly happiness. It thereby becomes complicit, as Adorno observes similarly of Hegel's *Philosophy of History*, with the ideological hegemony of the victors silencing the voices of the vanquished.[32] Precisely because spirit's struggle with itself is rendered uncritically into the a priori rational substance of history, the concrete relations underlying this substance must remain unscrutinized, glossed over by a series of all too harmonious "narratives."

This also occurs in Fichte at a more fundamental, more ontological level. For what is lost in the nebulous "struggle" of spirit with itself are the determinations of *nature* as an agent in human history; that biological needs, as Feuerbach and Freud both later emphasized, are no less constitutive of the anthropological and psychological dimension of human activity; and that the metabolism in which nature becomes society and society nature illuminates a richly biological dimension to a social history whose paved-over potentialities must not be overlooked. Yet in the last analysis, transcendental idealism develops only one side of the historical metabolism between nature and society; class relations, qua Fichte's "Ego," are hypostatized as the negating principle of a nature that is even more emphatically than Kant banished to the category of the accidental, the profane, that which is lacking in Spirit.

This culminates in one of the most ideological features of Fichte's philosophy: the notion that the Ego and non-Ego enter into "reciprocal determination." This is a most prominent theme, for instance, in the germinal work *The Science of Knowledge*. This work famously terminates with the Ego principle that has absorbed the otherness of the non-Ego and thus attained an identity between "Reason" and the fate of the world. Notably, the Ego does not arrive at a point in logic wherein the Ego and non-Ego actually coexist in a state of symbiosis or complementarity. Instead, "reciprocal determination" is construed in terms of actual domination: the "regulation" of the non-Ego by the Ego.

> For the knowledge of the sensuous world, that is to say, for natural sciences, philosophy is *regulative*, showing what we must require of nature, and how we have to question her. But

its influence on the sentiments of mankind in general consists chiefly in this, that it brings power, courage and self-confidence to man, by showing him that he and his whole fate depend solely upon himself, or by placing him on his own feet.[33]

What is obscured in this passage is that, contra the bourgeois deification of the unlimited expansion of labor, human activity does not depend entirely upon itself, does not stand entirely upon its own feet. It is limited rationally by the potentialities contained within its ecological context, within the possibilities of becoming latent within a given eco-community. In its obscuring of this, Fichte's rhetorical flourishes mask a subtle affirmation of ideological allegory: the basic logic of subordination and domination of nature is portrayed through a semblance of harmony and reciprocity with its other. The subordination and incorporation of the non-Ego beneath the authority principle of the Ego is portrayed not as a moment of suffering but, in line with official public relations, as a moment of triumph.

It was Hegel, despite his own allegiances to Fichte, who identified precisely this covert rationalization in the *Difference* essay:

> The non-Ego has no positive character, to be sure; but it does have the negative character of being something other, i.e., something opposite in general. As Fichte expresses this: intelligence is conditioned by an impact, but the impact is in itself entirely undetermined. Because the non-Ego expresses only the negative, something undetermined, even this character pertains to it only through the Ego's positing. . . . The positing of the opposite in general, the positing of something that is absolutely undetermined by the Ego, is itself a positing of [and by] the Ego.[34]

The positing of the opposite as dominated, therefore, is not a process of reconciliation or reciprocity but of conquest. The aggression directed toward nature and the dispossessed alike becomes an obscured moment in their "rational" integration with the authority principle of the ascendant class. Yet in a time when nature's biological integrity is threatened on a global scale, the cracks in this affirmative mythology of the bourgeois enlightenment are showing through its façade more than ever.

Enlightened anti-naturalism denies the possibility of a reconciliation between nature and humanity, a reconciliation premised not on ceaseless and boundless human activity but on its ethical integration with the biosphere. The hope for such integration runs up against the politically entrenched interest to preserve the material basis of a deeply riven society. The absolute abstractions of Ego, Spirit, and Reason constitute the false harmony of market society in the enduring, yet hypocritical pathos of the bourgeois enlightenment; a free and ecological society alone could resolve this pathos and free it from its contradictions. The echoes of Kantian and Fichtean epistemology endure within the cultural hegemony of late capitalism precisely because the historical moment that should have transcended them was aborted; because both enshrine the false reality principle according to which the bourgeois relation to nature, which aggressively appropriates its other, is itself "naturalized." But what appears in enlightened bourgeois society to be a rational freedom from nature's burdens remains blind to the concrete potentialities that exist within the material conditions of that society, and with them, humanity's salvation from a self-imposed ecological calamity.

Hegel's Critique of the Concept of Natural Law

> The significance of that "absolute commandment," know thyself—whether we look at it in itself or under the historical circumstances of its first utterance—is not to promote mere self-knowledge in respect of the particular capacities, character, propensities, and foibles of the single self. The knowledge it commands means that of man's genuine reality—of what is essentially and ultimately true and real—of spirit as the true and essential being.
>
> —G. W. F. Hegel, *Encyclopedia of the Philosophical Sciences* (1816)

One of the most remarkable works of Hegel is the youthful *System of Ethical Life* (1803), a work that contains the resolution of an immanent critique of natural law arguments (first initiated in an earlier critique of Kant's and Fichte's conceptualizations of natural law). Through a close examination of the contradictions of the bourgeois concept of "natural law," Hegel indicates the necessity of exposing the mystifying function of what Marxist theory would later designate in the form of "reification." This is to be achieved immanently: in revealing that bourgeois "natural law" arguments have their ultimate point of origin in actually existing social relations. Natural law, disrobed of its ideological raiment, is illuminated to be not a manifestation of an unchangeable "nature" but actually a series of mystifications rooted within a particular period of historical consciousness, the ideological hegemony of which is made to appear static, universal, and ultimately "natural." In so doing, Hegel begins to establish the possibility of a dialectical naturalism within its negative dimension: namely, as a self-reflective revelation of how present social relations become fixed in consciousness, and thereby the appearance of nature becomes false. Although Hegel did not develop the reconstructive dimension that accompanies such negativity in the later philosophy of Bookchin—indeed, the "positivity" of the Hegelian World-Spirit occludes the notional content of a harmonious reconciliation with the natural world—the young Hegel's revolutionary reformulation of the dialectic nonetheless elicits an intellectual tour de force marshaled against the colonization of bourgeois society's consciousness by reified thinking.

In her highly coherent commentary on the *System of Ethical Life*, Gillian Rose connects its themes to those of the earlier essay on natural law:

> It was suggested in the essay on natural law that the relations or lack of identity evident in Kant and Fichte's formal epistemology are correspondent to specific social relations or lack of identity. The *relations* (*Verhältnisse*) re-presented a *relative* part of ethical life which had been presented by Kant and Fichte as the whole, and that part corresponds to the relations (inequalities) of bourgeois private property.[35]

Indeed, as Rose suggests, Hegel shows that

> [t]he concept of equal persons, meaning equal right to own property, presupposes people without property. It presupposes people in all those relations which have not been taken up into the legal concept of 'person.' People who are not persons, who do not have even the right to property are, in Roman property law, things, '*res.*' The formal recognition of private property right presupposes this relation or subordination of others. One 'person' behaves as the 'cause,' 'concept,' or 'unity'

of the other. If this identity has no means (*Mitte*) to mitigate it and transform it, it is the relation of master to slave.[36]

In Rose's summary, this emphasis upon the "whole" exposes, in turn, the illusoriness of bourgeois society's

> . . . ideal of itself as a whole or identity. This unity is negative, for while it recognizes the relations or lack of identity, it only does so in order to dominate and suppress them. It is a moral ideal which subsumes and cancels nature, and hence it reconfirms the unjust property relations on which it is based. Hegel's argument is that any notion of freedom, whether Kant's moral autonomy or Fichte's legal freedom, which is opposed to necessity or the realm of nature, *justifies* the crimes which arise out of the real inequality presupposed by the formal equality of private property relations.[37]

Through this act of misrecognition early bourgeois society arrives at a distorted idea of what "nature" is that reflects far more closely the social ideology of its dominant class—founded on private property and a subsumption of natural potentialities under the capitalist mediation of the commodity form—than the life activity of the dispossessed. Throughout this jurisprudential and political-ideological edifice of misrecognition, Hegel observes, objective nature is never

> . . . present as ethical life; not even the family, far less still the subordinate levels, least of all the negative, is ethical. Ethical life must be the absolute identity of intelligence, with complete annihilation of the particularity and relative identity which is all that the natural relation is capable of; or the absolute identity of nature must be taken up into the unity of the absolute concept and be present in the form of this unity, a clear and also absolutely rich being, an imperfect self-objectification and intuition of the individual in the alien individual, and so the supersession of natural determinacy and formation, complete indifference of self-enjoyment. Only in this way is the infinite concept strictly one with the essence of the individual, and he [sic] is present in his form as true intelligence. He is truly infinite, for all his specific determinacy is annulled, and his

> objectivity is not apprehended by an artificial independent consciousness, nor yet by an intellectual intuition in which empirical intuition is superseded. Intellectual intuition is alone realized by and in ethical life; the eyes of the spirit and the eyes of the body completely coincide. In the course of nature the husband sees flesh of his flesh in the wife, but in ethical life alone does he see the spirit of his spirit in and through the ethical order.[38]

In attempting to sketch the potentialities of nature as distinct from the reified cover concept, Hegel envisions here the "notion" of ethical life as the negation of the partiality, or class character, of bourgeois property relations—a negation essentially founded upon the idea of substantive rather than formal equality.[39] Nevertheless, he stops short of a seemingly necessary further step, that is, to follow the context of this immanent critique more expansively into the possibilities of natural and social history that the "notion" of private property has repressed.

Nonetheless, Hegel reinvigorates a process of dialectic that yields fecund insights into the historical reality of the nature-concept. Unlike many baroque forms of reification, which according to Benjamin had the virtue of involving nature in a natural-historical continuum and thus passing over into the allegorical negation of mythology,[40] Hegel's immanent critique reveals that bourgeois reification is largely divested of its religious and historical antecedents; indeed, its subsumption of nature implies a break with much historical mythology, the forging of a new *mythos* within a constellation of Victorian and protestant images of nature. Were we to follow out this critique further than Hegel did in his time, we could attempt to identify the mythopoeic process in terms of the prevailing archetypes governing liberal ideology, such as those of individualism, negative liberty, and the sacrosanct function of the marketplace, in relation to the place that the nature-concept occupies within the rhetorical architecture of these tropes. In so doing we would be obliged to make a crucial further observation: namely, that in addition to the ideological concept of "natural law" that prevails in the form of bourgeois private property relations, this is only made possible in the first instance by the epistemological subsumption of nature beneath an ahistorical concept that sublimates beneath itself those discontents that might presage a more truly rational, more "ecological" relationship with the biosphere.

The Representation of Nature as Reification

Hegel's insights into bourgeois natural law frequently revealed the class basis of the universal claims of the bourgeoisie at the beginning of the nineteenth century. Yet for Hegel to have developed this observation more holistically would have been inconceivable in light of his failure to take the dialectic into the broader ideological myth of the bourgeois enlightenment: the denial of the ecological dimension of human history. We have already seen, by way of Kant and Fichte, how this denial takes place at the level of their epistemology. In the younger Hegel's case, the dialectic is often employed as the basis of immanent criticism of bourgeois "representations" or "misrecognitions" of the natural world, a theme that is carried through into his later *Lectures on Aesthetics*. In his *Philosophy of History*, however, nature is uncritically subsumed beneath the determinations of spirit in a form that seems to closely emulate Fichte's earlier schema in *Characteristics of the Present Age*. It is at this juncture that Hegel arguably turns his back on a genuine dialectic of nature and spirit—a defect that was to serve as a lodestone for the young Feuerbach's critiques of his teacher's philosophy. Regardless of the limitations of his immanent critique, however, Hegel's contrast of classical and romantic art reveals an important corollary of his critique of mythopoeic thinking.

The hallmark of Hegel's discussion of art is the historical contrast between Greek *Schein* presented as a "shining forth" of community relations, and the *Schein* of romantic art as "illusion" or "deception," a form of represented nature depicted as the purely abstract substance of the bourgeois subject's illusory sense of freedom.[41] The phenomenological basis of romantic art emerges historically as the culturally mediated *concept* of nature, the mythopoeic representation of nature-society relations. In the world of the Hellenes, by contrast, "individual life is substantial life," precisely because the Hellenes live in a world that is socially and politically integrated from the most basic administrative functions to the standards of social deliberation demanded by Pericles. The obvious model for Hegel's classical conception of art is free Athens, though one may wonder about how "substantial" life was for women and for the slaves. However, Hegel's emendations of what he calls the "Classical Ideal" cannot be read too cynically, for one must always bear in mind that they are grounded in the *ideal*, not merely the historical reality, of a democratic Hellenism. This ideal (it is contended) is inseparable from the art of the Hellenic period and "shines forth" in its depiction of the beautiful. The Classical Ideal corresponds with the concrete potentialities of the Hellenic world, a world in which, as Hegel was to phrase it in the introduction to the *Philosophy of History*, the Greeks had the virtue of knowing that some were free and others were slaves. The significance of this political consciousness cannot be overstated, not least because we still live in a world deeply immersed in the fictive, bourgeois mythology of subjective freedom: a world in which the many who are not free nonetheless believe, following the ideology of Kantian and Fichtean practical reason, that they are free.

Such an abstract and subjectivized conception of "freedom," Hegel suggests at many points in his canon, is a characteristic pathology of societies of objective unfreedom, an unfreedom that carries over and is reflected in the abstract subjectivity of romantic art. Such a pathological "representation"—in modern phraseology we would phrase this "ideology"—was purportedly unknown to the peoples of Hellenic Greece:

> Classical beauty with its infinite range of content, material, and form is the gift vouchsafed to the Greek people, and we must honour this people for having produced art in its supreme vitality. The Greeks in their immediate real existence lived in the happy milieu of both self-conscious subjective freedom and the ethical substance. They did not persist on the one hand in the unfree Oriental unity which has a religious and political despotism as its consequence; this is because the subject, losing his self, is submerged in the one universal substance, or in some particular aspect of it, since he has no right and therefore no support in himself as a person. Nor, on the other hand, did the Greeks make the advance to that deepening of subjective life in which the individual subject separates himself from the whole and the universal in order to be independent in his own inner being; and only through a higher return into the inner totality of a purely spiritual world does he attain a reunification with the substantial and essential. On the contrary, in Greek ethical life the individual was independent and free in himself, though without cutting himself adrift from the universal interests present in the actual state and from the affirmative immanence of spiritual freedom in the temporal present. The universal element in ethical life, and the abstract freedom of the person in his inner and outer

life, remain, in conformity with the principle of Greek life, in undisturbed harmony with one another, and at the time when this principle asserted itself in the actual present in still undamaged purity there was no question of an independence of the political sphere contrasted with a subjective morality distinct from it; the substance of political life was merged in individuals just as much as they sought this their own freedom only in pursuing the universal aims of the whole.[42]

As such, "the beautiful feeling, the sentiment and spirit, of this happy harmony pervades all productions in which Greek freedom has become conscious of itself and portrayed its essence to itself."[43]

For Hegel, then, there is an intimate dialectical connection between political life, ethical life, and the attainment or shining forth of the beautiful in art. It is difficult not to read phrases such as "the substance of political life" and "freedom only in pursuing the universal aims of the whole" as encomiums to a vibrantly democratic public sphere, Hegel's capitulation to monarchism in the *Philosophy of Right* notwithstanding. The beautification of nature by means of its mediation with the ethical life of "spirit" conveys a process of elicitation of potentiality and actualization, only made possible through the democratic life of the *polis*. Uniquely, the dialectical tension between individual freedom and the universal interest that was attained, at least for free male citizens, within the Athenian democracy produced that "deepening of subjective life" that made the highest achievements of art possible.

For Hegel, it is not, then, the mere representation (*Vorstellung*) of nature that embodies the highest forms of art, but its confrontation with the human mind. Most famously, in Hegel's theory of the landscape painting, the artist adds something that is lacking in the original landscape: the mood of the artist, his or her spiritual and ethical substance. Hence the landscape painting is superior to the original landscape.[44] Hegel's theory of the landscape is a potent allegory for the sort of dialectical naturalism that Murray Bookchin would, a little under two centuries later, develop in ever-greater degrees of sophistication. The artist, in mixing her or his creative and ethical foresight into the landscape, beautifies, restores, and accentuates its most pleasing potentialities. The artist draws out of nature particularities of shade, line, contrast, and perspective, allowing to shine forth certain features concealed or underplayed in the original, but still in a form that seeks to do it justice. Similarly, a dialectical naturalism would be a naturalism that acknowledged and protected the integrity of the biosphere—in particular its immense diversity—while accentuating the potentialities within it most pleasing and beneficial to humanity.

However, for Hegel, the great shining forth of art in the Hellenic period was to decline into merely representative and solipsistic tendencies in the feudal era. What Hegel terms "romantic" art reflects Western culture's long passage through Christendom, with its attendant deprecation of the world of "the flesh" and nature and its longing for a purely inner spiritual world of quietistic resignation. Hegel profoundly describes this acculturation of abstract subjectivity as a process of solipsism:

> At the stage of romantic art the spirit knows that its truth does not consist in its immersion in corporeality; on the contrary, it only becomes sure of its truth by withdrawing from the external into its own intimacy with itself and positing external reality as an existence inadequate to itself. Even if, therefore this new content too comprises in itself the task of making itself beautiful, still beauty in the sense hitherto expounded remains for it something subordinate, and beauty becomes the spiritual beauty of the absolute inner life as inherently infinite spiritual subjectivity.[45]

Placed within its proper historical context, this "infinite spiritual subjectivity" debases the relations between humanity and nature to the point that they are stripped of all objective ethical mediation. From its roots in late feudal Christianity, the early bourgeois configuration of culture, epitomized in both Luther's intuitionism and Kierkegaard's irrationalism, comes into its own in a certain sort of debasement of the ethical objectivity of the natural and social worlds, a denial of the very possibility of *an organic social totality*. Ethical life itself dissolves into a denatured social environment that is highly atomized, monadic, and preoccupied with the prerogatives of exchange value and private property relations. This colossal point of departure, which uprooted prebourgeois cultures in unimaginable ways, is a vital clue to understanding the radical import of Hegel's discussion of Romanticism.

In romantic art's disparaging abandonment of an ethical unity of nature and spirit is already contained the pathos of instrumental reason that Fichte had championed, and that Proudhon and the older Marx would later attempt to justify in an unreflective reification of bourgeois values. Yet as Hegel reminds us of the place of nature in the romantic form of art in a sense that keenly anticipates the subsequent novels of Dumas:

> The heroism which may enter here accordingly is no heroism which from its own resources gives laws, establishes organizations, creates and develops situations, but heroism of *submission*. It submits to a determinate and cut and dried [system of divine truth] and no task is left to it but to regulate the temporal order by that, to apply what is higher and absolutely valid to the world confronting it, and to make it prevail in the temporal. But since this absolute content appears compressed into one point, i.e. into the subjective heart, so that all process is transported into the inner life of man, the scope of the subject matter is therefore also infinitely extended again. It opens out into *a multiplicity without bounds*.[46]

It hardly seems coincidental that Hegel's depiction of the romantic form as a "multiplicity without bounds" connotes the decline of an earlier ethical unity that the emerging bourgeois order has corroded in the lives of women and men—a development registered sublimely in Balzac's *Human Comedy*. Protestant capitalism heralds the final dissolution of the social community of the *polis*, which despite official history's prejudicial "narratives" flourished in many of the free communes of the Middle Ages, into a strictly personal relationship with God and money. The ascent of romantic art thus expresses, in its negative dimension, the rationality of a society that has divested itself of an integrated social unity dissolved beneath class antagonisms—in its positive and most ideological dimension, the triumph of romantic transcendence in the form of the novel, "the disappearance of epic symbolisation, the disintegration of form in a nebulous and unstructured sequence of moods and reflections about moods, the replacement of a sensuously meaningful story by psychological analysis."[47] Its triumph signified emphatically what the young Lukács called the uniquely romantic "conflict" between the inner world of the subjective soul and "a world entirely dominated by convention, the full realisation of the concept of a 'second nature'; the quintessence of meaningless laws in which no relation to the soul can be found."[48] Thus in Romanticism "nature" and "spirit" can no longer be comprehended as ethical unity, as they were in the classical or integrated form of the Hellenes. To the extent to which this unity is sought, it is realized strictly within the solipsism of a transcendental subjectivity rather than the redemption of the social totality through its own concrete possibility.

In the unity of its contradictions, the romantic form therefore expresses dialectically both an ethical repugnance toward the alienation of humanity from nature and yet simultaneously, through its all-too-worldly hypostatization of a boundless subjectivity, the most subtle affirmation of this alienation. Turning inward, the "unhappy consciousness" of the romantic temperament finds beauty not in the concealed promise of an ecological society or shared ethical life but in the mystifying phantasmagorias of subjective bliss. Ironically, the perambulating subject of C. D. Friedrich's *Wanderer Above the Sea of Fog*, who is supposed to represent absolute freedom immersed in natural beauty, only serves to reinforce a denuded and reified concept of nature as a Hegelian "multiplicity without bounds." In the form of a hazy and indeterminate fog, "nature" provides no glimpse of the ethical unity of spirit and nature presaged by the social rationality of Hellenic democracy. To be floating free as a "consumer" in the apartments and offices of a totally bureaucratized mass society, a society stripped of all communal significance, is the Promethean curse of the bourgeois world; and yet its cultural counterpart, the neo-romantic dissolution of social relations into the substance of a vague unity between natural law and subjective freedom, serves only to reinforce the reality of social disintegration—and with it the fictive universality of private property and the fetish of the commodity.

Hegel could not have foreseen this development within its more contemporary mutations. Nonetheless, in his reproach of the "unhappy consciousness," the false reconciliations and universality of stoicism, skepticism, and positivism, and ultimately the solipsistic form of romantic art, he bitterly condemned the emerging bourgeois society for its systematic dissolution of *Sittlichkeit* into that battlefield of grasping, Fichtean Egos so devastatingly depicted in severe style by Balzac. This concealed moment of social criticism remains fruitful for an immanent critique of the concept of natural law, for it reveals the mythopoeic representation of nature that must be negated in order to regain a comprehension of nature on its own terms as an object that can be reconciled through an ecological ethics, rather than being subsumed into the cover concept of the non-Ego.

Hegel's Doctrine of the Notion

Hegel's *Science of Logic* further develops an analysis of the historically and socially conditioned process according to which a more dialectical and expansive concept of nature might be accommodated. What is most pertinent in reconstructing Hegel's *Logic* is to bring to life the centrality of his contention that reality is inadequate to its "notion," particularly inherent in the doctrine of "concrete potentiality." This aspect of Hegel's *Logic* forms a crucial cornerstone of a dialectical naturalism: for if the defining feature of dialectical naturalism is its break with bourgeois mythopoesis, then this could only occur in the context of a dialectical process that acknowledges not the merely given—which is always vulnerable to reification—but also the nonconceptual and often subterranean potentialities within the metabolism that conjoins natural history to social history.

In 1807 Hegel had opened the *Phenomenology* with a sustained critique of positivism, and with it the formal logic of identity, expressed as A=A. For Hegel, historical truth can only be represented partially, as a process of perishing and renewal, of becoming. It is only the individual as *conscious* subject who can make sense of the world and see beyond the commonsense view of the present to the all-embracing universal truths that constitute the notion of the objective world. Yet for all this faith in the subject, Hegel saw how, through Kantian philosophy, the duality between reason and social reality was to be preserved. In the words of Marcuse, "in Kant, Hegel declares, reason is limited to an inner realm of the mind and is made powerless over 'things-in-themselves.' In other words, it is not really reason but the understanding that holds sway in the Kantian philosophy."[49] Hegel sought to demonstrate that the world of sense-certainty, which can be readily perceived by human beings, "is an estranged and untrue world so long as man [sic] does not destroy its dead objectivity and recognise himself [sic] and his own life 'behind' the fixed form of things and laws," as Marcuse puts it.[50] Only through moving beyond commonsense understanding can consciousness break away from the false immediacy that becomes, by way of authority and tradition, the received wisdom of the times.

Within the context of the first few sections of the *Phenomenology*, Hegel advances a critique of positivism on the basis of its false representation of reality as the "dead objectivity" of the present. This dead objectivity inheres in the ossified images of tradition, which are "untrue" in that they do not express the potentialities and the contingencies of the thing (that is, its "notion"), but rather mistake the reified, accidental appearance of a given object for the universal form of the object in-itself. This kind of mistaken apprehension is the product of everyday common sense—what the logical positivists would call "ordinary language"—that Hegel characterizes derisively as the "common road" to philosophy, a road that can only give a distorted and necessarily incomplete account of reason.[51]

For Hegel, as opposed to the positivity of this identity thinking, knowledge begins with the senses that perceive a world seemingly of opposition and irreconcilable disunity and ends, through speculative philosophy and its *telos* of absolute knowledge, with recognizing the "logical form" that the notion takes.[52] Moreover, the term "truth," for the dialectical theory of society, captures not the accidental image of the here and now but also history's total movement, its holistic and evolutionary process. Accordingly, the movement of comprehension toward enlightenment is presented by Hegel in three progressive "phases" of consciousness: first, that of mere common sense; second, that of perception; and last, that of conceptual understanding, which can only be arrived at through philosophy.

Sense-certainty, the experience of daily life, is the most seemingly obvious experience of truth. For the Humean philosophy, sense-certainty was held to be the only authentic form of knowledge. Yet Hegel, in illuminating the temporality and ephemeral nature of sense-certainty, seeks to demonstrate that its representation of reality is one-dimensional. He illustrates that to surrender to the mere "here-and-now" of sense-certainty, as skepticism does, is not even logically consistent, for the only form of genuine unity within the diversity of space and time lies within the process of becoming. In Hegel's words:

> It is clear that the dialectic of sense-certainty is nothing else but the simple history of its movement or of its experience, the sense-certainty itself is nothing else but just this history. That is why the natural consciousness, too, is always reaching this result, learning from experience what is true in it; but equally it is always forgetting it and starting the movement all over again. It is therefore astonishing when, in the face of this experience, it is asserted as universal experience and put forward, too as a philosophical proposition, even as the

outcome of Scepticism, that the reality or being of external things taken as Thises or sense-objects has absolute truth for consciousness. To make such an assertion is not to know what one is saying, to be unaware that one is saying the opposite of what one wants to say. The truth for consciousness of a This of sense is supposed to be universal experience; but the very opposite is universal experience. Every consciousness itself supersedes such a truth, as e.g. Here is a tree, or, Now is noon, and proclaims the opposite: Here is *not* a tree, but a house; and similarly, it immediately again supersedes the assertion which set aside the first so far as it is also just such an assertion of a sensuous This. And what consciousness will learn from experience in all sense-certainty is, in truth, only what we have seen viz. the This as a *universal*, the very opposite of what that assertion affirmed to be universal experience.[53]

Therefore, in order to render something in language, tradition and authority constructs it in the false, "reified" form of a timeless and universal character; an *identity*, an essence, is forced upon it by the form-giving compulsion of the subject; it is imposed upon by a "*specific* unity in the diversity of its properties."[54] This denial of the negativity, or nonidentity, of the object is inherent in the formalistic drive toward identity that underpins positivism and other forms of "positive" philosophy. The characteristic ambiguity of dialectical philosophy resides in the omnipresent tension produced between, on the one hand, the identitarian yet false "whole" of the cover concepts, which it is obliged to employ as reference to social reality, and on the other the nonconceptual moments of that reality that stand ajar from its official concept. Without this moment of tension, dialectical philosophy would simply dissolve into the banality of empty tautologies, much like it did in the scholastic period and, more recently, in the treatises of analytic philosophy.

Insofar as this negativity is consistently developed through Hegel's philosophy, the subject's ability to reformulate concepts on the basis of the nonidentical content of objective reality shatters the illusion of common sense to which positivism and skepticism alike ascribe the definition of "reality." For what the subject has that mere empiricism lacks is the ability to ascribe reality to the potential—to that which inheres as a concrete potentiality in the actuality of the given social relations. In contrast, positivism, which would construe reality only in terms of sense-experience or, at most, through perception, is merely the image of an "estranged and untrue" world in Marcuse's summation:[55]

> Positivism, the philosophy of common sense, appeals to the certainty of facts, but, as Hegel shows, in a world where facts do not at all present what reality can and ought to be, positivism amounts to giving up the real potentialities of mankind for a false and alien world. The positivist attack on universal concepts, on the ground they cannot be reduced to observable facts, cancels from the domain of knowledge everything that may not yet be a fact . . . the potentialities of men and things are not exhausted in the given forms and relations in which they may actually appear; it means that men and things are all they have been and actually are, and yet more than all this.[56]

Hegel's holding fast to the universal, against positivism, was ironically to terminate in the mood of resignation to the given forms and relations—precisely under the guise of their identity with the universal concept—that characterizes much of the *Philosophy of Right*. What a dialectical naturalism draws from Hegel is therefore not the Pyrrhic striving for an image of social reality rendered harmonious with the "whole" of the concept. Most radically, rather, it represents the possibility of interrogating the nature-concept negatively, as a *historical* development, thereby liberating thought to be able to see *nature itself* as a history of eco-communities, each with their own compelling range of ever-evolving potentialities.

In elaborating this negative dimension of the nature-concept, a dialectical naturalism draws on Hegel's innovative extrapolation of the Aristotelean notion of potentiality into the phenomenology of history. A decisive feature of this extrapolation begins with Hegel's critique of the nihilism of "formal" or "abstract" potentiality, in which

> . . . possibility [potentiality] is the mere form determination of *identity-with-self* or the form of essentiality. As such it is the relationless, indeterminate receptacle for everything whatever. In the sense of this formal possibility *everything is possible that is not self-contradictory*; hence the realm of possibility is a boundless multiplicity. But each of these manifold entities is *determinate within itself* and *as against another* and contains negation; in general, indifferent *diversity* passes over into *opposi-*

tion; but opposition is contradiction. Therefore *everything* is just as much something contradictory and therefore impossible.[57]

It is evident here that Hegel anticipates the poverty of what one might call vulgar dialectics, that is, those shallow interpretations of the dialectic which perceive it as little more than the statement that "everything is contradiction." What is more, he shows how this primitive, Heraclitean conception of the dialectic, which Plato and Aristotle had already attempted to refute in their day, actually reinforces the philosophy of identity, the nemesis of all genuine dialectic:

> This merely formal predication of something—*it is possible*—is therefore equally as superficial and empty as the law of contradiction and any content that is admitted into it. *A is possible* means only that *A is A*. In so far as nothing is done to develop the content, this has the form of *simplicity*; not until it is resolved into the determinations does *difference* emerge in it. So long as one sticks to this simple form, the content remains something identical with itself and therefore something *possible*. But to say this is equally to say *nothing*, just as in the formal law of identity.[58]

Both positivism and skepticism can thereby be shown to agree with one another in their mutual denial of the moments within the A that point to something beyond itself, the sense in which A is not only equal to A but contains dimensions of B, C, and D within itself. While A's formal identity may simply mean that it is equal to A, it is also potentially the not-A. In the same way may an evolutionary genealogist hold fast to the formal identity of *Homo erectus* and yet completely overlook the fact that it is already potentially *Homo neanderthalis* and *Homo sapiens*, depending on the particular context of natural selection and the conditions of its becoming. In respect to this dialectical presentation of logic, A is still certainly equal to A—which is what is maintained by formalistic logic and by the scientific method—but, as Hegel demonstrates, A is also *not A*, it is *B*, which in turn is not merely *B* but itself contains moments of both *A* and *C*, and so on. Each thing contains aspects or moments that *point beyond itself*—to use the language of the *Phenomenology*, beyond a "being-for-self," and toward the realm of a "being-for-other"—and thus into the "organic unity" of the whole.

Hegel's ontology, following on from this core premise, assumes that the traditional presumption of formal categories of logic is a bad or shallow form of apprehending reality; mistaking what is immediate for what is mediate, mistaking sense-certainty or perception for the entire truth, it reduces the diversity and contradiction inherent in objects to their static equivalent in reified language. Contrariwise, Hegel's philosophy at least attempts to evoke what the philosophy of identity cannot through consciousness of the nonidentity that inheres in relations of identity. The formal law of contradiction, Hegel illustrates, is inadequate to the task of discerning concepts (including that of nature) in relation to their historical development. By holding fast to conceptual identity, prevailing images of nature present a reified positivity that involves nature with ideological prejudice either by severing it from the concept of society and labeling it with the capricious or the arbitrary (as in Hume, Kant, and Fichte), or valorizing an abstraction of "nature" as a moral absolute according to which all social institutions must be measured (as in much romantic philosophy, such as that of Schelling and also of Bakunin).

By contrast, a dialectical naturalism would be that which neither fixes the subject-object relation into antithesis, nor fixes them into a mystical oneness under a conceptual fetish of "nature." A dialectical naturalism, following from the premises of Hegel's critique of bourgeois natural law, must conceptualize "nature" in nothing less than the light of the developing potentialities of its history and its radical presence within the elaboration of human civilization. The very moment in which thought moves beyond the arbitrary limitations of formal identity, its nature-concept expands to accommodate what is not identical with itself. In this negative form, nature becomes more than a mere "is"; it becomes the *ought* of history, the Blochian "Not-Yet," the ecological attributes of a rational, ethical, and peaceable civilization.

According to Hegel, formal potentiality passes over into real potentiality when consciousness comes to comprehend "the in-itself as *pregnant with content*."[59] If we reflect upon the fact that the content of social actuality always contains moments of nonidentity within the totality, we are compelled to arrive at the notion of real or concrete potentiality, comprised of "the existing multiplicity of circumstances" that emerge from immediate existence.[60] In this sense, dialectical reason sublates formal actuality by educing its universal predication on the forms and content of contingency, necessity, and more generally, relation to what is not itself. In consequence what "vanishes" with the ossification of real potentiality into formal actuality, or the reified consciousness that renders the actual totality identical with its own false totality, is the awareness "that actuality was determined as the possibility or in-itself of an other, and conversely, possibility as an actuality which is *not that* whose possibility it is."[61] As such, absolute actuality and its sense of "necessity" exists only as the formalization of a real potentiality that existed within a constellation of other potentialities, transformed through the fabric of historical contingency into the enduring actual.

On this point of development Hegel's thought is truly propitious. To whatever extent we may interpret Hegel as a determinist in the manner of the theodicy of "World-Spirit," it nevertheless seems the case that he viewed "absolute necessity" in historical terms as a sort of animal myopia—an unconscious moment of formalization that lacked the vital determinations of human reason to sublate it into the forms of conscious and ethical spirit. Without this moment of reason, in which the "notion" of society is sublated through the determinations of its social and ethical "Idea"—in short, its *Sittlichkeit* or ethical life—history will remain forever blind to itself. What Hegel has to say on the subject of "absolute necessity" in the *Logic* is an unequivocal condemnation of this blindness of history:

> On the one hand, its differences do not have the shape of the determinations of reflection, but of *a simply affirmative multiplicity*, a differentiated actuality which has the shape of others, self-subsistent relatively to one another. On the other hand, since its relation is absolute identity, it is the *absolute conversion* of its actuality into its possibility and of its possibility into actuality. Absolute necessity is therefore *blind*.[62]

In order to emancipate thought from this barbaric state of necessitarian nature and necessitarian history, Hegel reflects on the possibility of the historical process as amounting to something more than blind necessity; in fact, contemplation of essence leads toward the final "Subjective" part of the *Logic*, the "Doctrine of the Notion." This is because, he asserts,

> [t]he general movement of Essence is a Becoming toward the Notion. In the Relation of Inner and Outer its essential moment emerges—namely, that its determinations are posited as being in negative unity in such a manner that each immediately is not only its other but also the totality of the whole.[63]

But what is "the notion" as Hegel conceives of it? We will avoid a lengthy foray into Hegel's own justification in lieu of Marcuse's more succinct formulation:

> According to Hegel, the notion is the subject's activity and, as such, the true form of reality. On the other hand, the subject is characterized by freedom, so that Hegel's Doctrine of the Notion really develops the categories of freedom. These comprehend the world as it appears when thought has liberated itself from the power of a 'reified' reality, when the subject has emerged as the 'substance' of being. . . . According to common-sense thinking, knowledge become the more unreal the more it abstracts from reality. For Hegel, the opposite is true. The abstraction from reality, which the formation of the notion requires, makes the notion not poorer but richer than reality, because it leads from the facts to their essential content. . . . The world of facts is not rational but has to be *brought* to reason, that is, to a form in which the reality actually corresponds to the truth.[64]

What most remarkably differentiates Hegel's formulation of the notion from transcendental idealism, however, is its distinctly Aristotelian orientation. In his *Physics*, Aristotle had advanced the concept of adequate end (*telos*) to denote what is good or rational within a given constellation of potentialities: "not everything that is last claims to be an end (*telos*), but only that which is best."[65] Hegel, too, is concerned with the adequate ends offered by history rather than, as the popular Fukuyaman vulgarization would have it, merely that which "is last." It is in this context that the doctrine of the notion provides an essential clarification of dialectical naturalism. For, if the notion is conceived of as social history's actualization of reason—social history's moments of utopian hope that could alone accommodate a reconciliation of nature and society—then it is precisely the dialectical tension of such historical "turning points" that a dialectical naturalism should be most intimately concerned with illuminating. These turning points are when social movements, perhaps, are best positioned to grasp the "adequate end" (most ethical and rational goal) within a particular moment of historical potentiality. This is even truer for the "vanquished" histories, or in Howard Zinn's terms "people's" histories, that official history would subsume beneath the distorted falsity of its own concept; for in these, we grasp a sense of what could have been, if different turns were taken in history. To ponder a more rational history than the present trajectory embodies the redeeming symbolism of what Hegel refers to as the notion: "being and Essence are the moments of its becoming; but the Notion is their foundation and truth, as that identity in which they have been submerged and are contained."[66] The notion is the identity of what could and should have been, not merely the accidental what-is.

This "notion" itself, despite its eventual subsumption beneath the formal and ideological drives of Hegel's philosophy, nonetheless illuminates itself as a negative concept, presaging an allegorical wellspring of ethical contact with nature. As the negative consciousness of this wellspring, a dialectical naturalism would be that which proceeded through a revelation of the possibilities of the prevailing forces of production and social relations that could plausibly rework future social development into a genuinely ethical interrelation with the biosphere. These potencies, however, remain forever grounded within the developing material, cultural, and psychological realities of civilization. If this historical-material reality is mythologized and thereby abstracted from history—which is precisely what occurs in Hegel's later lectures on the *Philosophy of History*—history is as forcibly alienated from itself as where hegemonic capitalism's positivistic claims to totality efface the truth of that totality.

The Anti-Naturalism of "Spirit" and the Limits of Hegel's Idealism

The *Philosophy of History*, as has often been observed, betrays many of the careful nuances of dialectic through its bombastic subsumption of humanity and nature alike beneath the cover concept of the "World-Spirit." Yet even the justly maligned *Philosophy of History* is not without its contradictions, not lacking in its moments of dissonance. The work cyclically presents a striking juxtaposition between the rational potentialities of historical periods, which in and of themselves suggest the social significance of human subjectivity, only to culminate most ironically in the methodical denial of this subjectivity—reason being coldly deprecated to supra-sensual process or blind agent ultimately beyond the comprehension of the subject. In Hegel's terminology, this supra-sensual "cunning of reason" presents humanity as "the instruments and means of the World-Spirit for attaining its object; bringing it to consciousness, and realizing it . . . those manifestations of vitality on the part of individuals and peoples, in which they seek and satisfy their own purposes, [which] . . . are the means and instruments of a higher and broader purpose of which they know nothing."[67] However, while the reactionary conclusions of Hegel's totalizing determinism could not be denied, he so often presents spirit in a rather different light: as the unfolding of consciousness and, particularly, as the awakening of *ethical life* and its sublation of blind instinct and tradition. This is characteristic of his statement on the emergence of subjectivity from nature:

> To the Ideal of Freedom, Law and Morality are indispensably requisite; and they are in and for themselves, universal existences, objects and aims; which are discovered only by the activity of thought, separating itself from the merely sensuous, and developing itself, in opposition thereto. . . . [it] must, on the other hand, be introduced into and incorporated with the originally sensuous will, and that contrary to its natural inclination.[68]

This formulation, despite its elements of truth, signals the resurrection of the reified anti-naturalism that was intrinsic to the ontology of the earlier idealism. In representing ethical progress via the formal, Kantian notion of antithesis leading to an allegedly necessary subsumption, it detaches "spirit" from its mediation through "nature" and thereby divests consciousness of what is *complementary* in the mediation of natural history through social history. The suggestion that thought develops itself "contrary to natural inclination" is, moreover, one of those rigid tropes of idealism that doubtlessly would have found favor with many of the bourgeois factory owners of French and English High Capitalism, forever lamenting the "natural indolence" of the workers. In assaulting the feudalistic idea of "natural relations," a new idealistic principle was asserted in line with the ideology of classical political economy—the triumph of labor-value over the realm of the sensuous, the life activity of the "work-shy," and the effacement of the restful, natural aesthetics of the rustic landscape and its "backward" population that had yet to be fully denuded into a toxic and inorganic ugliness.

This regression takes place not within the particularities of the spiritual-natural unity in the Hegelian analysis of Greek, Roman, and later European histories, but rather within the conceptual largesse that Hegel affirms as the identity of the World-Spirit. A characteristic example is presented in his racially charged assessment of Africa and its forced association with conditions of nature:

> In Negro life the characteristic point is the fact that consciousness has not yet attained to the realization of any substantial objective existence—as for example, God, or Law—in which the interest of man's volition is involved and in which he realizes his own being. . . . The Negro, as already observed, exhibits the natural man is his completely wild and untamed state. We must lay aside all thought of reverence and morality—all that we call feeling—if we would rightly comprehend him; there is nothing harmonious with humanity to be found within this type of character.[69]
>
> What we properly understand by Africa, is the Unhistorical, Undeveloped Spirit, still involved in the conditions of mere nature, and which had to be presented here only as on the threshold of the World's History.[70]

While Hegel's nauseating ethnocentrism is difficult to ignore here (along with his unjustly cynical deprecation of tribal society), his remarks on the later civilizations are even more implicitly ideological. We are told, for example, that Egypt occupies a "middle ground" between Nature and Spirit:

> If . . . we combine what has been said here of the peculiarities of the Egyptian Spirit in all its aspects, its pervading principle is found to be, that the two elements of reality—Spirit sunk in Nature, and the impulse to liberate it—are here held together inharmoniously as contending elements. We behold the antithesis of Nature and Spirit—not the primary Immediate Unity (as in the less advanced nations), nor the Concrete Unity, where Nature is posited only as a basis for the manifestation of Spirit (as in the more advanced); in contrast with the first and second of these Unities, the Egyptian Unity—combining contradictory elements—occupies a middle place.[71]

He then connects the rise of the Persian Empire with the "transition" to the Greek world:

> In Persia begins the principle of Free Spirit as contrasted with imprisonment in Nature; mere natural existence, therefore, loses its bloom, and fades away. The principle of separation from Nature is found in the Persian Empire, which, therefore, occupies a higher grade than those worlds immersed in the Natural. The necessity of advance has been thereby proclaimed. Spirit has disclosed its existence, and must complete its development.[72]

And finally:

> In the Idea of the Greek Spirit we found the two elements, Nature and Spirit, in such a relation to each other, that Nature forms merely the point of departure. This degradation of Nature is in the Greek mythology the turning point of the whole—expressed as the War of the Gods, the overthrow of the Titans by the race of Zeus. The transition from the Oriental to the Occidental Spirit is therein represented, for the Titans are the merely Physical—natural existences, from whose grasp sovereignty is wrested.[73]

Hegel's philosophy of history thus remained rooted in an idealism that was just as unequivocally to denigrate nature as incommensurate with "the Idea"—to present nature as a passive being-for-other—as it was to present the World-Spirit as the alleged harbinger of the rational becoming of nature. The contemporary ecological crisis demonstrates the falsity of this all-too-harmonious whole, this "destiny" of spirit. The young Marx, under the influence of Feuerbach, seizes upon this Hegelian falsity:

> *Externality* here [in Hegel's philosophy] is not to be understood as the *self-externalizing world of sense* open to the light, open to the man endowed with senses. It is to be taken here in the sense of alienation—a mistake, a defect, which ought not to be. For what is true is still the Idea. Nature is only the *form of the Idea's other-being*. And since abstract thought is the *essence*, that which is external to it is by its essence something merely *external*. The abstract thinker recognizes at the same time that *sensuousness—externality* in contrast to thought weaving *within itself*—is the essence of nature. But he expresses this contrast in such a way as to make this *externality*

of nature, its *contrast* to thought, its *defect*, so that inasmuch as it is distinguished from abstraction, nature is something defective. Something which is defective not merely for me or in my eyes but in itself—intrinsically—has something outside itself which it lacks. That is, its being is something other than it itself. Nature has therefore to supersede itself for the abstract thinker, for it is already posited by him as a potentially *superseded* being.[74]

The limits of the mature Hegel's dialectic lie precisely within his defective characterization of nature as "externality." On the one hand, in providing an account of dialectic that facilitated an immanent critique of mythopoesis (or in Marxian terms, the "reification of consciousness"), the younger Hegel shrewdly illuminated the ideological character of bourgeois representations of private property relations and a subjective romantic outlook as mythic distortions or false appearances. Notwithstanding this, he failed to take the dialectic into an interrogation of the *historical principle* of this mythopoeic naturalism: the extent to which the social mediation of nature's image had culminated in *the anti-naturalist outlook of the bourgeois enlightenment writ large.* This emerging bourgeois viewpoint displaced the "natural" foundation of human consociation with the abstract imperatives of moral idealism and the economistic reductionism of classical political economy. It was this primary act of representation that removed natural history from a peaceful accommodation within alternative possibilities of social freedom. The identity between bourgeois ideology and the events following in the wake of the French Revolution only gave further credence to the reactionary forces of the counter-Enlightenment, which held fast to a dogmatic, unreflective, and ultimately romantic idea of nature.

In the same decade of Hegel's death, one of his most promising students, Ludwig Feuerbach, came into prominence with a critical essay on Hegel's philosophy (published in 1839). It was the absence of a more complementary image of the mediation of nature through spirit in Hegel that formed one of the crucial points of departure for Feuerbach's own forays into dialectical thinking.

Feuerbachian Interlude

The philosopher Ludwig Feuerbach was one of the most significant socialist and dialectical philosophers of the nineteenth century to concentrate his attention upon nature as a substance of ethical and sensual mediation in the social constitution and critical reflection of humanity. Elaborating a radical critique of the Hegelian philosophy, in the 1830s and 1840s Feuerbach began to elaborate the foundations of an anthropological, materialist dialectic of Christian history. We will forgo a lengthy foray into Feuerbach's critique of Hegel here in order to emphasize the significance of one particular aspect of Feuerbach's philosophy—its insistence on the demystification of ideology in order to show what its mythopoeic identity denies.[75] Although he does not develop a concept of nature that locates nature within a truly historical continuum, Feuerbach nevertheless insists on the centrality of a dialectic between "I" and "thou"—between humanity and nature—as the developing substance of reason. This is what differentiates his more materialist and anthropological dialectic from that of Hegel's, and what provides another lodestone in the elaboration of a dialectical naturalism.

The following passages from Feuerbach's *The Essence of Christianity* demonstrate how Feuerbach immanently criticizes the supernatural metaphysics of Christianity, revealing their "natural" origins:

> Personality, individuality, consciousness, without Nature, is nothing; or, which is the same thing, an empty, unsubstantial abstraction. But Nature, as has been shown and is obvious, is nothing without corporeality. The body alone is that negativing, limiting, concentrating, circumscribing force, without which no personality is conceivable. . . . Flesh and blood is life, and life alone is corporeal reality.[76]
>
> Moral feeling can effect nothing without Nature; it must ally itself with the simplest natural means. The profoundest secrets lie in common everyday things, such as supernaturalistic religion and speculation ignore, thus sacrificing real mysteries to imaginary, illusory ones. . . . Water is the simplest means of grace or healing for the maladies of the soul as well as of the body. But water is effectual only where its use is constant and regular. . . . If in water we declare: Man [sic] can do nothing without Nature; by bread and wine we declare: Nature needs man, as man needs Nature . . . Nature gives the material, mind gives the form.[77]

Moreover, in *The Essence of Religion*, Feuerbach clearly admires the unity between nature and reason represented by the spiritualism of the Hellenic Greeks in a manner that draws upon Hegel's favorable appraisal of classical art:

> [The Greeks] . . . did not wish to be saved in heaven, only happy, only to live without trouble and pain; they did not sigh as the Christians do, because they were subject to the necessity of Nature, to the wants of sexual instinct, of sleep, of eating and drinking; they still submitted in their wishes to the limits of human nature; they were not yet creators from nothing, they did not yet make wine from water, they only purified and distilled the water of Nature and changed it in an organic way into the blood of the Gods; they drew the contents of divine and blissful life not from mere imagination, but from the materials of the real world; they built the heaven of the Gods upon the ground of this earth.[78]

What Hegel's philosophy lacked, Feuerbach observes, was what the Greeks possessed: *concrete* nature. Hegel lacked an appreciation for the extent to which "spirit" must realize itself within relations of ecological necessity, *complementing* the natural lifeways of the earth rather than constituting itself out of a repressive metaphysical antithesis to it. Feuerbach's great merit, echoing the evolutionary themes in his antecedent Gottfried Herder, was thus to try to illuminate the underlying reality of ecology in the determinations of social history (despite the fact that in Feuerbach this history is dissolved back into the "pure" abstractions of philosophy).

In his erudite work on Feuerbach's philosophy, Wartofsky has observed that Feuerbach attempts to

> . . . make philosophy self-conscious in a way that reveals its human foundations and its social and epistemological uses in a new way. . . . In short, Feuerbach provides the basis for a fuller epistemological critique of the nature and function of ideology.[79]

This demystification process was carried further by Marx into a critique of ideology, into a dialectic that emphasized the dependency of concepts on the historical contradictions of human species being and its relation to the natural world. Marx also criticized Feuerbach immanently, and with much justification, for construing "nature" in an ahistorical and abstract form. But for all that, the mature Marx was also to lose touch with a quintessential truth in Feuerbach's philosophy: the notion that humanity's mediation through nature had been distorted and represented in line with the epistemology of a protestant-bourgeois anti-naturalism that had sought to represent the emergence of spirit from nature, as in Fichte's and Hegel's philosophy, as a *sui generis* phenomenon, rather than one emerging from and acculturated within an ecological nexus. Yet Marx's disdain for the "romantic" or "backward" worship of nature—a lingering residue of the landed aristocracy of feudalism in nineteenth-century Germany—was comprehensible within his own time; ours, too, is not so distant from the reactionary spectacle of fascist ecologism that ecologically styled politics could cease to be suspected of a counterrevolutionary orientation. The principle of hope that sustains the dream of an ecological society could only be redeemed by a refusal to ontologize that which is historically determined.

CHAPTER TWO

Nature in Marx and Anarchism

Marx and the Historicization of Nature

The significance of Marx as a political thinker rests not only upon his relationship to communism, but also his theory of historical materialism, which insists upon the determined and historical character of "nature" by way of its mediation through social relations. In light of Marx's historical materialism, both the appearance and essence of nature are seen to be captured by the movement of history: its appearance a mirror of social ideology, its essence in the practical human activity according to which it is transformed into the substance of a human second nature. Hence, for Marx, unlike Rousseau and other figures of the romantic counter-Enlightenment, the concept of "natural law" or primordial moral order in nature is illusory: "the nature that preceded human history . . . is nature which today no longer exists anywhere (except perhaps on a few Australian coral islands of recent origin)."[1] Rather than seeking to derive, in the form of essentialism, a moral order from "nature," historical materialism emphasizes that moral order is always a *human* concept that is intelligible only with reference to a given historical constellation and its economic and political order:

> Each [historical] stage contains a material result, a sum of productive forces, a historically created relation to nature and of individuals to one another, which is handed down to each generation from its predecessor; a mass of productive forces, capital funds and circumstances, which on the one hand is indeed modified by the new generation, but on the other also prescribes for it its conditions of life and gives it a definite development, a special character. It shows that circumstances make men just as much as men make circumstances.[2]

More recently, several theorists of twentieth-century political ecology have sought to differentiate their own models of nature philosophy and attendant political theories from what they have construed as Marx's productivism or economic determinism. Andre Gorz, for instance, considers Marx's political project as an anti-ecological "creative objectification of man's domination of nature."[3] Similarly, in a critical essay, Murray Bookchin laments Marx as a figure of the Enlightenment "despiritization" of nature and humankind, a champion of the "conquest" of nature, and a stumbling block for the theorization of a veritably ecological ethics.[4] This negative appraisal of Marx in political ecology has contributed to a popular image of Marx as an anti-naturalist philosopher, an image also faithfully preserved in many orthodox Marxist writings, such as that of Schmidt.[5]

What follows seeks to clarify some of the ethical nuances of Marx's historicization of the concept of nature. In particular, it investigates the possibility that, although limited by the social climate of his day, and while Marx was by no means an ecologist, there is at least an implicitly ethical justification in the later Marx's "anti-naturalism" that has been somewhat obscured by his ecological critics. To some extent, indeed, the historicization of nature in Marx—that is, nature conceived as a reflection of human second nature and its evolving historic potentialities—can be defended in ethical terms. This possibility is hinted at, for example, through Antonio Gramsci's historical materialist interpretation of the concept of nature. As Giovanni Pizza stresses in his insightful analysis of this subject:

> According to Gramsci, 'second nature' is the internalization of what he calls *abitudini di ordinei*, 'habits of order,' . . . as hegemony is not to be understood only with respect to domination but also in regard of possible change, second nature is likewise always subject to possible transformation—one can rebel against it, in a self-reflexive process of dis-embodiment, with the creation of a new order in sight, and therefore of a new second nature.[6]

This is in reference to a passage of Gramsci's *Prison Notebooks*, in which Gramsci ponders the implications of Marx's historical materialism applied to nature:

> What does it mean to say that a certain action is 'natural' or, that it is on the other hand 'against nature'? Each of us,

deep within ourselves, believes that we know exactly what this means, but if we ask ourselves a direct question, we realise that it is not so simple to answer. In any case, we need to realise that we cannot talk of 'nature' as something which is fixed or objective; in this case 'natural' means right or normal according to our current historical conscience, which in turn is our 'nature.' The nature of humankind is a set of social relationships which determine an historically defined conscience, and it is this conscience which indicates what is 'natural' or not [and thus we have a human nature which is contradictory because it is the set of social relationships].[7]

Stated in this way, the transition from feudalism to capitalism, analyzed in so many of Marx's writings, speaks to the transition from one "historical conscience" to another, from one "nature" based on feudal social relationships to a "nature" that originates from and is reproduced within capitalistic social relationships. Therefore, regardless of the extent to which more contemporary history has vitiated Marx's idea of progress, it may be shown that Marx's "anti-naturalism" remains intelligible in ethical terms insofar as Marx considered the transition from feudalism to capitalism as opening a landscape of ethical potentialities that were unavailable to feudal society and its various configurations and representations of "nature." Accordingly, rather than an unequivocal champion of the conquest of the natural world and as a representative of the instrumental reason of the Enlightenment,[8] it is possible, and arguably more consistent with Marx's theory of historical materialism, to view Marx's position as a more contradictory, equivocal, and perhaps even ethical one. This requires, however, as Smith and O'Keefe have emphasized, that one "look[s] [in Marx] not for a 'concept of nature' per se but for an understanding of the *relation* of human societies with nature," a social and ethical context "not inherent in nature but rather . . . embedded in the human relation with nature."[9]

The Younger Marx's Naturalism

There are no explicit references to ecology or an ecological society anywhere in Marx's writings, notwithstanding the implicitly "naturalistic" passages in the more youthful and Feuerbachian *1844 Manuscripts*. Nevertheless, and although for Marx nature did not constitute a substance of social determination in its own right, the mediation of nature's image through the historical constellations of society can be shown to be an essential element of his thought. It is, therefore, within the careful reexamination of the nuances of Marx's historical materialism that the philosophical origins of a genuinely dialectical naturalism might be recovered, as distinct from both the anti-naturalism of the bourgeois enlightenment and many of the official doctrines of orthodox Marxism.

Much of the preexisting commentary on the ecological aspects of Marx's writing tends to diverge either into an undialectical hostility to Marx's professed "productivism" or an equally undialectical and anachronistic "Marxology," which dresses up Marx in the attire of a twenty-first-century ecologist with twenty-first-century concerns and knowledge.[10] Alternatively, commentators have often put stress upon the differences between the younger, Feuerbachian Marx, who was, it is contended, concerned with the society-nature relation from a humanistic and ostensibly "ecological" perspective, and the more mature Marx, who is asserted to have advanced a basically inorganic notion of "nature" as the raw materials of human sovereignty, coexisting in an apparently antithetical relation with its other. According to Schmidt's view of this chronological change in his well-known work on the subject:

> In the Paris Manuscripts [of 1844], while under the influence of Feuerbach and Romanticism, Marx portrayed labour as a process of progressive humanization of nature, a process which coincided with the naturalization of man. He therefore saw in history, stamped as it is with the imprint of human labour, a clearer and clearer equivalence between naturalism and humanism. The later, and more critical, Marx of the economic analyses took the view that the struggle of man with nature could be transformed but not abolished.[11]

Schmidt's distinction here contains its moments of truth. Indeed, the young Marx had begun to see, through Feuerbach, the social accommodation of the sensual and organic world as a potentially rational one: a mediation made on the side of human liberation through what Hegel might have expressed as the being-for-self-and-other of ethical life. Yet this more accommodating understanding of nature, as the ethical corrective of social pathologies, is absent in his later works, such as the three volumes of *Capital*. Marx never gave any substantial justification for abandoning this viewpoint, nor for adopting what Schmidt appropriately characterizes as an essentializing ontology of "struggle" with nature. In the affirmation of such an ontology, Marx's mature theory risks acceding to a restoration of the abstract nature-concept of Fichte and Hegel: nature qua the mere materials to be worked up by the World-Spirit. Indeed, there has been no shortage of orthodox apologias for this kind of instrumental interpretation of Marx's understanding of nature.

However, despite this abstract interpretation being revived under various orthodox tendencies in twentieth-century Marxism, the transformation from the young Marx's humanistic naturalism to the elder's alleged anti-naturalism contains an implicit ethical justification, without acknowledgment of which no account of his writings could do them justice. The origins of Marx's nature-concept can be sought after in the *1844 Economic-Philosophic Manuscripts*, while the foundations of his later anti-naturalism can be elucidated within his middle- and late-period writings. It is primarily within the early and middle periods of his writing that the following analysis will be concentrated.

The younger Marx articulates the emerging potentialities of a democratic communist association of labor in a form that is clearly favorable to the perspective of a dialectical naturalism, or historical conception of nature:

> Association, applied to land, shares the economic advantage of large-scale landed property, and first brings to realization the original tendency inherent in land-division, namely, equality. In the same way association re-establishes, now on a rational basis, no longer mediated by serfdom, ownership and the silly mysticism of property, the intimate ties of man with the earth, for the earth ceases to be an object of huckstering, and through free labor and free enjoyment becomes once more a true personal property of man.[12]

Nature, no longer itself a product of huckstering and the accumulation of capital, would merge with the substance of free human enjoyment, of desire, of aesthetic pleasure. Nature would perhaps come to resemble an equilibrium between uncultivated wilderness and its ecological riches and a humanized landscape, transformed with the discrimination of an architectural and aesthetic eye, and yet also with an eye conscious of the integrity of ecological relationships. Thus, the reworking of nature, on nonbourgeois and noninstrumental terms, may be conceived not as antithetical to the earth's ecology but rather as its ethical acculturation within the substance of a rational society. This distinction forms the essential qualification of Marx's youthful humanism, which would distinguish it from the instrumental reason of the bourgeois enlightenment. This ethical orientation of reason, for Marx, forms the humanist undercurrent of humankind's "species being":

> It is just in the working up of the objective world . . . that man first really proves himself to be a *species being*. This production is his active species life. Through and because of this production, nature appears as *his* work and his reality. The object of labor is, therefore, *the objectification of man's species life*: for he duplicates not only in consciousness, intellectually, but also actively, in reality, and therefore he contemplates himself in a world that he has created.[13]

Through its mediation within the rational potentialities of labor, nature no longer appears as that wild otherness, threatening and foreign to human needs and human pleasure, but is integrated within a renewed ethical substance. This dialectic of subject and object, in which human second nature reproduces itself in the midst of its transformational integration of natural history, is carried through by Marx to two diverse moments of the historical transformation of nature that took place during the nineteenth century. Nature is actualized both instrumentally, that is, as "human use,"[14] and yet also noninstrumentally in a sense that Marx describes as "humanized nature."[15] Thus, while nature may be first apprehended in the guise of the mere reduplication of the Fichtean Ego, "[man's] object,"[16] this reduplication is then sublated into the *emancipation* from mere "utility" and "practical need."[17] Hence the significance of the second negation, which was so sorely lacking in the bourgeois concept of labor in Fichte's philosophy: nature's emancipation from an object of human egotism becomes synonymous with humanity's emancipation from conditions of social domination. This early Marxian image of nature's mediation through human species life presents us with the beginnings of a model for a dialectical naturalism: a naturalism that presents nature within the developing whole, or relative unity, of its ethical mediation through the more rational potentialities of humanity.

The Concept of Nature in Marx's Middle Period and the Ethical Dimension of Marx's Anti-Naturalism

In the later writings Marx begins to emphasize the dialectical synthesis of natural and human history as terminating in human second nature: the supersession of what is natural. Does this indicate a "new" period in Marx's thought, a turn toward a more instrumental concept of labor in which it is seen as merely determined, as the "materials" of labor? Schmidt indicates as much in his statement on the primary thread of the mature Marx's nature-concept: "Nature, as the material with which men are faced, can only be regarded as *unformed material* from the point of view and the purposes of human activity."[18] This, however, strikes one as synonymous with the outlook of bourgeois political economy and its instrumental conception of natural potentiality, which Marx subjected to devastating criticism both in the *Grundrisse* and throughout the three volumes of *Capital*. In fact, this statement seems to reify the historical reality of the bourgeoisie's simplification of the biosphere into mere "unformed materials" or "resources" for the purposes of exchange into an *ontological essence* of "human activity." In the same way that vulgar scientism dissolves the world into a crude "matter" to be appropriated by avaricious corporations with few ethical scruples, so does Schmidt's Marx seem to become subtly captured by the abstract, instrumental orientation of the political economist toward nature. What could have led to this contradiction between the younger and older Marx, if not misinterpretation on Schmidt's part, and what were the justifications provided by Marx for his doing so?

The reasons for this unresolved contradiction in Marx's thought can only be discerned succinctly here; nevertheless, we may at least point the way to their resolution. An essential point of reference is, aside from the *Grundrisse* and Marx's journalistic writings, the historical prognostications that underlie the structure of the third volume of *Capital*. A close study of these volumes reveals that Murray Bookchin's vociferous denunciation of Marx's concept of nature as an acquiescence to "bourgeois sociology"[19] is not necessarily incorrect in light of much orthodox Marxism today; it is however lacking in a fuller examination of Marx's own *historical* justification for doing so, which could have led to a more sympathetic analysis of Marxism within the development of Bookchin's social ecology. Bookchin, along with other ecological critics of Marx, tends to obscure the significance of the dialectical justification in Marx's middle period, in which his writings endorse the social transformation of the bourgeoisie from what he conceives as mystifying, unethical, and nature-worshipping feudal societies into "progressive" realizations of the capitalist mode of production. *The Manifesto of the Communist Party* emphasizes that the bourgeoisie "has created enormous cities, has greatly increased the urban population as compared with the rural, and has thus rescued a considerable part of the population from the idiocy of rural life."[20] Regardless of the extent to which this generalization does justice to the geographic nuances of feudal society and the relationship between town and country in feudal Europe, one cannot fail to observe that for Marx the nature-concept is always a potential product of *reification* according to which irrational and hierarchical social relations, be they emerging from religion or from a political class, are mystified into "the idiocy of rural life." From the fantastical heavenly hierarchy of the celestial empire of China to the naturalistic ontologies of the caste system and Hindu animal cults in India, Marx repeatedly expresses a deep disdain for the reactionary appeal to "nature," particularly in his writings for the *New York Tribune*. The characterization of Marx as a mechanist or productivist, made by many of his ecological critics, is therefore erroneous, for there is indeed a decisive historical and even ethical justification for Marx's sometimes exaggerated emphasis upon the instrumental reworking of nature at the hands of human labor. From the viewpoint of Marx's period in the nineteenth century, it is at least understandable that ecology would appear to him as a largely reactionary concept, and that by contrast the revolutionary transformation of the *relations* of production at the hands of the bourgeois *forces* of production would appear as the most progressive, potentially rational phenomenon of his time—not in terms of its actuality, but rather in terms of the social potentialities to which it would give birth.[21]

Bookchin's analysis is nevertheless *not* incorrect because, from the viewpoint of the twentieth and twenty-first centuries, this situation has been fundamentally reversed. The bourgeoisie no longer act as the universal champions of technological progress, but—as witnessed in their regressive influence upon renewable energy investment in various instances of contemporary national politics and by the broader phenomenon of planned obsolescence—also often act in their class interest to stagnate and retard technological progress, while continuing to support productive forces that are wasteful, unnecessary, and ecologically destructive. Moreover, a great quantity of "work" today no longer fits Marx's description of socially necessary labor, but is socially unnecessary or even socially harmful.

Marx did not foresee Keynesianism, corporatism, fascism, or capitalism's thriving in historic moments of creative destruction—all phenomena that seriously jeopardize the "declining rate of profit" prognostication that is at the core of Marx's prediction of capitalism's downfall. And, contrary to Marx's time, ecology—despite its capture by various reactionary and liberal political movements—has emerged as a more *radical* concept insofar as it raises human awareness of the ecological destructiveness of the status quo and impels it toward the imagination and practical realization of a more rational, ecological society. This dialectical transformation into opposites, which separates Marx's time from our own, renders Marx's notion of a "progressive" subsumption of nature under capitalist relations of production no longer tenable. However, this voiding of the progressive implications of Marx's analysis of capitalism does not alter the basic implications of Marx's historical materialist understanding of nature. Its historicization of nature continues to provide a sound theoretical basis for the critique of the *hegemonic distortion* of nature's image under capitalism and an awareness of the historical becoming of alternative potentialities within a given historic nexus of society and nature. In this sense, Marx's middle period of writings remains a vital lodestone in the philosophical outlook of dialectical naturalism. Rather than constructing an essentialist concept of "natural law" or "nature," Marx's historical materialism insists upon the constructed and mediated character of what is considered to be nature.

In one of his most embittered essays on Marx, the tone of which was softened in his discussions on Marx fifteen years later,[22] Bookchin repeatedly laments Marx's "subversion of the ethical content of law" and "the way in which [for Marx] domination is annexed to liberation as a precondition of social liberation."[23] As evidence of what Bookchin interprets as Marx's "dismissal" of "moral boundaries of action,"[24] he cites passages from works such as *The Future Results of British Rule in India* (July 1853):

> Bourgeois industry and commerce create these material conditions of a new world in the same way as geological revolutions have created the surface of the earth. When a great social revolution shall have mastered the results of the bourgeois epoch, the market of the world and the modern powers of production, and subjected them to the common control of the most advanced peoples, then only will human progress cease to resemble that hideous pagan idol, who would not drink the nectar but from the skulls of the slain.[25]

There is, however, precisely an *ethical* nuance here that seems to have escaped Bookchin and many of Marx's other detractors. In order to grasp it, one must strive to understand that for Marx, there is another immanent moment in the historical development of nature that is not identical with the pathology of bourgeois enlightenment (that is, the conversion of nature into a merely instrumental means of exchange value). This other moment is referred to by Rose as the "history of culture" (in relation to Adorno, who inherited the notion from Lukács).[26] To conceive of nature as the "history of culture" does not mean that nature is made to become identical with cultural "superstructure," nor that nature as a concept is merely an empty signifier for relations of production. Nature as the "history of culture" refers to the dialectical process wherein nature, along with its distorted image, is constantly reproduced within a specific, cultural continuum of relations of production. According to the basic tenets of Marxian theory, such relations of production always rest upon technological forces of production that determine their concrete possibilities and their historic limits.

Holding fast to this dialectical character of Marx's nature-concept can help make sense of the apparent transition from Marx's earlier naturalism to what Schmidt regards as his later, often exaggerated, anti-naturalism. For Marx, the genesis of concrete possibility for the realization of communism rests upon the "revolutionary" role that *both* capitalist forces of production (i.e., their rapid technological progress) and capitalist relations of production (their "collectivization" of the proletariat in factories and the economic compulsion underlying the proletariat's pursuit of class struggle) come to realize.[27] However erroneous this prognosis might seem from the viewpoint of the twenty-first century, it need not be interpreted as a renunciation of the dream of an ethical or ecological society within socialist thought, nor as an abnegation of the boundaries of moral action. A more sympathetic observation would envision Marx's increasing anti-naturalism as the *ethical dimension* of his preoccupation with the historical dialectic of *concrete possibility* that capitalism has awakened in exploding the rustic, feudal image of "nature" and—however destructively, however lamentably—transforming "nature" into a class struggle in which all of "the old shit" of feudal traditions no longer exerts a hold over the fate of humanity.[28] Capitalism's concrete awakening of the possibility of a technologically advanced and egalitarian future, under this more sympathetic reading of Marx's "anti-naturalism," becomes not merely an economic but also an ethical landscape of possibility, freed from the various social mystifications of the feudal era based upon a distortion of nature's image.

To be sure, there are many justifiable criticisms that may be leveled at elements of Marx's historical hubris, not least his and Engels's sometimes dubious anthropology in *The German Ideology* and his projection of many tacit assumptions of bourgeois political economy over the past, as Bookchin lays bare in his critique of Marx's anthropology.[29] But such a critique, if it is to be genuinely immanent, must not overlook the often implicit ethical rationale that sustains Marx's critique of naturalism. Far from repeating tropes concerning the "reverence" for nature that utopian thinkers often read back into feudal relations—a reverence not without its truth but often also placed in the service of reactionary politics—Marx tends to emphasize what romantic thinkers may neglect in their Scottish "golden age" image of medieval naturalism, namely, feudalism's abhorrent lack of social equality, its needlessly destructive wars over landholdings, the social evils of its religious hierarchies, and the perennial vulnerability of many of its villages and townships to waves of barbarian incursions (one could indeed also add the repeated waves of plague, such as the black death, to the image of medieval naturalism). Given the prevalence of such phenomena, Marx not merely argues against precolonial society in India and its reified image of nature on economic or technical grounds, but he argues against it on *ethical* grounds:

> English interference having placed the spinner in Lancashire and the weaver in Bengal, or sweeping away both Hindoo spinner and weaver, dissolved these small semi-barbarian, semi-civilized communities, by blowing up their economical basis, and thus produced the greatest, and to speak the truth, the only *social* revolution ever heard of in Asia. Now, sickening as it must be to human feeling to witness those myriads of industrious patriarchal and inoffensive social organizations disorganized and dissolved into their units, thrown into a sea of woes, and their individual members losing at the same time their ancient form of civilization, and their hereditary means of subsistence, we must not forget that these idyllic village communities, inoffensive though they may appear, had always been the solid foundation of Oriental despotism, that they restrained the human mind within the smallest possible compass, making it the unresisting tool of superstition, enslaving

it beneath traditional rules, depriving it of all grandeur and historical energies. . . . We must not forget that this undignified, stagnatory, and vegetative life, that this passive sort of existence evoked on the other part, in contradistinction, wild, aimless, unbounded forces of destruction and rendered murder itself a religious rite in Hindostan. We must not forget that these little communities were contaminated by distinctions of caste and by slavery, that they subjugated man to external circumstances instead of elevating man the sovereign of circumstances, that they transformed a self-developing social state into never changing natural destiny, and thus brought about a brutalizing worship of nature, exhibiting its degradation in the fact that man, the sovereign of nature, fell down on his knees in adoration of Kanuman [Hanuman], the monkey, and Sabbala, the cow.[30]

This inspired passage of Marx's middle writings perhaps best evinces the ethical nuances underlying Marx's turn toward an "anti-naturalism." Nature is no longer canvased as a relation of coproductivity, or mediation in human species life, nor does one encounter any references to the naturalization of humankind. Rather, "nature worship" and other forms of the historical mystification of nature are presented as hindrances to ethical progress, hindrances to be overcome in the future achievement of human "sovereignty."

However, there are at least two aspects of this turn that are by no means complementary, despite what Marx himself may have believed—on the one hand, an incisive critique of the mystification of nature, or of "never changing natural destiny," which exist in order to benefit dominatory social and religious hierarchies; on the other, an exaggerated (and with the benefit of hindsight, arguably false) edification of bourgeois instrumental reason as "revolutionary," including the notion of the instrumental manipulation of nature as a *precondition* of human sovereignty. This is the side or moment of Marx that his political ecology critics, with a good degree of overemphasis, deploy to arrive at their image of an anti-ecological Marx. Yet the contradiction remains. Where one moment seems to be defined by an ethical impulse—bestowing to human societies the freedom of self-determination, free from the capricious inhibitions of nature such as disease, or "nature" and its social diseases—the other closely follows the hubris of Fichte's and Hegel's construct of the World-Spirit. In so doing, it seems to abnegate the ethical conscience that would give birth to both a naturalized humanity and a humanized nature. In light of this instrumentalism, we once again seem to arrive at the antithesis of Fichte between a wholly positive, ethical human sovereignty and a wholly negative and merely determined nature. Such an antinomy is erroneous, for it obscures what was potentially rational in the human reverence for nature under earlier periods of history, and it badly misconstrues the humanity-nature relation into an ontological master-slave dialectic that humanity, in the course of its historical progression of the relations of production, merely reverses, and thus preserves rather than abolishes.

Regrettably, what has come down to us in the form of "Marxism," perhaps not least owing to its twentieth-century distortions, has generally favored the highly instrumental moment of the nature-concept in Marx rather than its more ethical and possibly "ecological" alternative. In this sense, in a form reflective of the ideology of state capitalism, Marx has been rendered as merely another representative for the Stalinist mantra of ever-increasing production for production's sake rather than as a philosopher of ethical or ecological socialism. Aside from a few notable exceptions, such as Antonio Gramsci and Georg Lukács (who more rigorously sought to redevelop the dialectical impulses of Marx's nature-concept qua "the history of culture"), the "orthodox" Marxism of our time seems to be remarkably shorn of the ethical nuances underlying Marx's concept of nature.[31] Such a transformation of Marx's historical concept of nature into a doctrine of anti-naturalism, a transformation already carried out in certain passages of Schmidt's analysis, signals the transformation of Marx from a historical thinker limited by the historic scope of his age into the supposed prophet of a ready-made system:

> Marx's own concept of matter [is] the dialectical-materialist view that men, whatever historical conditions they live in, see themselves confronted with a world of things which cannot be transcended and which they must appropriate in order to survive.[32]

Rather than the naturalized humanity of the *1844 Manuscripts*, for Marxian orthodoxy, "humanism" seems to acquire the form of the cunning of instrumental reason. This was made possible, nevertheless, by the residue of an instrumental image of nature that plagued Marx's later writings. The subject-object relation between labor and nature, as Schmidt summarizes it, indeed often remains fixed in antithesis for the later Marx: "sundered into two parts, man and material to be worked on, nature is always present to itself in this division."[33] Similarly, Gillian Rose has observed of Marx's thought more generally that it holds fast to a Neo-Fichtean form.[34] In the reified form of "material to be worked on" Marx's concept of nature is, according to Rose, already permeated by the *socially mediated* concepts of the bourgeois Ego, in turn uncritically appropriated by Marx as a transcendental immediacy. The very formulation of nature existing in "two parts," moreover, is a patently epistemological dualism that originates in the prevailing social order. It is what Hegel called, criticizing Fichte in the *Differenzschrift*, a "subjective subject-object." A subjective subject-object is already complicit with ideological hegemony insofar as it delivers the object over to the domination of its reified concept, rather than indicating the possibilities of the object that reside beyond it. Yet it would be a misreading of Marx to posit that he was not aware of this problem of the reification of nature, or that his image of nature was entirely devoid of an ethical basis. A great deal of Marx's later hostility to images of "nature" can be seen to emerge from his disdain for reactionary social constellations of the nineteenth century that appealed to the mythopoeic image of "nature" in order to preserve hierarchical political traditions.

Beyond the Limits of Marx's Nineteenth Century

Arguably, most if not all shortcomings of Marx's anti-naturalism can be traced to his failure to transcend the "subjective subject-object," or distorted image of nature, that characterized his historic period. To provide one concrete example: as early as in *The German Ideology* Marx and Engels seemingly essentialize the liberal anthropology of Locke, which has as its defining feature that private property is held to be the timeless a priori relation of "man" to biological nature (and thus that competition for the appropriation of nature gives rise to a "legitimate" conflict between competing class societies).[35] Nature-as-property is in fact conceived as the ontological foundation of social relations as such, a glaring contradiction to the very premises of historical materialism:

> The only barrier which the community can encounter in relating to the natural conditions of production—the earth as to *its own property* (if we jump ahead to the settled peoples) is

another community, which already claims it as its own inorganic body. *Warfare* is therefore one of the earliest occupations of each of these naturally arisen communities, both for the defence of their property and for obtaining new property.[36]

This depiction is highly anachronistic. The prevailing conceptions of "property," "competition," and even "the State" have their origins in modern bourgeois society and would have been utterly foreign to the idioms of many earlier peoples, even many of the settled peoples of early Bronze and Iron Age civilizations. In this rather careless passage, Marx and Engels do history a great disservice by representing propertarian relations as a timeless, a priori, and "natural" fact, as if human communities have never organized themselves on any different basis than the capitalistic "appropriation" of the "ready-made fruits of the earth."[37]

A similarly careless passage with essentializing implications can be encountered in volume 3 of Marx's *Capital*. It is with no small irony that here Marx seems to transform the possibility of reconciliation between humanity and nature into a frozen Fichtean antinomy:

> Just as the savage must wrestle with nature to satisfy his needs, to maintain and reproduce his life, so must civilized man, and he must do so in all forms of society and under all possible modes of production.[38]

The only way this passage could make sense, within the historical understanding of nature advanced by Marx, would be to view Marx's choice of verbs, such as "wrestle," very metaphorically, perhaps poetically. "Wrestling" with nature, under this interpretation, would become a metaphor for its rational and ethical integration into human social life. Only this interpretation is in accord with Marx's Hegelian belief in a progressive World-Spirit and the downfall of capitalism at the hands of the proletariat, a philosophy of history that still may have seemed plausible within Marx's viewpoint of the nineteenth century. Why else would he quote so approvingly, in discussing the breakup of feudal India under colonialism, the words of Goethe's *An Suleika*?

> Should this torture then torment us
> Since it brings us greater pleasure?
> Were not through the rule of Timur
> Souls devoured without measure?[39]

The domination of nature and the suffering of the oppressed under capitalism are innately justified, for the later Marx, because the capitalist mode of production and its instrumental rationality are viewed as inherently redemptive. The "immiseration thesis" of *Capital* volume 3, in which the declining rate of profit heralds the immanent decline of capitalism, suggests that capitalist relations of production are supposed to produce the indefatigable conditions for its own negation, the liberation of its forces of production for rational human ends. But what if such conditions are not produced, or are subverted? When much of Europe was reduced to rubble in the second world war, what was brought about was not the end of capitalism but rather an even more entrenched and more global capitalism that could ensure soaring profits through Europe's reconstruction, and even—via the welfare state and other social-democratic measures—integrating the proletariat's apparent, short-term material interests within the apparatuses of production and consumption. These events, and others since then, continue to compel a radical rethinking not only of Marx's theoretical premises but particularly of his implacably affirmative philosophy of history—a theoretical crisis well understood and responded to by the first generation of the Frankfurt School.

Similarly, Bookchin's social ecology, through a careful reading of more recent anthropology and of classical and medieval history, carries out such a radical rethinking and arrives at two essential differences from the later Marxian nature-concept. First, the relationship between humanity and nature is by no means metabolized as an ontological "struggle"; rather, Bookchin's exploration of "organic society" illuminates how different civilizations possessed a more reciprocal and ecological image of nature.[40] Second, far from being "inevitable" or "natural," social hierarchies and the legacy of social domination are shown to have originated in a complex, dialectical "metabolism" between the social structure of tribal society and the natural conditions of its becoming, which were favorable in many respects to the rise of elder rule and male warrior societies.[41] Consequently, Bookchin reverses Marx's progressive philosophy of history that would place the domination of nature within a spectrum of preconditions for freedom, instead attempting to locate the genesis of instrumental reason not in terms of an ontological historical necessity but rather as one among many possible pathways elaborated by specific, historical systems of domination/hierarchy. This reversal, while requiring a proper reconstruction of social ecology itself and various qualifications that would emerge from it, only gives stronger emphasis to the leitmotifs in Marx's historical materialism that would construe the prevailing images of nature as products of a specific social history, of specific potentialities of a given historical period and its acculturation of its surrounding ecology. It is this materialist understanding of history, propelled by the foundations of Marx's thought, that ultimately furnishes the possibility of a critical analysis of the prevailing images or concepts of nature in terms of "reification" or "hegemony." Without such theoretical foundations, a dialectical naturalism would be unthinkable.

Post-Proudhonian Anarchism and the Persistence of Mythopoeic Naturalism

Since the emergence of anarchism in the form of Pierre-Joseph Proudhon's (1809–1865) political theory, it has become common, no less among the Left than elsewhere, to regale anarchism as a doctrine of little more than chaotic, individualist protest, culminating in its most infamous associations with the acts of terrorists and vagabonds. Certainly the element of exaggeration present in this caricature, which has always smelled of the burning wick of sectarian conspiracy, cannot be readily dismissed, for nineteenth- and early twentieth-century anarchism had a vibrant communistic thread that placed stress upon the utopian ideal of a nonhierarchical society, determined by the allegedly "natural" relations of mutual aid.[42] Yet in no small part even anarchism's social dimension, which has long since given up its ground to the cultural colossus of liberal individualism, tends to remain captive to the mystique of a concept of "natural law" that supplants historical materialism's emphasis upon mediated character of what appears as "nature." Herein lurks anarchism's allegiance with the "bad infinity" of a utopianism that devolves into the empty worship of the natural and a concept of revolution closely bound up with a sentiment of restorationism: the recovery of a mythopoeic "natural society," as opposed to the creation of a new political order.[43]

An immanent critique of anarchism's concept of nature—insofar as a continuity of sorts exists across the diffuseness of its theory—must therefore begin by examining the contradictory body of values that makes up the appeal of various anarchist theorists to the "natural" or to relations of "natural law." Ironically, despite the political diversity that is often celebrated by adherents of anarchism as a token of virtue, the recurring appeal to "natural" law or "natural" society forms one of the most cohesive leitmotifs across all of the major anarchist thinkers of the nineteenth and twentieth century. It is Proudhon alone, the founder of modern anarchism, who is the exception to this rule. Despite what Pritchard calls Proudhon's "natural ontology,"[44] it is evident throughout his large canon of writing that Proudhon remained highly skeptical of various appeals to "nature," tending to see them, in a spirit later echoed by Marxian theory, as mere rationalizations or reifications of ideological hegemony. As Pritchard observes:

> . . . for Proudhon there is no natural transcendental order to society either 'domestic' or 'international.' Social order is produced over time precisely because what is just at any given moment is only relative to human intelligence, our desires and passions and *drive*. Society is continually seeking order in this anarchy and consecrating new world orders according to new, emergent norms of global justice *and* in response to material change.[45]

Indeed, Proudhon seems to have regarded the concept of nature as solely applicable to social constellations of spontaneous association. Such associations, in his words, "willy-nilly impose upon themselves some conditions of solidarity . . . which soon constitutes itself into a city or a political organism, affirms itself in its unity, its independence, its life or its own movement (*autokinesis*), and its autonomy."[46] These "natural groups," giving birth as they do to a "political organism," bring about their own distinct bodies of values and relations; in essence, they are *historical* phenomena. The dialectic of ecology and human history is thus conceived within the conditions of a determinate potentiality. The question of nature, for Proudhon, must always be redirected back to the question of social relations and the dialectic between different political "organisms" that emerge in given historical circumstances.

The picture that emerges from post-Proudhonian anarchism, however, is rather different.[47] Post-Proudhonian anarchism drew from Romanticists such as Rousseau in arguing for the restoration of a more authentic, basically unchanging "natural" society. This fascination with "natural law" redolent within the Romantic movement can be read in historical terms, as Lukács suggests, as both an instinctive reaction against the consequences of the capitalist despoliation of nature and as a confused repository for all of the utopian dreams of reconciliation that bourgeois ideology taboos.[48] However, one must seriously question whether Rousseau's faith in the instinctivism of a "natural" morality is really a repudiation of the historical values of bourgeois society and the negative concept of nature it mythologizes.[49] What is in fact historical—human relations with nature and the moral vocabulary prevailing political structures weave into the *appearance* of nature—may be subtly obscured by a system of thought that imbues nature with an ahistorical, "perfect" substance, reducing the content of social pathologies into a jargon of natural authenticity. "Yet," as Adorno notes, "history does intrude on every word and withholds each word from the recovery of some alleged original meaning, that meaning which the jargon is always trying to track down."[50] Post-Proudhonian anarchism may be shown to err precisely insofar as it seeks to *recover* an allegedly original and basically static nature, as distinct from the dialectical imagination that would elucidate how "nature" has been continually transformed within its historical matrix of potentialities.[51]

Nature Against Itself: The Contradictions of Bakunin's "Natural Human Society"

The first major anarchist thinker to follow in Proudhon's footsteps, chronologically, was Mikhail Bakunin (1814–1876).[52] Bakunin advances a pivotal concept of "natural human society" and deploys it as a substance of cooperative universal morality, against all notions of government, laws, and political order. Thus liberty, for Bakunin, consists in the pursuit of the laws of nature or in the restoration of natural society. Liberty is

> based upon the respectful observations of the laws of nature . . . it is finally the well thought-out and free organization of the social environment in conformity with the natural laws inherent in every human society. The first and last condition of this liberty rests then on absolute submission to the omnipotence of nature.[53]

From the outset, this statement is startlingly ambiguous. How may we ascertain, we may ask, the natural laws inherent in every society? Furthermore, are such laws unchanging throughout every society, or does every society have its "unique" natural laws, and therefore is nature to be conceived on a relativistic basis? His further sentiments on natural law only seem to add another dimension of vagueness:

> ... the harmony of the forces of nature only appears as the actual result of that continual struggle which is the very condition of life and movement.... If order is natural and possible in the universe, it is solely because this universe is not governed according to some system imagined in advance and imposed by a supreme will.[54]

Already, we may note a glaring contradiction: nature should be "respectfully" observed, yet its content to be observed is "that continual struggle which is the very condition of life and movement." This would seem to be a classical statement of social Darwinism, and one potentially inclined to fascistic conclusions. But then, he also adds the sentiment that it is necessary for human beings "to make their social environment moral" by bringing it into conformity with "justice," which is "complete liberty of everyone in the most perfect equality of all."[55]

Yet one cannot help but to observe here that "justice," making the social environment moral, would seem to be in clear conflict with "liberty" insofar as liberty is "based upon the observation of laws of nature" that are *in conflict* with prevailing social morality. Because Bakunin fails to substantiate or clarify what these "laws" may be, or how they may be recognized beyond subjective judgment, one could easily assume, for example, a social Darwinian pathos of "continual struggle" and "movement" that is in conflict with the requirements of justice. Liberty—respectfully observing these brutal laws of nature—would then be in open conflict with "justice," or attaining "complete liberty of everyone in the most perfect equality of all," in contradistinction to natural law. But then, liberty would be in conflict with liberty! If we were to instead eliminate this contradiction by presuming that nature assumes the dimensions conducive to liberty—a conclusion that seems to be more congenial to Bakunin's denial of free will and championing of materialism—then we have a concept of "natural society" that is synonymous with egalitarian "justice." However, it is precisely here that we meet with another terminal contradiction: for, as we shall soon see, Bakunin asserts that natural law is alone that which can be recognized by the judgment of a subject free of all external authority (Bakunin's included). Consequently, a subject could choose to agree with Bakunin that natural society was equivalent with egalitarian justice; but one could just as freely consent to a fascist or anarcho-capitalist "imaginary" of nature deeply at odds with any socialist conception of egalitarian justice.

Murray Bookchin has suggested that such moments of incoherence within the development of anarchist theory are a result of its failure to resolve the historical tension between socialism, with its belief in an *institutionalized* society and some measure of political authority, however democratic, and liberalism, with its unrelenting ethos of individual freedom from authority, regardless of its degree of democratic justification.[56] An awareness of this unresolved contradiction helps to make sense of much in anarchist theory, especially with regard to its often incoherent conception of "natural society." Indeed, this contradiction is apparent in Bakunin's work, beginning with his reformulation of the "social problem" posed by the great French Revolution: "To organize society, in such a manner that every individual, man or woman, should, at birth, find almost equal means for the development of his or her various faculties and the full utilization of his or her work."[57] Bearing this in mind, it is not difficult to see why Bakunin openly condemns the anarchist individualists in emphasizing the "natural" context in which individuality comes into its truth:

> Society antedates and at the same time survives every human individual, being in this respect like Nature itself. It's eternal like Nature, or rather, having been born upon our earth, it will last as long as the earth. A radical revolt against society would therefore be just as impossible for man as a revolt against nature, human society being nothing else but the last great manifestation or creation of Nature upon this earth. And an individual who would want to rebel against society . . . would play himself beyond the pole of existence.[58]

Furthermore, Bakunin goes so far as to set out the basic features of what he calls "the new revolutionary State," which is not a "State" inasmuch as it is a core principle of communal self-administration:

> Since the revolution must everywhere be achieved by the people, and since its supreme direction must always rest in the people, organized in a free federation of agricultural and

industrial associations, the new revolutionary State, organized from the bottom up by revolutionary delegates . . . will have as its chief objective the administration of public services, not the governing of peoples.[59]

Thus, the *socialist* dimension of Bakunin's philosophy. Such would seem to indicate an unambiguous embrace of a *political* theory, with its concomitant view of the *politicized* context of "natural society" (as for Proudhon).

However, this superficial emphasis upon public administration and organization begins to unravel upon closer examination. Bakunin's image of nature, notwithstanding its Hegelian trappings, actually moves in the opposite direction of Hegel's sublation model carried out in the *Philosophy of History* lectures. Rather than championing the historical emergence of spirit from nature, Bakunin seeks to dissolve spirit's substance back *into* natural law. Blurring the distinction between biological first nature and human second nature allows Bakunin to equivocate them in a concept that he refers to as "natural human society."[60] Although evoked in progressive, Hegelian terms as the "starting point" of civilization contrary to the state, Bakunin's "natural human society" nonetheless projects an image of social institutions as essentially innate, or transcendentally preconditioned, rather than consciously or purposively created by human reason. This distinction between institutions emerging from specific social relations and a transcendental "natural human society" may seem insignificant at first glance, but it becomes decisive in the context of political theory. If morals are envisioned to unconsciously emanate from a benign "nature," even a directly democratic government or democratically administered judiciary are appraised as *obstacles* to the realization of "natural human society." In other words, "natural society" presumes a state of harmonious free agreement between individuals; individual liberty is held to be sacrosanct, and of greater worth in the "triumph of justice" than the democratic administration of justice: "There may be many unarticulated laws that rule [society], but these are natural laws, inherent in the social body . . . it follows that they are not to be confused with the judicial and political laws proclaimed by some legislative authority."[61] It appears to have not occurred to Bakunin that what appears as "natural" to one social group, for example a ruling class, will likely resemble nothing of the "natural" laws of the group it is oppressing. "Natural laws, inherent in the social body," substantiate nothing more than a vague universalism, a reformulation of liberal-individualist consensus ideology qua the reification of "natural society."

This is the point at which Bakunin's anarchism dissolves into an irretrievable individualism. For "the liberty of man," Bakunin asserts, "consists solely in this; that he obeys natural laws because he has himself recognized them as such, and not because they have been externally imposed upon [him] by any extrinsic will whatever, divine or human, collective or individual."[62] And yet, "the first and last condition of liberty rests then on absolute submission to the omnipotence of nature."[63] The contradiction here is that one must submit to an "omnipotence" whose ground is nevertheless that one *recognizes* it as "nature." If we resolve this contradiction, we are then left with *subjectivity* as the ontological determinant of "nature" and "natural society." The Bakuninist image of society is essentially dissolved into an autarchy, in which presumably sovereign egos seemingly determine their own "nature" within the limits of subjective recognition.

However, this abstract construction bears little resemblance to the notion of a historically mediated subjectivity, nor to that of a universal natural law; in fact, it is glaringly incoherent and at odds with itself. In the first instance, individuals would have to exist in a social vacuum, in which their daily habits, opinions, and prejudices were not shaped by the social psychology of a given political order, in order to recognize nature free of reification; moreover, individuals would need to be of the psychological type of the freethinker, a specimen that is reasonably rare even within the most spirited of revolutionary periods and has as its precondition a long period of gestation in the form of prerevolutionary reading groups and other forms of consciousness raising. This raises the question of the concrete, historical *reality* of subjectivity, which allegedly freely determines the laws of nature. Here, Adorno's discussion of the category of narcissism within the psychological framework of fascism is a powerful rejoinder to Bakunin:

> It is precisely [the] idealization of himself which the fascist leader tries to promote in his followers, and which is helped by the Führer ideology. The people he has to reckon with generally undergo the characteristic modern conflict between a strongly developed rational, self-preserving ego agency and the continuous failure to satisfy their own ego demands. This conflict results in strong narcissistic impulses which can be absorbed and satisfied only through idealization as the partial transfer of narcissistic libido to the object. . . . This pattern of identification through idealization, the caricature of true

conscious solidarity, is, however, a collective one. It is effective in vast numbers of people with similar characterological dispositions and libidinal leanings. The fascist *community of the people* corresponds exactly to Freud's definition of a group as being 'a number of individuals who have substituted one and the same object for their ego ideal and have consequently identified themselves with one another in their ego.'[64]

Accordingly, it is more than plausible that significant numbers of individuals, under the dominion of bourgeois liberal society and its constant pressure of individual competition in the marketplace, would consent to give up their liberty in pursuit of the psychological security of the collective, to jettison individual responsibility amid its dissolution into herd conformity, and to derive a measure of psychological satisfaction from the collective idealization of the authoritarian leader; the creation of a culture industry under capitalism anticipates this, fascism completes it. Perversely enough, here fascism resembles socialism insofar as it abolishes (albeit illusorily) the rugged and often painful struggle for existence that market society embellishes as "nature." Instead, the masses take refuge, under fascism, in a collective idealization of a "nature" that is the embodiment of blood and soil nationalism and authoritarian realpolitik. Such forces become the literal embodiment of what Bakunin calls "omnipotent" nature—not ontologically, to be sure, but certainly ideologically. "While the masses think of themselves as the creators of their own destiny," observes Horkheimer of late capitalism, "they are the objects of their leaders."[65] The premature celebration of the capacity of individuals to judge natural laws for themselves, a common theme in both anarchism and liberalism, complacently overlooks the culture industry's and fascism's dissolution of true subjectivity; precisely this is what is affirmed as the democracy of subjective judgment in late bourgeois society.

Bakunin's assertion of the "omnipotence of nature," therefore, readily collapses beneath the relativism that his "recognition" thesis presupposes. What the masses may in greater likelihood submit to, under the reification of natural society, is a framework of domination, culturally and psychologically immersed within the continuity of its historical positivity. Indeed, that which Bakunin champions as "nature" would be frankly unrecognizable to a people long subjected to the positive institutions of hierarchical society. What is recognized as nature by the slave is the well-tread path of habit and native custom; nature is not truly known but only well known. Here, one cannot overlook the compelling dialectic of Étienne De La Boétie's 1548 essay:

> It is true that in the beginning men submit under constraint and by force; but those who come after them obey without regret and perform willingly what their predecessors had done because they had to. This is why men born under the yoke and then nourished and reared in slavery are content, without further effort, to live in their native circumstance, unaware of any other state or right, and considering as quite natural the condition into which they were born. There is, however, no heir so spendthrift or indifferent that he does not sometimes scan the account books of his father in order to see if he is enjoying all the privileges of his legacy or whether, perchance, his rights and those of his predecessor have not been encroached upon. Nevertheless it is clear enough that the powerful influence of custom is in no respect more compelling than in this, namely, habituation to subjection. It is said that Mithridates trained himself to drink poison. Like him we learn to swallow, and not to find bitter, the venom of servitude. It cannot be denied that nature is influential in shaping us to her will and making us reveal our rich or meager endowment; yet it must be admitted that she has less power over us than custom, for the reason that native endowment, no matter how good, is dissipated unless encouraged, whereas environment always shapes us in its own way, whatever that may be, in spite of nature's gifts. The good seed that nature plants in us is so slight and so slippery that it cannot withstand the least harm from wrong nourishment; it flourishes less easily, becomes spoiled, withers, and comes to nothing. Fruit trees retain their own particular quality if permitted to grow undisturbed, but lose it promptly and bear strange fruit not their own when ingrafted. Every herb has its peculiar characteristics, its virtues and properties; yet frost, weather, soil, or the gardener's hand increase or diminish its strength; the plant seen in one spot cannot be recognized in another.[66]

When Bakunin, therefore, argues that "natural laws . . . are not fixed by any authority,"[67] he fails to distinguish between his own ideological abstraction and the concrete historical trajectory in which the natural is mediated and reflected back upon itself. It is arguable that the subject of totally administered capitalism, acculturating the seeds of an original nature within its own soil of mediation, could no longer recognize what Bakunin endorses as an act of subjective recognition. In his attempt to lend this liberal abstraction the aura of facticity, his philosophy dissolves into the inevitable incoherence that accompanies the championing of free subjectivity within a concrete historical society that has denuded subjectivity into the ideology of its own absence—the mere object of administered manipulation. Only a society free of domination would be capable of recognizing the substance of the liberated ecological; moreover, through the exertion of its capacity for reason, it would no longer feel bound to the mystifications of tradition or ideological hegemony in the form of "natural society."

The Ambiguities of Kropotkin's Concept of "Anarchist Morality"

The anarchist-communist Peter Kropotkin (1842–1921) is chiefly known for his biological studies of animal behavior, his political polemics, and his renowned work on "mutual aid" as a factor of Darwinian evolution. He is also known, to a lesser extent, for a number of pamphlets elaborating the political philosophy of anarchist communism. Kropotkin's writings also illustrate sensitivity to the reciprocal determinations of ecology and society, a sensitivity that is often present in his intriguing studies of the relationship between the anthropological development of ethical conceptions and the influence of Darwinian natural selection. Influenced greatly by Bakunin, Kropotkin nevertheless endeavored to furnish Bakunin's vision of natural human society with greater precision, political form, and scientific objectivity. It is in this sense, among others, that Kropotkin's works are worthy of extended study. Nevertheless, it is true that he, too, could not sublate the theoretical stasis of a mythopoeic naturalism.

The reasons for this vary and must be illuminated in greater detail. In general terms, owing to his distrust of "institutions" and his faith in a positivistic "natural law," Kropotkin's theory of morality tends to dissolve into a simplistic endorsement of a benevolent Darwinism. Kropotkin simply does not ponder the question of whether human second nature *could* be unproblematically rendered into the first nature of Darwinian "laws," nor to what extent humanity's technological, cultural, and psychological nuances have to some extent transcended the laws of biological evolution to which they were once far more directly captive. For this reason, history's equivocal relationship between conscious and unconscious behavior, first and second natures, and structure and agency tends to be blurred by Kropotkin into the implacably positive identity of Darwinian "mutual aid." Mutual aid thus functions as the conceptual identity that obscures any distinction between forms of social cooperation that are basically instinctive, genetic, and fortuitous, and forms of social cooperation that emerge out of the ethical life of concrete social relations. Social mediation retains its "natural" character in Kropotkin precisely by his obscuring its differentiation *from* nature, and in the end human second nature is reduced into the conduit for an inevitable outgrowth of natural "instincts" and "laws." In a tendency inherited from Condillac, which Herder had already seen through in his critique of romantic anthropomorphisms,[68] Kropotkin lavishes upon humanity and animal life alike an undifferentiated instinctivism—the validation of an allegedly prepolitical biological drive.

Manifest under such a positivistic orientation, Kropotkin's theory of mutual aid as a factor of evolution remains dubious in its application to human history: for, as many of its bourgeois opponents have rightfully pointed out, it is woefully one-sided to tautologically posit an ethical substance as "nature" and then seek out examples. Here, the contrast between anarchism and social ecology could not be more dramatic. Where one posits from a cover concept of "sociability" the mythical substance of "nature," the other explores speculatively, within a historical continuum, the origins of ethical life as a result of history's emerging, self-determining potentialities. Such potentialities must be seen to give rise to actuality strictly within the conditions of development unique to a given historical period and its *concrete* configuration of a nature-society metabolism. Where a mythopoeic naturalism forever seeks out a metaphysical preconditioned, and uses natural phenomena selectively as a form of hypothesis validation, a dialectical naturalism holds fast to an image of nature that is always in some way conditioned, mediated, and thus acculturated within the history of human civilization. Because of this it is a dialectical naturalism alone that retains traces of the non-conceptual, the differentiated, and the concrete particular, as against the reifying tendencies that would subsume them.

For these reasons, it is at the outset by no means certain that Kropotkin escapes the very same charge that he levels at the bourgeois philosophy of history, particularly that of Hobbes: namely, that it is a one-sided doctrine that selectively confirms itself through historical examples and then passes itself off as a metaphysical absolute. The thesis that human ethics are rooted in animal instincts of mutual aid or self-sacrifice that are practically universal in nature is itself merely the absolute opposite, equally unmediated form of the Hobbesian dogma of the universal egoistic instinct inhering in human psychology.

Having placed the following analysis in such general outlines, let us now turn to consider Kropotkin's nature-concept more closely. A fitting place to begin is with Kropotkin's most renowned work, *Mutual Aid: A Factor of Evolution.* In his evaluation of Darwinian evolution, which forms the central thesis of this work, the tension between biological first nature and human second nature is omnipresent. His account of the universality of mutual aid based on his observations in Siberia is a case in point. While studying animal behavior in Siberia, he remarks, he

> . . . saw Mutual Aid and Mutual Support carried on to an extent which made me suspect in it a feature of the greatest importance for the maintenance of life, the preservation of each species, and its further evolution. And finally, I saw among the semi-wild cattle and horses in Transbaikalia, among the wild ruminants everywhere, the squirrels, and so on, that when animals have to struggle against scarcity of food . . . the whole of that portion of the species which is affected by the calamity, comes out of the ordeal so much impoverished in vigour and health, that *no progressive evolution of the species can be based upon such periods of keen competition.* Consequently, when my attention was drawn, later on, to the relations between Darwinism and Sociology, I could agree with none of the works and pamphlets that had been written upon this important subject . . . to admit a pitiless inner war for life within each species, and to see in that war a condition of progress, was to admit something which not only had not yet been proved, but also lacked confirmation from direct observation.[69]

To give Kropotkin his due here, there remains a ring of truth, to this day, to Kropotkin's rebuff that the Hobbesian conception of nature rests upon little more than pseudoscience, lacking any plausible confirmation in studies of animal behavior. For example, even the famous Neo-Darwinist and evolutionary biologist Richard Dawkins (b. 1941), who entitled his most renowned book *The Selfish Gene*, has voiced support for the thesis that altruism and cooperation are often more effective genetic "pathways" for natural selection than Malthusian competition.[70] Similarly, the evolutionary biologist Stephen Jay Gould (1941–2002) has more recently constructed a highly sympathetic account of Kropotkin's observations.[71] To extrapolate from the studies of animal life a totalizing philosophical anthropology, however, already betrays the presence of a reifying mentality that seeks to reduce the diversity of human history to the abstraction of universal laws of nature. Such an analysis distorts human history, insofar as it fails to register how that history has gradually become captive to forces qualitatively different from merely *natural* selection. Mutual aid may well be a tendency or principle of the natural world; indeed, Darwinian science may well confirm its presence as

> . . . a feeling infinitely wider than love or personal sympathy—an instinct that has been slowly developed among animals and men [sic] in the course of an extremely long evolution, and which has taught animals and men alike the force they can borrow from the practice of mutual aid and the joys they can find in social life . . . the unconscious recognition of the force that is borrowed by each man [sic] from the practice of mutual aid; of the close dependency of everyone's happiness upon the happiness of all; and of the sense of justice, or equity, which brings the individual to consider the rights of every other individual as equal to his own.[72]

Yet a truly dialectical account of human history would only be complete with an earnest look at the countervailing historical "forces" that construct a realm of domination that severs the dependency of human beings upon one another, that disfigures justice into authoritarian dictation, and that deforms the individual into a monad that pursues her or his self-interest at the expense of all others. One need only look at the neoliberal cult of the entrepreneur, at the facial gestures of a fascist mob following the mere mention of Jews, or at the vast historical limitations that cosmopolitan ethics must grapple with (most recently in the form of nationalism) to conclude that the allegedly universal "feeling" of mutual aid is not so infinitely wide as Kropotkin may have believed.

Yet his only refrain is to return, somewhat dogmatically, to the supposed purity of nature. We are told:

> It is evident that it would be quite contrary to all that we know of nature if men [sic] were an exception to so general a rule [of mutual aid]: if a creature so defenceless as man was at his beginnings should have found his protection and his way to progress, not in mutual support, like other animals, but in a reckless competition for personal advantages, with no regard to the interests of the species.[73]

This is a direct allusion to Rousseau, who also noted (in his *Discourse on the Origins of Inequality*) the basically defenseless physiology of *Homo sapiens* in his ridiculing of Hobbes.[74] Yet inasmuch as the romantic imagery of the "noble savage" justifies itself in the idyllic life of certain tribal institutions, it was arguably by no means so universal a rule in the life of tribal humanity as Rousseau and Diderot tended to suggest. Kropotkin shows some regard for this, albeit at the expense of subsuming it once again under the cover concept of mutual aid. He remarks that the "primitive" tribalist

> . . . is not an ideal of virtue, nor is he [sic] an ideal of "savagery." . . . the primitive man has one quality, elaborated and maintained by the very necessities of his hard struggle for life—*he identifies his own existence with that of his tribe; and without that quality mankind never would have attained the level it has obtained now.*[75]

It is evident in passages such as these that Kropotkin has failed to consider whether tribalism is to be regarded simply as a biological instinct of "mutual aid" as he positivistically asserts, or rather whether the identification of existence with the tribe is the product of a mediation through a *distinctly human* second nature. Notwithstanding humanity's omnipresent reliance upon biological nature, the tendency to transform it into the mere object of a "natural law" obscures the dialectical turn in evolutionary history according to which humanity has gradually distinguished its own social culture from a merely instinctive nature. With this distinction comes not only the potential for more sophisticated forms of cooperation, but also the outgrowths of a hierarchical and dominatory social history, with which the emergence (and more recently reemergence) of popular fascism bring about a regression behind "the level it has obtained" ethically.

A degree of recognition of human second nature is nonetheless concealed in a contradictory and irresolute form beneath the positivism of Kropotkin's analysis. At best, however, it remains implicit, undeveloped, an essence that does not appear; it is recognized only through what Kropotkin terms developing "conceptions," conceptions that are once again subsumed under an allegedly instinctive "nature":

> When the clan organization, assailed as it was from within by the separate family, and from without by the dismemberment of the migrating clans and the necessity of taking in strangers of different descent—the village community, based upon a territorial conception, came into existence. . . . The conceptions of a wider union, extended to whole stems and to several stems of various origin, were slowly elaborated. The old conceptions of justice which were conceptions of mere revenge, slowly underwent a deep modification—the idea of amends for the wrong done taking the place of revenge. The customary law . . . [constituted] a system of habits intended to prevent the oppression of the masses by the minorities whose powers grew in proportion to the growing facilities for private accumulation of wealth.[76]

For Kropotkin, then, it seems that it was enough to merely prove that "feelings" of mutual aid and instinctive communism existed side by side the official histories of church, state, and the burgeoning egoism of bourgeois society. It was enough, that is to say, to prove that an ethos of mutual aid had manifested historically as an outgrowth of the solidarity of the oppressed, irrespective of the countermanding forces that all too often frustrated it.

Nevertheless, this coexistence does not justify the imperiousness of Kropotkin's declaration that mutual aid is literally the "predominant fact" of nature.[77] Indeed, while perhaps an accurate enough statement when applied to nonhuman nature, it becomes a distortion if carelessly applied to the social relations of human history. It is precisely this polemical moment—the embrace of a reified instinctivism and its grandiose application to human history—that has had the most unfortunate consequences for the development of anarchist political theory. Precisely because of Kropotkin's failure to distinguish the presence of social mediation from Bakuninist instinct or "sociability" in his analysis of human history, the concept of "mutual aid" posits a psychologically *passive* concept of freedom in which "nature" must merely be allowed to take its course.

The resulting idea that humanity's various pathologies of domination can be resisted by merely affirming humanity's substance as one of mutual aid not only acts as a daily apologia for the inhumanity in which humanity is immersed; it gives way to a dangerous passivity that may complacently disregard the sober imperative to *transform* "nature" in the midst of social revolution, whether that be first or second nature. Perhaps not least among the reasons why there is, to this date, no compelling anarchist analysis of fascism resides in anarchism's inability to come to terms with human behavior that rests outside of the assumption of a benevolent universal naturalism. By point of contrast, it is by no means a coincidence that those psychoanalytic theories that have taken seriously the mediation of sexual biology through social and economic relations, be they bourgeois in the form of Freud or socialist in the form of Wilhelm Reich and the Frankfurt School, have also developed the most far-reaching analyses of fascism.

None of this is to deny that Kropotkin does acknowledge the limits of mutual aid in his more carefully worded passages, wherein he admits that two contradictory developments may coexist simultaneously in particular historical circumstances. However, it would be most erroneous to consider this a dialectical awareness. From "the lowest stages of the animal world," we are told, "we can follow [mutual aid's] uninterrupted evolution, in opposition to a number of contrary agencies, through all degrees of human development, up to the present times."[78] Like Fichte and Hegel's ultimately positive World-Spirit, mutual aid is made to appear as the metaphysical absolute toward which an allegedly progressive history marches: "Each time . . . that an attempt to return to this old principle was made, its fundamental idea itself was widened."[79]

This temerity is sometimes weakened in Kropotkin's later works, however, particularly the *Ethics: Origin and Development*. He observes there, with a drastic yet unexplained qualification, that the supreme task of ethics is to find a rational synthesis between individuation and the common welfare of all "in the form of the potentialities concealed in modern society."[80] Here we gain a glimpse of the idea of a developmental theory of morality—a vision that moves the notion of mutual aid beyond the egregious cover concept of "natural law," though by no means consistently. In this work, Kropotkin resolves the ambiguities of the historical development of morality into an ever-present dialectical conflict between the dominatory forces of social development, which always aim at the fortification of particular interests against the whole, and the liberatory forces of social development, which strive for the freeing of universal humanity from the yoke of domination through social forms of solidarity, mutual aid, and radical egalitarianism. The latter is grounded in the increasing sophistication of mutual aid from a mere instinct to a conscious ethical life; to the former, however, he gives the dignity of its own distinct history and trajectory of development, a dignity he was not willing to extend to it in the earlier *Mutual Aid*. It is only, therefore, in his twilight years, and within the pages of an obscure work, that Kropotkin concedes the possibility of a human second nature not identical with a mythopoeic instinctivism.

For the mature Kropotkin, in contrast to the earlier themes of *Mutual Aid*, the progress from morality to ethics and its peculiar social determinations are products of historical determination, aided by the growth of human sociality and consciousness of freedom. Thereby do the historical essences of ethical life, which are by no means reducible to the mythopoeic nature-concept of *Mutual Aid*, come to be smuggled into his theory of society:

> Throughout the history of mankind [sic], from the most primeval times, there is a conflict between these two elements: the striving for justice, i.e., equity, and the striving for individual domination over others, or over the many. The struggle between these two tendencies manifests itself in the most primitive societies. The "elders," in their accumulated wisdom of experience, who saw what hardships were brought upon the entire tribe through changes in the tribal mode of life, or who had lived through periods of privation, were afraid of all innovations, and resisted all changes by force of their authority. In order to protect the established customs they founded the first institutions of the ruling power in society. They were gradually joined by the wizards, shamans, sorcerers, in combination with whom they organized secret societies for the purpose of keeping in obedience the other members of the tribe and for protecting the traditions and

the established system of tribal life. At the beginning these societies undoubtedly supported equality of rights, preventing individual members from becoming excessively rich or from acquiring dominant power within the tribe. But these very secret societies were the first to oppose the acceptance of equity as the fundamental principle of social life . . . [and] that which we find amongst societies of primitive savages . . . has been continued throughout the entire history of mankind up to the present time. The Magi of the East, the priests of Egypt, Greece, and Rome, who were the first investigators of nature and of its mysteries, and then the kings and the tyrants of the East, the emperors and the senators of Rome, the ecclesiastical princes in Western Europe, the military, the judges, etc.—all endeavoured . . . to prevent the ideas of equity, constantly seeking expression in society, from being realized in life and from threatening their right to inequality, to domination.[81]

Against the dogmas of the moral relativists and sophists, the deontological intuitivists (such as the Neo-Kantians and, more broadly, the religious metaphysical schools), and the utilitarian moralists, Kropotkin espouses what might be termed a developmental notion of ethics in which we can trace a historical movement from primitive conceptions to more sophisticated ones, all the while determined by a relation of historical necessity—a development, in other words, embedded in the dialectical interrelation between social history and its natural conditions of becoming.

The elderly Kropotkin's developmental naturalism is arguably nothing less than a more abortive and self-contradictory form of dialectical naturalism. If it is admitted that ethical conceptions have developed through the particularity of a given social period, this educes the possibility that it is not purely a benevolent "natural law" or instinct to which humanity owes its ethical progress but rather *specific constellations* of social relations that have directly facilitated its institutional development. This, in turn, gives birth to a vital distinction between biological nature, governed by instincts and drives, and that of a differentiated human second nature, in which is enclosed the development of ethics. Nevertheless, these late innovations remain unfortunately obscure, and the legacy of Kropotkin's anarchism today rests almost solely upon the conclusions found in *Mutual Aid*.

Digression: On the Historical Scars of Nature Philosophy

The specifically mythopoeic, or reified character, of Kropotkin's naturalism emerges from the limits of the Darwinian concept of nature when applied to *human* history. As a cover concept of natural history, natural selection is always prone to distortion or oversimplification if it refuses to come down into the concrete ecological situation in which a given species finds itself: a sentiment at the very heart of Darwin's *On the Origins of Species* that many of his most zealous self-styled followers blindly disregard. For this reason, evolutionary theory can only expand to encompass the totality of world history if it does not fail to account for the role of species differentiation, choice, and self-determination in natural evolution. A dialectical naturalism would alone be that which apprehends "nature" not merely as that which confers survival value, but in terms of a social organism's increasing differentiation and diversity in light of its overall potentiality. By contrast, a cover concept of nature that holds fast to an undifferentiated "sociability" or "cooperation" as a ubiquitous law of social development is a form of identity thinking that fails to grapple with the problem of differentiation—specifically, of *human* differentiation, which renders survival of the organism contingent upon the peculiarities of civilization's laws and social relations, not merely the tribal procuring of food, water, and shelter in a mythologized state of nature.

This problem is epitomized in Kropotkin's highly ambiguous concept of morality. To render moral feeling equivalent with "nature" is one of the most sweeping forms of argumentation frequently adapted by Kropotkin in seeking a universal grounding for mutual aid. Such a formulation appeals to the intuitive, to the mediated that passes itself off as the immediate, and therefore to the false. Moral feeling, as Nietzsche laid bare in great detail, is a product not only of nature but of social environment; for this reason, it bears all of the scars of history. Radical feminism in particular has drawn attention to this in its far-reaching analysis of the prevailing concept of sexuality.[83] Precisely what is popularly affirmed as the natural is what most of all should be held in suspicion of being something more than it appears to be. In other words, one might say the *object* of nature and the *cover concept* of nature refer to phenomena of a different order and cannot be intuited without violence to the former. Where one leaves open the possibility of giving voice to the potentialities of the natural world, and thereby the possibility of an alternative configuration of ecological relationships, the other is little more than a reified implement of ideological hegemony.

His failure to make such a distinction is where Kropotkin most often runs aground. This failure to distinguish between object and representation is, however, redolent of much of the history of nature philosophy. The fallacious attribution of nature to what originates in the determinate conditions of human history is a problem repeated ad infinitum in many system-building attempts to formulate a concept of "nature." Hence the perspicacity of Marx's notion of "historical materialism," which firmly asserted the *historical* basis of truth against the reifying tendencies of formal philosophy. The problem of reification in philosophy lies not in the content of its various formulations but in the nature of the thing itself: for as both Feuerbach and Adorno observe, philosophical truth must remain one-sided so long as its subject remains trapped in idealist abstractions, in the traditional formalities of logical propositions. Conceptual identity always retains a certain distance from the thing represented: an important insight of Hegel's early philosophy, albeit one that was glossed over by the later Hegel and subsequently only revived by Adorno.

It is precisely the ambiguity of what is celebrated mythopoeically as "nature" that lends strength to those forces that would celebrate barbarism as the halo of natural authenticity. "Mutual aid" in its linguistic immediacy calls to mind the gloss of an advertising slogan that papers the image of social harmony over the underlying reality of mass suffering and wretchedness. Just as the assumed immediacy of language, frequently taken up in the textbooks of logical positivists, betrays precisely the historical character of language, so too does the assumed harmony between mutual aid and natural law threaten to come to the aid of what exists. In the spate of floods and cyclones that regularly afflict northern Australia, for example, various news anchors invoke the all-too-valorous spirit of "mutual aid" in their uplifting tracts about the goodness of humanity and its national spirit. One does not have to delve too deeply to discover that the meaning of this "goodness" is the harmony between instinctive responses to suffering and the preservation of the prevailing power structure. When in need of visual imagery, the news industries have not infrequently shown video footage of flood and cyclone victims banding together to rebuild the small businesses of the petty-bourgeois and to help restock their wares for future custom.

In the case of Marx, as we have observed earlier, the relationship of natural to social history was construed in a dialectical form—by referring all appeals to "nature" to the presence of social mediation. But this insight remains inadequate if not sublated by a more heightened ecological sensibility and quickly regresses into the type of anti-naturalism often on display in vulgar Marxism. For natural history gives form, substance, and limitation to human history, and the study of ecology is not exhausted in the pragmatic concerns that occupy botanists or scientists. The cosmological scope of the natural world, including its almost limitless potential for diversity in the evolution of life on other planets and in solar systems and galaxies, challenges humanity to see in nature not merely its own self-reflection but also the potential for something other than what is.

The Self-Contradictory Historicism of Kropotkin's "Mutual Aid" Thesis

This distinctive divide between a mythopoeic and a dialectical naturalism is reflected in the political and philosophical implications that emerge from them. Where Kropotkin and other anarchists tend to conflate instinct with ethics and nature with a positivistic and unchanging "law," a dialectical naturalism regards mutual aid as little more than a *potentiality* that must be actively developed through the mediations of social institutions—be they revolutionary or otherwise—and the directiveness and intelligibility that they provide to history. This insight finds its aesthetic parallel in the work of the nineteenth-century symbolists and, later, the surrealists.

Kropotkin's positivism goes some way toward elucidating these differences in outlook. So much is indicated in his appraisal of Comte:

> [Comte's] main conclusion was that the social tendencies of man can be explained only by inherent quality, i.e., by instinct and by its urge toward the social life. As a contrast to egoism, Comte called this instinct *altruism*, and he regarded it as a fundamental property of human nature; moreover, he was the first to point out boldly that the same innate tendency exists in animals. . . . Moral tendencies are observed also amongst social animals, but morality as the joint product of instinct, feeling, and reason, exists only in man.[83]

The linguistic structure of Comte's concepts that Kropotkin glowingly recapitulates here betray a stress on fixity and law-like development, which leaves very little room for social determination in human history. Comte's employment of concepts of quality, property, force, and so forth, to connote human characteristics imply that animal and human nature are static, unchanging things, much akin to the laws of physics; but the dialectical truth of such conceptions is that they are the product of a particular social environment, a particular form of subjectivity, and a particular trajectory of social development, as Hegel illustrates so eloquently in the course of his *Phenomenology of Spirit*. Regardless of the binding framework of physical laws, the scope of diversity and potentiality in natural evolution is arguably wide enough to permit the differentiation and dialectic that suggest little in nature is permanently frozen into the unchanging moral sensibility that Kropotkin would imagine.

Despite Kropotkin's positivistic language of "instinct," "mental bent," and "sociality" however, there is a hidden, historical truth to his observations about the characteristics of mutual aid. This historicism comes to the fore in the midst of his analysis of the late feudal era. Here he observes that by failing to expand mutual aid beyond parochial limitations and by failing to spread over the landscape the principles of federation and decentralized communal governance, the freedom movements of the late feudal era allowed sufficient space for the reactionary regimes of centralized statism to develop again, modeled on the pathos of imperial Rome.[84] Even worse: through the economic, social, and ecological disruptions endemic to the early Renaissance era, they paved the way for the breakdown of communal life and the unbridled individualism of bourgeois society. What this seems to illustrate is that while mutual aid is often confused for a mythical and universal "instinct" of humanity, it is also grasped by Kropotkin in a self-contradictory way as *potentiality*, as that which must be actualized by the ethical progress of communitarian institutions.

Kropotkin's analysis of the late feudal era sheds so much light on its transition to capitalism, and with such a nuanced sensitivity to historical mediation, that it singularly seems to stand ajar from the mythopoeic naturalism that he elsewhere espouses. He says of the free communes of that era, for example:

> The life of a medieval city was a succession of hard battles to conquer liberty and to maintain it. True, that a strong and tenacious race of burghers had developed during those

fierce contests; true, that love and worship of the mother city had been bred by these struggles . . . but the sacrifices which the communes had to sustain in the battle for freedom were, nevertheless, cruel, and left deep traces of division on their inner life as well. Very few cities had succeeded, under a concurrence of favourable circumstances, in obtaining liberty at one stroke, and these few mostly lost it equally easily; while the great number had to fight fifty or a hundred years in succession, often more, before their rights to free life had been recognized, and another hundred years to found their liberty on a firm basis—the twelfth century charters thus being but one of the stepping-stones to freedom. In reality, the medieval city was a fortified oasis amidst a country plunged into feudal submission, and it had to make room for itself by the force of its arms.[85]

To survive these daunting pressures, the cities were obliged to form "leagues" for mutual protection and defense from the prey of feudal armies. However, these were eventually to succumb to the absolute monarchies that began to centralize political and economic power in the late medieval period. Accordingly, Kropotkin asks:

> Why did these centres of civilization, which attempted to answer to deeply-seated needs of human nature, and were so full of life, not live further on? Why were they seized with senile debility in the sixteenth century? And, after having repulsed so many assaults from without, and only borrowed new vigour from their interior struggles, why did they finally succumb to both?[86]

His answer points to three factors: the manifestation of new forms of social hierarchy, advanced by the emerging centralized states; a neglect of agriculture; and the influence of "ideas," what would in more contemporary terms be termed ideology. None of these, ironically, inherently affirm Kropotkin's cover concept of nature; rather, they emphatically establish the presence of historical mediation, the reworking of "nature" according to the concrete possibility of social forces.

The foundations of a new form of social hierarchy had thus been laid as a result of the social contradictions peculiar to that era and its social relationships. It was, Kropotkin suggests, the desperation of segments of the peasants for material needs and freedom (neglected by the feudal lords) that drove them to sanctify a new (yet ultimately illusory) faith in the powers of the centralized State.[87] Here the secret of mutual aid discloses itself, behind Kropotkin's back as it were, as a de facto negation of a mythic and undifferentiated natural law. In allowing such historicism into his analysis, Kropotkin allows for precisely the logic of social mediation, the play of forces that inhere in material circumstances and that crystallize into a human second nature—the very same second nature that Kropotkin would ironically attempt to dissolve into concepts of "sociability" and "cooperation" as transcendent "natural" laws.

This self-contradictory historicism can result in nothing else than a rejection of the supposed transcendentalism of "mutual aid" in the face of customs and institutions that are adapted out of the power structures of hierarchical rule. Nature can no longer be regarded as a transcendental and universal basis for ethics, as the cover concept of mutual aid would pretend. Rather, it is seen to contain within its moments of historical reflection the basis of a developing and mediated second nature, without which human history could never be coherently differentiated from biological nature. To admit of this influence of statist or hierarchical ideology upon social development is precisely to admit of the untruth of the cover concept of mutual aid: to reveal immanently that there exists a layer of historical mediation that the reification of nature dissolves into a mythopoeic, ultimately distorting instinctivism. The retreat into mythopoesis could only terminate in a tautological political doctrine that asserts that there is nothing to do in the building of a revolution except to let nature take its course. Such a politics could only questionably be called radical, let alone revolutionary; and perhaps this is why, even at the high-water mark of anarchist sentiment in revolutionary Spain, one could only with great difficulty point to an anarchism distinct from syndicalism and the latter's far more assertive interpretation of social mediation in nature.[88]

Naturalism as Politics

Orthodox reception practices, not least because of their subsumption beneath the academic division of labor, have traditionally obscured the extent to which a given nature philosophy is pregnant with political implications. This is nowhere more true than in the case of anarchism, which has long been ignored by the academic mainstream and yet treated rather uncritically by its adherents on the academic periphery, who tend to take its naturalism for granted.[89] A fitting point to begin an analysis of the political implications of mythopoeic naturalism would be the aporias of the anarchistic notion of a "stateless society," founded on the concept of "civil" or "natural" society.[90]

What is often considered to distinguish the libertarian dimension of socialism from the authoritarian is the theory of the state. For the latter it is characteristically viewed as an opportune means to an end, to be put in the service of socialist revolution. Yet, for the former, the very appeal to the state has always been treated with deep suspicion, as exemplified by Bakunin's prescient warnings against possible interpretations of Marxism and his entreaties that its realization would culminate not in free communism but rather in a state dictatorship masquerading as "socialism."[91] Libertarian socialists since the Enlightenment have similarly drawn attention to the repressive, aggressive, and destructive characteristics of the state. While not all have advocated its total abolition, libertarian socialism, and more specifically anarchism, is decidedly characterized by a distrust of the motivations and functional necessity of governments. Charles Fourier, by no means a socialist, articulated an important principle of libertarian socialism in his endorsement of the federative principle (a deeply libertarian doctrine aimed at limiting and decentralizing political power) and advocated face-to-face and humanly scaled communes as the best means to actualize the benign potentialities of nature, exemplified in the natural passions and drives. An early clue to the formulation of modern anarchist thought is evident here. It is the intrinsic conviction that human gregariousness has a "natural" rationality of its own; that the spirit of mutual aid is innate in the psychic structure of human biology, and takes on the role of an active and determining agent; and finally, that a preconditioned "nature" does not drive humanity into a war of each against all but contains the very seeds of freedom, egalitarianism, and reason, which can even be observed in many respects in the deeply social life of "primitive" humanity, and which can only be properly developed and elaborated further in a form of society free from the constraints of hierarchical power. From this principle, it is but a very small step to draw the conclusion that the state is an "unnatural" development and that the very progress and enlightenment of humanity can only be achieved with its abolition.

As Kropotkin and most other anarchists define it, "the state" is a distinctly modern development, spanning a life of only a few centuries;

thus, it is by no means to be falsely equivocated, in the manner of Hegel for example, with historical forms of civil society in toto. To conflate the state with society is, in Kropotkin's words,

> . . . to overlook the fact that Man [sic] lived in Societies for thousands of years before the State had been heard of; it is to forget that so far as Europe is concerned the State is of recent origin—it barely goes back to the sixteenth century; and finally, it is to ignore that the most glorious periods in Man's history are those in which civil liberties and communal life had not yet been destroyed by the State, and in which large numbers of people lived in communes and free federations.[92]

While Kropotkin, unfortunately, does not concretely address the *social structure* of these "societies," he nonetheless suggests that the idea that the state is a "timeless" social construct is thoroughly misguided. And indeed there are vast differences between the modern, centralized state and a federative structure of self-governance espoused by libertarian socialists, in which social and political administration becomes the task of decentralized communes federated into an interregional nexus. Significantly, he remarks:

> What we find today among the Kabyles, Mongols, Malays, etc., was the very essence of life of the barbarians in Europe from the fifth to the twelfth and even until the fifteenth century. Under the name of *guilds, friendships, brotherhoods*, etc., associations abounded for mutual defence, to avenge affronts suffered by some members of the union and to express solidarity, to replace the 'eye for an eye' vengeance by compensation, followed by the acceptance of the aggressor in the brotherhood; for the exercise of trades, for aid in case of illness, for defence of the territory; to prevent encroachments of a nascent authority; for commerce, for the practice of 'good neighbourliness'; for propaganda—in a word for all that Europeans, educated by the Rome of the Caesars and the Popes, nowadays expect from the State.[93]

Given such examples, Kropotkin rejoins that the state is not merely unnecessary to the progress of human affairs but deleterious to them. State law, for example, "originated in established usage and custom, and . . .

from the beginning it has represented a skillful mixture of social habits, necessary to the preservation of the human race, with other customs imposed by those who used popular superstition as well as the right of the strongest to their own advantage."[94] This raises the question of the basic characteristics of a stateless or "natural" society.

On this point an irresolvable aporia is met. Social ecology and anarchism may well be united in their bifurcation of "state" and "society"—a distinction with a significant historical pedigree in Gerard Winstanley and the French sansculottes more generally. Both may also, to be sure, oppose themselves to the prevailing "natural law" theory of the state, as so influentially espoused by the Right-Hegelian Lorenz Stein and still taught at many universities today. Nonetheless, on the notion of a stateless society, social ecology and anarchism are inviolably divided. Where the former seeks to constitute political authority out of a federated direct-democratic power structure of "communalism," the latter seeks to dissolve political authority into a mythic "consensus" and is often characterized by an innate distrust of political institutions as such.[95] Even as one of the most social of all the anarchists, Kropotkin's idea of a stateless society, founded in the presupposed universality of "mutual aid," is mired in a nebulous terminology of "free agreement" and "free association"—phrases so ambiguous that they could connote anything from liberal contract theory to anarcho-capitalism. Moreover, as we have discussed previously in the context of Bakunin, anarchism is marked by a resounding failure to specify the social or political forms toward which its praxis is oriented; even the syndicalist "worker's councils" remain economic rather than truly civic institutions, and many interpretations of anarchism lack, in contradistinction to Marxism, the clarity of a specific social stratum or class that is to bring about its realization. Thus, unsurprisingly, when Kropotkin comes to discuss the characteristics of his vaunted "free association," he tends to discuss them as purely "natural," spontaneous outgrowths of a "sociability" instinct, rather than as outgrowths of institutions or social strata:

> The Dutch settled matters in a more practical way, long ago, by founding guilds, or syndicates of boatmen. These were free associations sprung from the very needs of navigation. . . . Obstruction was thus avoided, even though the competition between the private owners of the boats continued to exist. . . . The boatmen did not wait for a great Bismarck

to annex Holland to Germany . . . they preferred coming to an international understanding. . . . Maybe the syndicate has also a tendency to become a monopoly, especially where it receives the precious patronage of the State that surely did not fail to interfere with it. Let us not forget either, that these syndicates represent associations whose members have only private interests at stake, and that if at the same time each shipowner were compelled—by the socializing of production, consumption, and exchange—to belong to federated Communes, or to a hundred other associations for the satisfying of his [sic] needs, things would have a different aspect.[96]

Kropotkin's stress here on "syndicates" and "communes" is a welcome contrast to the outlook of the lifestyle anarchism that often prevails in our own era. However, Kropotkin tends to assume that a spontaneous "free association" emerges as a fact of natural human society—and thus that a hierarchical second nature is untrue to nature. He even uses vague statements like "international agreement" to make it seem like mutual aid and free communism are simply matters of popular consent. Can it really be believed, however, that in the wake of a class-riven society, "agreement" between fractured classes would be possible or desirable? And what of the transitional forms between a state society and a stateless society? Kropotkin's anarchism, like that of Bakunin, is lacking in any determination of these forms and as a result falls back into a highly romanticized naturalism. Yet if history has proven anything, it is that those people that have managed to most effectively resist social domination and create more or less free and egalitarian societies have only done so on the basis of well-organized and self-disciplined institutions of self-government. The most sustained victories in revolutionary history were not arguably "natural" outgrowths inasmuch as they were the inevitable outcome of a distinct and pervasive institutional nexus—from the Hellenic *ecclesia* and its emphasis on *paideia* to that of the Parisian sansculottes and revolutionary study groups, to the CNT-FAI, which as Sam Dolgoff has shown in his illuminating work on Cuban history, was the achievement of a sophisticated matrix of underground syndicalist institutions that extended their reach as far as the Spanish Americas in the nineteenth century.[97]

In contrast to anarchism, Murray Bookchin has outlined the juxtaposition between the state and a stateless society in terms more favorable to a dialectical naturalism:

> There can be no society as such without institutions, systems of governance, and laws. The only issue in question is whether these structures and guidelines are authoritarian or libertarian, for they constitute the very forms of social existence. The state is an ensemble, not of institutions as such, but of authoritarian institutions (usually controlled by classes), which is where anarchism gets lost in a tangle of highly confused individualistic concepts.[98]

This distinction parallels (to be discussed later) communalism's basis in majoritarian direct democracy and the possibility of minority dissent—an idea Bookchin contrasts emphatically to the "mythic Oneness" of consensus in anarchist circles, which often relies, in his estimation, on the intimidation of dissenting persons and a degree of groupthink.[99] The most significant relationship here is that between naturalism and a theory of political institutions. In resting upon the theoretical laurels of a benevolent natural law, anarchism's concept of "natural society" tends to become an unexamined dogma that profoundly fails to explicate any meaningful institutional forms for its realization. Lost in this development was anarchism's promise to bring about a radical political theory capable of adequately theorizing the transition from a dominatory to a nondominatory and ecological society. This much was at least more earnestly attempted by twentieth-century libertarian Marxism and by the radical feminism of the 1960s and 1970s; and both council communism and second-wave feminism, despite their various failings, evinced concrete plans for new social institutions, rather than falling back upon the conceptual reifications of "spontaneity," "sociability," "mutual aid," or "natural society."

The Determinate Negation of Kropotkin's Theory of Society

The possibility of negating a mythopoeic naturalism is present in Kropotkin not so much in what was explicit in his notion of an instinctivist "mutual aid" but rather in what was an undeveloped theme of certain passages of his writings—notably, the revelation that mutual aid takes place within a dialectic of becoming, a presentiment that nature contains the embryo for social differentiation, and above all the suggestion that "ethics" as such is the culmination of a socially mediated subjectivity and sublation of purely unconscious or intuitive instincts. Later in the twentieth century, Bookchin's social ecology took it upon itself to liberate this germ of a dialectical naturalism from the shell of the static positivism and Romanticism in which Kropotkin had enfeebled it. A dialectical naturalism could thereby be expressed in the following thesis: in order to redeem the historical potentialities of nature, revolutionary thought must emancipate itself from the reified consciousness that would reduce the struggle between revolution and counterrevolution to a crude dualism of nature and culture. Both nature and culture, in reality, bear the historical imprint of human domination; what a true revolution would suggest is not a restoration of the one and the subjugation of the other, but a qualitatively new social order that would come to see both in a different light.

This would require the abandonment of any arguments from a "natural law" position. Even the historian Peter Marshall, who is by all means sympathetic to anarchism, sees through to this necessity:

> By drawing moral conclusions from observations of natural phenomena, [Kropotkin] committed the 'naturalistic fallacy,' that is to say, he unjustifiably inferred an 'ought' from an 'is,' a statement of how things should be from a statement of how things are. Human values are human creations, and even if nature operates in a particular way it does not necessarily follow that we should follow suit.[100]

As Marshall suggests, the very notions of "good" and "bad" are themselves only intelligible as outgrowths of a socially mediated linguistic history. The question of to what extent human differentiation from nature serves the cause of social freedom and equality, then, must never lose sight of the dialectical play inherent in this differentiation: the activities and problems of humanity are always grounded in its natural environment. In the most intimate ways, our species continues to be at the mercy of nature and remains dependent upon the stability of the biosphere to sustain its species life. However, this process is not one-sided. Human life in turn, bound up with the material contradictions of its own and unique second nature, comes to determine external nature and acculturates it within its own sphere of relationality.

The Necessity of a Dialectical Naturalism

The best of nineteenth-century anarchism occupied itself with what was often called the "social question"—the functionally appropriate metabolism between the individual, society, and nature conceived on an ethical basis. Kropotkin's idea of mutual aid, which remains influential within anarchist political philosophy, asserted the reality of a purely instinctive "natural law" against the presence of historical and social mediation. The political implications of this form of mythopoeic naturalism became clearer, however, in the subsequent history of anarchism. With the increasing incursions of the culture industry into popular consciousness, the reified nature-concept, which erodes the need for institutions of government and law in anarchist thought, began to assume features of the ideological individualism that, under the prevailing ideological hegemony, masquerades as "nature." Particularly in the case of anarchism's liberal assumption of an antithesis between the individual and society, a reified naturalism, not penetrated by the negativity of critical reflection, passes over into the unreflective affirmation of subjective liberty in the midst of its objective dissolution.

In order to go beyond the limitations of this reification, what was necessary was already articulated, albeit irresolutely and implicitly, in certain passages of Kropotkin's writings. The notion that nature's image is mediated through social institutions, and that human history is not reducible to the merely instinctive or biologistic but is possessed by the distinct qualities of spirit, is an insight that was at best well concealed in his mature work, the *Ethics*. The task that was never adequately undertaken by either Bakunin or Kropotkin, nor arguably by their contemporary followers, is the determinate negation of an undialectical naturalism, which would reveal the extent to which human second nature acculturates its "natural" context within its own pathologies, and thus the extent to which social relations move within a peculiar dialectical logic that can under no circumstances be simplistically reduced to questions of natural authenticity.

The characteristic naivete of much of post-Proudhonian anarchist politics and its complacent reliance upon a mythopoeic naturalism was probably criticized most elegantly by Bookchin in one of his last essays:

> It remains to ask: how are we to achieve [a] rational society?
> One anarchist writer would have it that the good society (or

a true "natural" disposition of affairs, including a "natural man") exists beneath the oppressive burdens of civilization like fertile soil beneath the snow. It follows from this mentality that all we are obliged to do to achieve the good society is to somehow eliminate the snow, which is to say capitalism, nation-states, churches, conventional schools, and other almost endless types of institutions that perversely embody domination in one form or another. Presumably an anarchist society—once state, governmental, and cultural institutions are merely removed—would emerge intact, ready to function and thrive as a free society. Such a "society," if one can even call it such, would not require that we proactively *create* it: we would simply let the snow above it melt away. The process of rationally creating a free Communalist society, alas, will require substantially more thought and work than embracing a mystified concept of aboriginal innocence and bliss.[101]

A crucial point of departure from this "mystified concept" was made by Bookchin himself in the 1980s and 1990s. Works such as *The Ecology of Freedom* attempted to articulate the dialectical contradictions of nature's mediation through social history, and in turn, the violence that the history of a hierarchical civilization has done to nature, in a manner perhaps more evocative of the libertarian dimensions of Hegel and Marx than of anarchism. The anthropological study of nature's image compelled Bookchin to focus his attention upon the historical potentialities of direct democratic and libertarian socialist institutions, governance, and the dispersal of power in order to apprehend the developing concrete possibility of an ecological society, a society premised on the mediation of nature through what Hans Jonas has termed an "ethics of responsibility."[102] This required nothing less than a clear break with the reified naturalism to which anarchism has remained captive.

CHAPTER THREE

Recovering a Dialectical Naturalism

The Basis of a Dialectical Naturalism

Under the conditions of the cold war it may have seemed that a revolutionary politics directed against the ecological implications of late capitalism was without philosophical foundation. The Eastern Bloc had only consolidated Marx's theory into a stale dogma, aspects of which originally had the merit of residing in a state of dialectical tension with the young Marx's notion of a naturalistic "species being." For its part the West, while witnessing the promising birth of the ecology movement in the 1960s and 1970s, has nevertheless remained culturally captive to the bourgeois and romantic images of nature that have been analyzed previously. To show what both a reified anti-naturalism and a romantic naturalism have missed, nothing less would be required than a kind of dialectical naturalism that, in revealing what is immanent to history, would simultaneously illuminate how history has betrayed that immanence.

This possibility meets with a promising accommodation in Bookchin's formulation of a "dialectical naturalism." Its negative dimension has already been foreshadowed in the form of an immanent critique of the ideological implications of both the mythopoeic dualism of the bourgeois enlightenment and the equally mythopoeic naturalism redolent of anarchist political philosophy. What remains is to demonstrate how a philosophy of dialectical naturalism has developed in the twentieth century, most prominently throughout Murray Bookchin's work. A thorough explication of Bookchin's "social ecology" is, to be sure, quite outside of the limits of scope required by this book.[1] Nevertheless, to the extent that the politics of social ecology can be shown to emerge from the foundation of a dialectical naturalism, they are inexorable from both its form and content.

A dialectical naturalism has several historical precedents in Hegelian and Marxian theory, as we have seen earlier. Here, building on the foregoing analysis of these precedents, three fragmentary, precursory models in socialist thought are presented. These fragments, it is hoped, serve to reinforce the notion that a dialectical naturalism continues to develop in socialist theory, rather than something that should be regarded as a closed or dogmatic system. To the extent that Bookchin failed to live up to the implications of a dialectical naturalism, or did not carry them out immanently, there is some scope for criticism. Of greatest uncertainty in this regard, perhaps, is the relationship of a dialectical naturalism to Bookchin's political program of communalism. This is particularly so because it is here that one of the most essential questions of political praxis must arise from the preceding philosophical foundations: namely, how to transform ecologically destructive capitalist institutions into revolutionary institutions capable of bringing about a genuinely ecological society.

The development of Bookchin's thought, which spanned several decades and multiple volumes, makes the question of what the presentation of dialectical naturalism should begin with a perplexing task. The author's presentation of dialectical naturalism here does not attempt anything like a chronicle or inventory of Bookchin's thought, for the main interest is to illuminate how a dialectical naturalism is closely bound up within the creation of ethical social institutions.

Precursory Models of Dialectical Naturalism

The Nature Dialectic of Fourier's Utopia

The writings of Charles Fourier (1772–1837) were, in a certain sense, a continuation and progression of those made by the most radical proponents of French materialism. Despite their much maligned "utopian" contents, they emerge historically as the spirit of a searching social critique that, by way of Fourier's working insights into the emerging capitalist system, counterpose to bourgeois mores the intricate image of a more ecologically harmonious reality principle, founded on gregarious social conditions, in which utopia takes the form of conceptual allegory. Precisely in the allegorical form of passions, institutions, and utopian imagination does history unfold, including natural history, and merge itself into the continuum of the social.

Historical evil does not take the form of an ahistorical "civilization" or "authority," much less a recalcitrant "nature," in the words of Fourier. Rather, he conceives that the historically immanent "commercial mechanism" is responsible for the social maladies of smuggling, usury, speculation, hoarding, parasitism, cheating of the law, and all of the other pathologies he condemns; all result from the underlying rationality of the emerging bourgeois order, the profit of one being intimately yoked to the exploitation of the many.[2] He suggests that it is a hallmark of the rationality of economic liberalism that "according to the rules of commercial liberty the company has the right to refuse to sell at any price, to allow the wheat to rot in its granaries while the people are starving."[3] This practice was as common in Fourier's time as in the twenty-first century, with acute precedents such as the potato "famine" in Ireland. And of the general spirit of the age, Fourier observes, "the mercantile spirit has shown its profound malevolence. The mask has fallen; monopoly and deceit are now revealed. Philosophy can no longer deceive itself about the infamies of the serpent with which it has been associated."[4]

The serpentine implications of bourgeois political economy were, to be sure, far more systematically exposed in the later writings of Marx. But what counts is that Fourier does not "naturalize" bourgeois second nature by rendering its private property relation equivalent with "natural law," nor champion the conquests of its industry against nature, nor blindly dissolve social conditions into a mythopoeic natural law. Nothing could be further from Fourier than the ontologization of what is ultimately historical. He sees beyond the false dichotomy of civilization and nature. This insight is achieved through his holding fast to the dynamic processes of institutions, which in aiming to adequate human passions to their rational end, have for their object the achievement of a public sphere that meets the needs and desires of all rather than allotting them only to a privileged few. By revealing institutions as social structures of change and rational determination, Fourier indicates the possibility of a nature-society relation that is fundamentally divergent from that which has become hypostatized into bourgeois ontological need. Accordingly, while Fourier was by no means a socialist, there is nonetheless a concealed socialist ethic at the heart of his utopian sketches. This element manifests within the institutional nexus in which nature is, at least potentially, ethically mediated.

In comparison with the malevolence of the emerging market society, Fourier juxtaposed his utopian sketch of the "phalanstery," founded on the idea of a rational social order that satisfies human passions. In itself this already implies an idea of civilization decidedly foreign to the most undialectical formulations of Freud regarding the antithesis between nature and repressive civilization. As Fourier remarks, "morality," by which he clearly means the repressive "second nature" underlying the long span of hierarchical civilization,

> . . . teaches man [sic] to be at war with himself, to resist his passions, to repress them, to believe that God was incapable of organizing our souls, our passions wisely; that he needed the teachings of Plato and Seneca in order to know how to distribute characteristics and instincts.[5]

At this point, Fourier has not yet gone beyond the romantic tendency of condemning the mores of civilization. However, what distinguishes him from such a tendency is his effort to imagine an alternative institutional nexus that develops directly out of natural history's potentialities and fulfills them within the social. In his nuanced reversal of the Freudian foundation myth, social diversity, variation of labor, and composite social bonds are presented not as boundaries to civilization but as the most rational forms of their becoming. Human history is seen not as the cynicism that confirms the sadomasochistic and patriarchal-acquisitive attributes of that which is last through that which was first, but as the faulty alchemy of a human potency that always possesses the possibility of exploding the continuum of wayward civilization and restoring it to its most rational and ethical state of becoming.

It is therefore unsurprising that Fourier regards vice as a negative consequence of the repression of "natural" passions and drives. The failure of the bourgeois moralists is interpreted not in their own terms as a defect of nature, but rather as a failure of the oppressive social organization that market society solicits. The shortcomings of hierarchical civilization are thus resolutely distinguished from the shortcomings of nature:

> It is true that these impulses [of vice] entice us only to evil, if we yield to them individually; but we must calculate their effect upon a body of about two thousand persons socially combined, and not upon families or isolated individuals; this is what the learned world has not thought of; in studying it, it would have recognized that as soon as the number of

associates (*societaires*) has reached 1600, the natural impulses, termed attractions, tend to form series of contrasting groups, in which everything incites to industry, becomes attractive, and to virtue, become lucrative.[6]

On this basis Fourier attempted to provide a quantitative outline of what he considered to be the most vital of the human passions, and to explain, in abundant detail, how the ideal community would function on the basis of face-to-face governance and would be strictly limited according to the dictates of human scale. These notions are essentially Aristotelean and not without certain practical aporias and limitations. But they are also more intricate than what Aristotle could imagine in his time, filled to the brim with exhaustive digressions on the exigencies and idiosyncrasies of human socializing, habits, customs, and calculations as to the most convenient arrangements conceivable for satisfying them. While we cannot possibly go into the requisite detail regarding these features here, perhaps most noteworthy of all is that Fourier places much emphasis on "cabbalism" as the fabric of social association. Cabalism is, in his terms, "the passion that, like love, has the property of confounding ranks, drawing superiors and inferiors closer to each other."[7] Thus, he observes,

> [t]he cabalistic spirit is the true destination of man [sic]. Plotting doubles his resources, enlarges his faculties. Compare the tone of a formal social gathering, its moral, stilted, languishing jargon, with the tone of these same people united in a cabal: they will appear transformed to you; you will admire their terseness, their animation, the quick play of ideas, the alertness of action, of decision; in a word, the rapidity of spiritual or material motion.[8]

The formation of social clubs or cabals was for Fourier an essential prerequisite to the achievement of individual pleasure, along with other passions such as alternation and the composite stimulation of the senses. What is most essential to his theory of natural history, however, is that it does not involve the subsumption of human institutions beneath a reifying nature. Rather, natural history is only redeemed in and through the human imagination, its benign hedonism, its practical reason; the human social character is held to be capable of grounding natural history in an ethical and life-affirming institutional context.

Such institutions would realize what the repressive morality of the protestant ethic taboos: the possibility of rescuing a participatory public sphere from its subsumption under the private interest, reviving humanity's "passions," orienting them nonrepressively around the organization of all work according to the desiderata of pleasure and attractiveness rather than of mere exchange value. Marx and Engels's exhortations against its "utopian socialism" notwithstanding, Fourier's thought contains within its most social categories the negativing principle of bourgeois society: the "natural" forces of pleasure and desire that its political economy treats as alien to all "rational" society. By desublimating these potencies through the realization of humanly scaled communities, the irrational distinction between work and play would be abolished:

> In order to attain happiness, it is necessary to introduce it into the labors which engage the greater part of our lives. Life is a long torment to one who pursues occupations without attraction. Morality teaches us to love work: let it know, then, how to render work lovable, and, first of all, let it introduce luxury into husbandry and the workshop. If the arrangements are poor, repulsive, how arouse industrial attraction?[9]

Such ethical critiques are also immanent ones, for they measure up the claims of bourgeois ideology surrounding work against the degrading reality of the factory system. As its rational end, Fourier suggests the significance of *variety* in the rational organization of labor. Here, he departs from the earlier philosophy of the French materialists, which viewed sensation and matter as the only organizing basis of reality. For Fourier, in contrast, this empirical reality is intricately inflected, in its most rational determination, with the distinct judgments of human reason. This reason seeks to organize human affairs not on the bourgeois ground of purely technical needs and consumption, premised on the reifying "negation" of nature, but rather in the *sublation* of natural needs and passions into an integrated, organic totality. Such a form-giving totality, as Fourier hints at, would emerge in the midst of a society in which the living quarters of human communities are adequately scaled and constructed in architectural forms that are symbiotic with the surrounding ecology rather than antagonistic toward it. Fourier's utopia was planned out according to such principles, with an efficient utilization of living space, the organization of architecture subject to communitarian rather than private desiderata, and the prudent restrictions on living populations along the lines of human scale and face-to-face democracy. This is illustrated in passages such as the following:

> In work, as in pleasure, variety is evidently the desire of nature. Any enjoyment prolonged, without interruption, beyond two hours, conduces to satiety, to abuse, blunts our faculties, and exhausts pleasure. A repast of four hours will not pass off without excess; an opera of four hours will end by cloying the spectator. Periodical variety is a necessity of the body and of the soul, a necessity in all nature; even the soil requires alteration of seeds, and seed alteration of soil. The stomach will soon reject the best dish if it be offered every day, and the soul will be blunted in the exercise of any virtue if it be not relieved by some other virtue.[10]

Fourier's use of ecological metaphors here is indeed strikingly dialectical. Variety is read into the social body as a "natural" necessity; yet in dialectical contradiction with this, human institutional configurations introduce an unprecedented reality of social complexity, intelligibility, and creative articulation into its actualization. Read as conceptual allegory, the concept of "variety" appears in Fourier not as merely unconscious or merely given but as the consciousness of nature fulfilled only within an adequate social context. This distinction between biological nature and its social adequation would later be taken up by Bookchin and developed into an anthropological-historical outlook he would come to call "social ecology."

Perhaps the greatest commentary on the incipient development of a dialectical naturalism in Fourier was unwittingly penned by Walter Benjamin:

> One of the most remarkable features of the Fourierist utopia is that it never advocated the exploitation of nature by man, an idea that became widespread in the following period. Instead, in Fourier, technology appears as the spark that ignites the powder of nature. Perhaps this is the key to his strange representation of the phalanstery as propagating itself

"by explosion." The later conception of man's exploitation of nature reflects the actual exploitation of man by the owners of the means of production. If the integration of the technological into social life failed, the fault lies in this exploitation.[11]

In this holistic vision of an ecological reconciliation, the Fourierist utopia prefigures Bookchin's essay on "Liberatory Technology" by over a century and shows how an immanent critique of bourgeois life—namely, through an analysis that reveals its inadequacy from an ecological and biological standpoint—might illuminate the dialectical relationality between humanity and nature, in a form conscious of the "Not-Yet present" that is so necessary, as Ernst Bloch intimated, to the challenges of the revolutionary moment.

Lukács's Critique of the Concept of Nature in Bourgeois History

Lukács's *History and Class Consciousness* (1921) is a remarkable work of Hegelian Marxism; its greatest achievement remains its presentation of a phenomenology of proletarian consciousness, which in negating the immediacy of bourgeois rationality comes into knowledge of its own historical potentialities. Through this process, class consciousness acculturates nature as a three-sided phenomenon. Within these three stages of reflection, nature is presented in line with what Lukács envisions to be the historical experience of the proletariat. Because of this holding fast to the historical basis of the nature-concept and its mediation through the power relations of society, *History and Class Consciousness* presents an exemplary early model for a dialectical naturalism. In the development of three successive stages of reflection, nature is finally revealed as shorn of its reified cover concepts and expressed directly in the notion of its ethical reconciliation with the social totality. Yet Lukács leaves the concrete, practical context of this reconciliation unexplored. The critique itself remains an abstract one, concerned purely with a critique of reified consciousness in the circumstances of ideological concept formation.

For Lukács, the concept of nature under the conditions of bourgeois society is articulated in a typically Kantian form: as riven into a duality between the understanding (theoretical reason) and the acts of consciousness (practical reason). Within this twofold form, however, bourgeois society

> . . . generates very important and unavoidable problem-complexes and conceptual ambivalences which are decisive for the way in which bourgeois man understands himself and his relation to the world. Thus the word 'nature' becomes highly ambiguous.[12]

Lukács subsequently delineates the phenomenological understanding of nature into three concepts. The first is that of "the idea, formulated most lucidly by Kant but essentially unchanged since Kepler and Galileo, of nature as the 'aggregate of systems and laws' governing what happens."[13] This conception is extremely one-dimensional and positivist in its reduction of ecology to mere "laws": it merely seeks to explain instrumentally "what happens" in a quantitative sense, rather than a qualitative one. This purely positivist conception of nature remains within the orbit of Engels's reductionistic "dialectic of Nature"—a reductionism that reintroduced metaphysics in the guise of science (such as the infamous "iron law" of the transformation of quality into quality pilfered from Hegel).

However, Lukács shows a more nuanced side in his presentation of the first concept of nature. Its "development," we are told, arises "out of the economic structures of capitalism, [which] has been shown repeatedly . . ."[14] In the manner of a genuinely dialectical historicism, Lukács does not fix the purely quantitative conception of nature into an unchangeable universal but rather conceives of it in historical-material terms—as emanating from the instrumental rationality ushered forth by capitalism.

The second conception of nature is decisively ideological. It is "a *value concept*, wholly different from the first one and embracing a wholly different cluster of meanings."[15] This "value concept" crystalizes into the potentialities of a socialist humanism that capitalism emphatically denies. Thus, the reference to Rousseau here is both crucial and illuminating:

> A glance at the history of natural law shows the extent to which these two conceptions have become inextricably interwoven with each other. For here we can see that 'nature' has been heavily marked by the revolutionary struggle of the bourgeoisie: the 'ordered,' calculable, formal and abstract character of the approaching bourgeois society appears natural by the side of the artifice, the caprice and the disorder of feudalism and absolutism. At the same time if one thinks of

Rousseau, there are echoes of a quite different meaning wholly incompatible with this one. It concentrates increasingly on the feeling that social institutions (reification) strip man of his human essence and that the more culture and civilisation (i.e. capitalism and reification) take possession of him, the less able he is to be a human being. And with a reversal of meanings that never becomes apparent, nature becomes the repository of all these inner tendencies opposing the growth of mechanisation, dehumanisation and reification.[16]

The first two concepts then, which at first seemed riven and dualistic, are in fact mediated through one another in the bourgeois consciousness. In its capacity of revolutionary negation, "nature thereby acquires the meaning of what has grown organically, what was not created by man, in contrast to the artificial structures of human civilisation."[17]

Lukács does not fail to omit that nature is at the same time *second* nature: the metabolism through which human community finds both its preformation and ultimate completion, all the while, in a future rational society, "humanizing" its landscape in accordance with human needs, desires, and most importantly ethical life. In fact, this is the implicit premise of the third and final conception of nature:

At the same time, [nature] can be understood as that aspect of human inwardness which has remained natural, or at least tends or longs to become natural once more. "They are what we once were," says Schiller of the forms of nature, "they are what we should once more become." But here, unexpectedly and indissolubly bound up with the other meanings, we discover a third conception of nature, one in which we can clearly discern the ideal and the tendency to overcome the problems of a reified existence. 'Nature' here refers to authentic humanity, the true essence of man liberated from the false, mechanising forms of society: man as a perfected whole who has inwardly overcome, or is in the process of overcoming, the dichotomies of theory and practice, reason and the senses, form and content; man whose tendency to create his own forms does not imply an abstract rationalism which ignores concrete content; man for whom freedom and necessity are identical.[18]

Yet Lukács leaves unexplored the practical, revolutionary implications of this negative dialectic. He expostulates, to be sure, that nature "does not exist as a 'fact of the soul,' as a nostalgia inhabiting the consciousness, but it also possesses a very real and concrete field of activity where it may be brought to fruition, namely art."[19] But beyond some further remarks on Schiller and a critique of the denuded concept of nature to be met with in Hegel's *Philosophy of History*, he does not probe any deeper into the concrete relation between nature and humanity.

Consequently, we are left with a political prescription of the highest form of the understanding: the overcoming of "reified existence." The concrete forms that such an overcoming would take remain to be elucidated in the contemporary context. Suffice it to say that such transformations would speak to more than simply art, more than simply the unity of theoretical with practical activity. They betoken an as-yet unrealized totality of liberated social life that is pervaded with values that we might call "ecological." Lukács gives conceptual form to these potentialities, but our period is perhaps too distantly removed from the revolutionary context of the 1920s and 1930s to articulate them in the same way.

Bloch's Notion of "Technological Contact"

It is difficult to appreciate the finer points of emphasis in Bookchin's discussion of the "social matrix" of technology without recourse to Bloch's thematic exploration of "technological utopias," "technological contact," and the bourgeois appropriation of technology in his sublime work *The Principle of Hope* (1959). What Bloch's analysis elucidates are the utopian possibilities incumbent upon the historical development of technology to reconcile the humanity-nature relationship. The bourgeois myth of scarcity, still prevalent today despite its technological abolition, only serves to reinforce the dominion of the antithetical nature-concept; in order to shatter its illusory universality, it is necessary to confront the drive toward social rationality with its more subversive potentialities.

Bloch had evidently taken from Marx his finer points on the "metabolism" between society and nature, including Marx's sublime point in the *1844 Manuscripts* that society embodies the most "natural" metabolism between nature and the individual. Nonetheless, he had also reworked them into something that went beyond Marx's late notion of an ontological "struggle" with nature. This is nowhere truer than in Bloch's consideration of the historical dialectic of technological development.

Bloch's passage on the potentially cooperative metabolism between nature and technological innovation, as an underlying precondition of its dialectical wholeness, shines forth the concrete possibilities of technology that bourgeois society, in its drives toward a domineering quantification and mechanism, would deny us:

> It is part of mechanistics to confine itself to beginnings which are kept isolated, and it is all the more a part of it to forget the original relation to production itself in face of the product and its relations. But that which objectively corresponds to the technological world change must be founded for concrete technology in an objective production tendency of the world, just as, mutatis mutandis, it is founded for concrete revolution in the objective production tendency of human history. Co-productivity of nature is required, that which Paracelsus himself had in mind when his nature already appeared to him as friendly or capable of being befriended in a utopian way, 'inwardly full of remedies, full of prescriptions and one big chemist's shop,' a cosmos in which man opens up, just as the microcosm of man causes the world to come to its senses.[20]

Not only has bourgeois society forgotten the Renaissance image, which Bloch draws upon by way of one of Goethe's poems, of a "coproductivity" with nature, a cooperative and symbiotic image embodied in the Hellenic and Fourierist image of technology. The bourgeois commodity economy has utterly twisted the very modus operandi of technology itself into the demonic forms of the war economy, artificial scarcity, technology as a model for social psychoses. In this sense, as Bloch describes it, emerges the phenomenon of the late bourgeois "curbing of technology, apart from the military kind":

> Before the last crisis too much was produced for capital to be able to cope with it. Famine began, not because of crop failure as in earlier times, but because the granaries were too full. As is evident and well-known, the private capitalist economy has itself become a chain for the production which it once

unchained. Only new means of death are interesting, shortly before and during the war, war technology is booming, the peaceful kind follows in its wake.[21]

This lucid historical observation informs Bookchin's trenchant analysis of the late bourgeois image of technology, an image that has completely forgotten its origins in the symbiotic metabolism between humanity and nature, and thus with it the very notion of a qualitative nature not reduced to a crude mechanism or abstract quantity. And with it, of course, has also departed the very conception of ethical life in the sense of its late medieval era and Renaissance association with the organic (one thinks especially of John Ball, and much later of William Morris). In fact, as Bloch observes, this very outlook is utterly alien to the late bourgeois way of thinking:

> Bourgeois thinking as a whole has distanced itself from the materials with which it deals. It is based on an economy which, as Brecht says, is not interested in rice at all but only in its price. . . . Thus a non-organic, de-qualifying spirit has been spreading ever since the end of the original accumulation of capital, and hence since the concentrated production of commodities and the corresponding commodity-thinking. From the seventeenth century on, the qualitative concepts of nature disappear which had still been cultivated by Giordano Bruno and even by Bacon himself in places.[22]

With the prospects of a better world come those of both a new "metabolism" with technology and with nature. It is precisely these enchanting, utopian potentialities of a "kindness" that "beats in the works of technology"[23] that a dialectical naturalism aims to free from the shackles of a reified consciousness that holds fast to the one-dimensionality of the given—to the denuded and purely instrumental image of technology as a realm of quantification, mechanism, and dehumanization. In order to undertake this, it would be required, in defense of the radicalism of its political conception, to show how the prevailing forms of nature philosophy are still entrenched on the bourgeois ground of reification. Although this necessity has been demonstrated earlier in this book, Bookchin's own critique of prevailing nature philosophy is an essential point of departure for his elaboration of a dialectical naturalism.

Murray Bookchin's Social Ecology

Murray Bookchin (1921–2006), a Russo-American socialist who was influenced by currents of both Marxism and anarchism, began his intellectual life as a young Trotskyist in the 1930s and had probably earned the right to be regarded, by the time of his death, as one of the most radical thinkers to emerge from the United States ecology movement. Bookchin gave his philosophical and social views the appellation of "social ecology." A crucial aspect of social ecology is Bookchin's attempt to formulate a dialectical naturalism. His interpretation of a dialectical naturalism is no mere exercise in traditional theory, however, for it is essential, as Bookchin endeavours to show, to the coherence of a humanistic and libertarian socialism that is the core of his social ecology. This emerges decisively in the context of his late writings on the politics of communalism.

The core leitmotif of social ecology, which distinguishes it most clearly from earlier forms of nature philosophy, is the dialectical mediation of nature's image through society. Social ecology contends that reason has emerged out of a natural history that, dispossessed of anthropomorphic and mythopoeic projections, can be seen to be guided by an evolutionary natural history of increasing complexity, directiveness, and even a semi-conscious, participatory "choice" in a given eco-community's determination of their surrounding environment. These concepts, despite their highly speculative and sometimes discrete character, can be read as a journey of exploration, aiming to recover those potentialities left by the wayside of bourgeois development.[24]

The Critique of Neo-Kantian Philosophy

Bookchin's formulation of dialectical naturalism, although prefigured by much of the content of his earlier writings, emerged in the early 1990s out of a sustained criticism of contemporary trends in nature philosophy. Neo-Kantian nature philosophies, particularly those influenced by Bateson and Habermas, are singled out by Bookchin as retaining the dualism and subjectivism of Kant's epistemology at the expense of historical concretion. Nonetheless, Bookchin's own critique is specifically directed against the epistemic reductionism intrinsic to the centrality of cognition in Kant's philosophy. Echoing Adorno's *Metacritique of Epistemology*, Bookchin conceives of the turn toward subjectivism in nature philosophy as redolent of the subject-oriented ideology of the capitalist marketplace. The implications of this for nature philosophy are insidious. Nature appears to align itself with the accidental and contingent quality of the individual, rather than with an ethical potentiality grounded socially. For if nature cannot be grounded in institutional terms—indeed, based within the nexus of its social mediation—its image reduces to the static Kantian cover concept of transcendental subjectivity. Thus for Bookchin it was Kant, rather than Descartes, who

> . . . finally denatured nature of its Presocratic remnant by removing the material "grade of being" altogether. Things-in-themselves ceased to be things at all for cognitive purposes, and one grade of Being effectively ceased to exist. Kant left us alone with our own subjectivity.[25]

In Bookchin's appraisal, therefore, any resurgence of Neo-Kantianism is a tangible obstacle to bourgeois society's consciousness of the relation between natural and social history: Neo-Kantianism wholly lacks an outlook that extends beyond the basic configurations of subjectivity and into the historic *objectivity* of nature-society relations. Accordingly, it reproduces ahistorically (i.e., "transcendentally") the ideology of the bourgeois enlightenment—nature as a dualistic, antagonistic otherness to be incorporated within the Ego's interiorized thought-forms.

If such "subjectivistic approaches to nature and those based on systems theory must be challenged," Bookchin expostulates, "we are obliged to formulate new premises that provide coherence and meaning to natural evolution."[26] The "first" of these carefully chosen presuppositions, according to Bookchin, is that "we have the right to *attribute* properties to nature based on the best of our knowledge, the right to assume that certain attributes as well as contexts are *self-evident* in nature."[27] He suggests that while "this assumption is immediately problematic for a vast number of academic philosophers . . . ironically, it is no problem for most scientists."[28] Yet whereas in Kropotkin such scientific attributes are subsumed under the mythopoeic cover concept of "mutual aid," Bookchin's own formulations involve social history within a process of dialectical relationality to a much greater degree.

Habermas also falls under criticism as an adherent of Neo-Kantian dualism. Bookchin suggests that Habermas's communication theory tends to present nature as a Fichtean otherness within a nexus of subjectivity rather than as a developing historical substance in its own right:

"Intersubjectivity" and "intersubjective relations," for their part, cannot explain in any meaningful way *how* humanity is rooted in biological evolution, or what we broadly call "Nature," least of all by deftly using the phrase "social construction" to bypass the very objective evolutionary reality that "Nature" connotes. Just as a subjectivized nexus of "intersubjective relations" dissolves the objectivity of social phenomena, so a subjectivized nexus of "social construction" dissolves the objectivity of natural evolution, as if neither social phenomena nor natural evolution had any actuality, aside from being a pair of simplistic epistemological categories. Here Kant reappears with a vengeance, with the possible difference that even his noumenal or unknowable external reality has disappeared.[29]

The criticism of Habermas provides some further insight into what specifically Bookchin is defining his formulation of dialectical naturalism *against*. Bookchin's objection to Neo-Kantian dualisms is founded solely upon "their claim to universality, since their *presuppositions* provide an inadequate framework for understanding natural history and apprehending its ethical implications."[30] This raises the question of what he conceives to be a more adequate basis for comprehending natural history and its complementarity with social relations.

Recovering Reason and the Bookchin-Eckersley Debate on Ecological Ethics

Like those of other near-contemporary humanists such as Carl Sagan, Bookchin's writings from the 1990s are characterized by an attempt to defend the possibility of a rational and intelligible account of natural history that neither dissolves it into a Kantian "thing in-itself" nor into an incoherent intuitive mysticism. Bookchin's defense of reason is principally addressed to the prevalence of eco-mysticism within the ecology movement. This is a form of mysticism that, in his terms,

> . . . generally celebrates its very imperviousness to rational analysis. Explicitly *anti*-rational, it makes its strongest appeal to the authority of belief over thought. Reason, mystics usually tell us, is cold, objective, indifferent, and, according

to some of its feminist critics, even masculine. Not so with mystical outlooks, we are told, which are warm, subjective, caring, and feminine. . . . *Eco*mystics, in particular, tend to add a quasi-ecological dimension to mysticism by imparting a preternatural dimension to the interconnected natural world.[31]

A foremost example of this, relevant to Bookchin's mature writings, was the phenomenon of "deep ecology." Largely a product of the New Left counterculture in the American West Coast, deep ecology has sometimes been proffered in academic circles as a radical school of thought opposed to the "shallow" ecology of liberal environmentalism. Bookchin, however, is quick to draw attention to its debasement of the rational premises of science.[32] Through these defects deep ecology can be revealed to subtly invalidate both the notion of a rational, ecological *society* and its material institutionalization in an ecological ethics, which both depend on scientific processes of objective verification of the natural world.

One might take issue with Bookchin's somewhat narrow conflation of the "methodology of modern science" with reason as such here. As, for example, those of the earlier Frankfurt School have demonstrated abundantly, positivistic science remains vulnerable to criticism for its tendency to subtly reproduce as "objective" the ideological hegemony of the status quo. Nevertheless, the notion that "modern science" constitutes a homogenously narrow methodology in its own right is demonstrably false, and for Bookchin this myth tends to perpetuate the falsehood that mystical forms of thinking retain a certain sense of coherence or objective validity.

The implications of this attempt to resurrect irrationalism in the midst of nature philosophy becomes, for Bookchin's dialectical naturalism, a crucially negative point of departure. In defense of science, for all of its positivistic failings, Bookchin presents a timely reminder that "the methodology of science constitutes a minimal objective criterion by which we may judge ideas on the basis of *reality* and not on the basis of the self-proclaimed insights of spooks."[33] Moreover science, taken as a whole, is hardly a dogmatic repository of "mechanistic assumptions" founded on a "narrow" definition of data, as the deep ecologists would have it. "Cosmology today," he observes, "is such a sweeping, extravagantly creative, and even dialectical field of study that to call its methodology narrow is, to put it gently, evidence of gross ignorance."[34]

This is not merely an epistemological criticism. Bookchin stresses the historical significance of upholding the legacy of the Enlightenment and humanistic science in the face of the contemporary reaction against both. A defense of reason thus becomes a guiding element of dialectical naturalism, not least because a dialectical naturalism is founded on the notion that natural and human history can be rendered as both an intelligible and coherent whole.[35] Such intelligibility and coherence, what is more, are

> . . . no trivial matter. It took thousands of years for humanity to begin to shake off the accumulated 'intuitions' of shamans, priests, chiefs, monarchs, warriors, patriarchs, ruling classes, dictators, and the like—all of whom claimed immense privileges for themselves and inflicted terrible horrors on their inferiors on the basis of *their* 'intuited wisdom.'[36]

The defense of reason must therefore be grounded, he insists, in the evolutionary differentiation of human second nature from merely biological "first nature." This distinction, advanced in a somewhat bombastic form by Fichte and Marx, nonetheless becomes for Bookchin the negation of the negation that must be directed against the romantic ideology of "natural law." The deep ecologist assertion that there is "no ontological divide" between "the human and non-human realms," accordingly becomes the target of Bookchin's criticism of the historically immanent differences between first and second natures that the ontological need of a monistic "oneness" would deny:

> In fact, the ontological divide between the non-human and the human is *very* real. Human beings, to be sure, are primates, mammals, and vertebrates. They cannot, as yet, get out of their animal skins. As products of organic evolution, they are subject to the natural vicissitudes that bring enjoyment, pain, and death to complex life-forms generally. But it is a crucial fact that they alone *know*—indeed, *can* know—that there is a phenomenon called evolution; they *alone* know that death is a reality; they *alone* can even formulate such notions as self-realization, biocentric equality, and a 'self-in-Self'; they *alone* can generalize about their existence—past, present, and

future—and produce complex technologies, create cities, communicate in a complex syllabic form.[37]

In failing to appreciate the fecund process of gradation that subtly leads from natural to social evolution, deep ecology, in Bookchin's appraisal, simply sidesteps any rational consideration of the dialectical complementarity—which by its very definition includes differentiation—between social and natural evolution, substituting it with a purely intuitive conception of "nature." So lacking is deep-ecological monism in a sense of the concrete that it even fails to grasp that the technological and scientific "satisfaction of needs," which deep ecologists and primitivists rail against, so often itself cannot be satisfied within the primitive conditions of first nature alone. This absence of a historical materialism in deep ecology's hostility to technology obscures precisely how the capitalist mode of production represents, via the fetishism of the commodity, an estranged and untrue form of the potential for "kindness" that Ernst Bloch held to be the beating heart of technology.

A more precarious but nevertheless defensible element of Bookchin's critique of deep ecology resides in his famous debate with Robyn Eckersley in the early 1990s on the subject of imparting "values" to nature.[38] At least three dimensions of this debate are worthy of note in relation to a dialectical naturalism: the possibility of objectively ascertaining "natural" values, the concrete source and characteristics of such values, and the institutional parameters necessary for fostering a more "ecocentric" or ecologically harmonious valuing of the biosphere.

The first dimension of this debate, as highlighted by Bookchin himself, concerns a crucial contradiction at the heart of attempts to assign inherent worth to particular forms of life in the biosphere. This contradiction is illuminated in one of Robyn Eckersley's contributions to the debate, when she attempts to argue from a Humean or Kantian position that we can never with any certainty "know" nature:

> *Can we really be sure* that the thrust of evolution, as intuited by Bookchin, is one of advancing subjectivity? In particular, is there not something self-serving and arrogant in the (unverifiable) claim that first nature is striving to achieve something that has presently reached *its most developed form* in us—second nature?[39]

An outstanding irony of this claim is that it obscures the *human origins* of the concept of "eco-centrism" or "biocentrism" advanced by deep ecologists such as Eckersley. Biocentrism is an ethical concept that assumes an ontology of "inherent worth" intrinsic to everything that exists in the natural world.[40] However, as Bookchin suggests in a way very reminiscent of Nietzsche, it is simply a mystification to assume an immediacy or self-evident ontology of "inherent worth" without acknowledging precisely that such values are *human* values arising out of the historical mediations of a particular social valuing of nature, and thus that such "intrinsic worth" is simply a reification of a given constellation of values as "natural." This is not necessarily an argument against the ethical principles of biocentrism in toto, but at the very least an important rejoinder that the foundations of ethical traditions must always be grasped in terms of their social and historical mediacy.

A further irony of Eckersley's claims in the debate is that she does not recognize that for Bookchin, and indeed for a dialectical naturalism, human second nature is, as Adorno once remarked of intelligence, a potentially *moral* category. As Bookchin expresses this: "animal intention and will are too limited to produce an ethics of good and evil or kindness and cruelty . . . even among the most intelligent animals, the limits to thought are immense in comparison with the extraordinary capacities of socialized human beings."[41] The evolutionary process of acquiring the traditions and institutions of a system of morality emerges as a historical fact of anthropology, far from an allegedly "unverifiable claim," by contrast to the mere instinctivism redolent of a good degree of nonhuman nature. To attempt to make humanity ethically equivalent with nature, as deep ecology's concept of "biocentrism" would have it, is to sweep away the profound history of a specifically *human* evolution with the stroke of a pen, ignoring the remarkable advances in human history that have rendered it qualitatively unique in the biosphere.

This leads to a second point of contention in the deep ecology debate, namely, the extent to which purportedly ontological values can be derived from what Bookchin refers to as the "grounding" of nature. His essay *Recovering Evolution* emphasizes repeatedly that deep ecologists have misconstrued his nature-concept by assuming a rigid hierarchy of "worth" culminating in humanity, where for Bookchin the ethical ground of nature is solely and exclusively one of *nascence*, that is, of what Hegel called concrete potentiality:

> By using the term grounded in relation to ethics, I am trying to say, following a long philosophical tradition, that values are implicit in the natural world, not that first nature is an arena for ethical behavior. There is no ethical nonhuman nature as such. To validate this point would require a full-length article in itself. The difficulty deep ecologists are likely to have with my view that ethics is "grounded" in nature stems from the static image they have of nonhuman nature. Accordingly, from their standpoint, nature either "is" or "is not" an arena of ethical action. That it can be a nascent arena for the emergence of ethics seems beyond them. By contrast, my view is evolutionary—that is, I am concerned with how an ethics evolves through the gradual emergence of human agency over aeons of evolutionary development. Insofar as the evolution of human beings from a nonhuman nature is simultaneously a continuum and disjunction, one can argue philosophically from a developmental viewpoint that the human ability to function as moral agents has its objective origins in their evolution from nonhuman nature. Hence, nowhere do I speak of an "ethics in nature" but rather of a nature that forms the ground for a human ethics.[42]

One might sense that, at certain points here, Bookchin is a little unfair to his critics: the connectedness of biological evolution, central to deep ecology, does not necessarily constitute a "static" image of nonhuman nature, nor should human agency be considered the sole arena for the evolution of ethics in historical terms. Indeed, as Kropotkin emphasized in *Mutual Aid*, many communities of animal species have developed moral habits and instincts, however more primitive they may appear when compared to the evolution of ethical institutions in human history.

On the other hand, for Bookchin's concept of dialectical naturalism, ethics can only be spoken of within conditions of a temporal emergence, not posited as an ahistorical ontology, as something existing innately in the natural world. There must be a *social* referent, a discernable logic of social and moral development that underlies an ethical perspective on nature. And yet misapprehensions of this position remain prominent in the secondary literature—for example, in White's interpretation:

One of the problems with Bookchin's holistic metaphysics is that the desire to present a determinate and singular reading of 'nature' ensures that the specificity of the insights of the natural sciences, at their different levels of analysis, are essentially collapsed together. Thus, it is assumed that because ecology and evolutionary biology display certain properties, so must it be with all of nature. Consequently, while Bookchin's ontological writings are suffused with rhetoric on the value of holism, the end result is reductionist.[43]

Yet Bookchin's writings, far from advancing a "singular" reading of nature, always stress that nature can only be conceived of through a process of social valuation, and thus in the last analysis a multiplicity or diversity of "readings":

Life-forms that create and consciously alter their environment, hopefully in ways that make it more rational and ecological, represent a vast and indefinite extension of nature into fascinating, perhaps unbounded, lines of evolution which no branch of insects could ever achieve—notably, the evolution of a fully *self-conscious* nature.[44]

Bookchin's deep ecologist critics seemed to have remained blind to the dialectical play in passages such as these, and this is not least of the sources for their confusion of Bookchin's dialectical naturalism. A "fully self-conscious nature" expresses both the relations of identity and non-identity, or the negative unity, of biological nature and human second nature in historical terms. Likewise social crises, in the terms of Bookchin's dialectical naturalism, must cease to be considered *merely* social, as if they were bereft of an ecological context; while natural crises must no longer be reduced to the purely intuitive relation of the romantic form, that is, between the monadic bourgeois "self" and unconscious nature, the Hegelian "multiplicity without bounds," into which its alleged uniqueness is to be dissolved.

These two dimensions of the deep ecology–social ecology debate—namely, the possibility of objectively ascertaining "natural values" and the concrete source of such values—both culminate in a third dimension, specifically the institutional parameters necessary for actualizing a more ecologically ethical civil and political society. Moving forward in time beyond the 1990s, and putting aside crucial ideological differences from

Bookchin, it is interesting to note that Eckersley's views have increasingly edged closer toward an acknowledgment of the *social mediation* of ethics in nature, at least insofar as her more recent writings on ecological intervention and geopolitan democracy are concerned.

In a recent piece, Eckersley has advanced two arguments for an international agreement on the use of force for environmental protection, namely, to forestall ecological catastrophes in the face of state inaction and the probable increasing rate and severity of environmental disasters in the future.[45] Eckersley also appeals to the authority of international law and the UN security council in advancing a case for human intervention to prevent ecocide:

> Insofar as ecocide also produces direct, immediate, and grave consequences for humans, involving large numbers of deaths and/or significant human suffering on a par with genocide or crimes against humanity, then the moral case for ecological intervention need only ride on the coattails of the moral case for humanitarian intervention.[46]

Finally, Eckersley also considers arguments for interventions to protect nonhuman nature from harm and seems to endorse the notion that some degree of moral consideration for nonhuman species should be embedded within the prevailing international system.[47] Similarly, in a recent piece exploring the concept of the Anthropocene, Eckersley seeks to anchor the quest for ecological ethics in the wake of the ecological crisis in what she terms "geopolitan democracy." Such a democracy would be defined, among other traits, by an attempt to cross the divide between public and lay knowledge, culminating in a highly educated democratic polity:

> A necessary but by no means sufficient step towards closing this gap is greater public dissemination and translation of science (broadly construed here to include the natural and social sciences and humanities) related to the effects of Earth systems changes on particular communities, alongside critical reflection on the effects of local practices on ecological and larger Earth systems. This includes, for example, connecting changes to the Earth's carbon, hydrological, nitrogen and phosphorus cycles, and the loss of biodiversity, to local climates, food systems, human health, safety and well-being, economies and life-worlds.[48]

It would seem from the preceding that, in the time since the deep ecology–social ecology debate, Eckersley has come much closer to Bookchin in accepting that human agency and intervention in nature are the key grounds for determining an objective ecological ethics. Indeed, the belief in the need for an informed populace, faith in democratic reason, and a focus upon the institutional nexus according to which nature is valued and moralized, would all now seem to be crucial points of agreement between Eckersley and Bookchin. Accordingly, the grounds of the debate have shifted in a way that is decisive for dialectical naturalism and will eventually lead to our succinct consideration of the politics of communalism. They now turn upon the character of the institutional nexus itself according to which an ecological ethics is defined, understood, and advanced, and what kind of institutions both theorists advance as those with the greatest hope of counteracting the ecological crisis.

Despite her varied and apt criticisms of liberal democracy, Eckersley's preoccupation with rights regimes, the UN, and incorporating environmental concerns within the prevailing international system seems to color much of her analysis with a liberal-internationalist perspective. The overbearing pragmatism of her fixation on the state and merely formal rights tends to obscure the question of whether the ideological hegemony of liberal democracy and its capitalist economies are even *capable* of advancing an ecological ethics to the point that the ecological crisis will actually be averted. By contrast, Bookchin's lifelong fascination with radical alternatives to the status quo connects to his elaboration of a dialectical naturalism through a core premise: that the prevailing images of nature and possibilities for an ecological ethics is a product of the character of society and its civil, economic, and political institutions. For Bookchin, capitalism and its attendant liberal democracy becomes ecologically ruinous because it lacks a power structure governed by real democracy, which would hold out far better hope of averting the crisis through the utilization of democratic reason. Therefore, liberal-internationalism's ethical development, such as it is, remains formal, stunted, and abortive under the dominion of a small concentration of political and economic elites. In Jessica Dempsey's phrase, this "tragedy of liberal environmentalism" is embodied in the paralysis of meaningful global progress on environmental protection and the "Sisyphean" nature of international environmental reform attempts.[49]

It is, thus, not so much the ethics of "biocentrism" but rather the premise that a genuinely ecological ethics can be successfully cultivated under a global liberal capitalist hegemony that remains the abidingly relevant point of difference between Bookchin and Eckersley. For a dialectical naturalism that inquiries into ecological ethics, rather than assuming absolutist ontological positions, must be redeployed into the question of *how* a given society reifies the natural world, and whether or not such mythopoesis is aerated by a spirit of reason, self-awareness, and social reflection. In Bookchin's view, as we shall see later, it is a direct democratic reason that is advanced as the most realistic possibility for developing an ecological ethics capable of halting the ecological crisis.

On the other hand, there is at least one aspect of their interpretation in which Eckersley and White have hit upon a poorly theorized element of Bookchin's dialectical naturalism, although it remains obscure because of their general misreading of Bookchin's concepts. This is the sense in which Bookchin's attempt to impart values such as differentiation and complexity to the process of natural evolution remains unsubstantiated in his work, beholden to his dialectical naturalism as more of an unexamined presupposition than a carefully qualified attribution derived from a scientifically verifiable process. This is not to say that Bookchin is simply mistaken in reading these values into nature; in fact, a cogent argument could be made to the effect that differentiation *is* a nascent attribute of Darwin's principle of natural selection. Nor is it to condone White's assertion, drawing on Stephen Jay Gould and Steven Rose, that "no level [of nature] is an ultimate reality or a reference point for extrapolation—'all are legitimate aspects of our natural world.'"[50] Perhaps it is fairest to remark that Bookchin's assumption of an increasing differentiation or complexity as an inherent tendency of nature rather amounts to a gap in his writings that lacks the crucial substantiation necessary to properly defend it.

ECOLOGIZING THE DIALECTIC

Despite their holding fast to dialectical philosophy, and in this sense their philosophical superiority over the one-sided conceptions of ecologism, both Hegel and Marx nonetheless failed to extend the dialectic to the subject of society-nature relationships. As we have already observed, Hegel sought to segregate "spirit" from nature in his *Philosophy of History*, thus hypostatizing an impenetrable and ultimately undialectical dualism, whereas the later Marx, at times, had a tendency to reduce nature into a lifeless plasticity preformed and negated by labor power. How exactly does Bookchin's dialectical naturalism conceive of society-nature relationships differently?

Bookchin's presentation of the historicity of society-nature relations, in contrast to the traditional Marxian image of a nature "subdued" by humanity, places much more stress on the underlying "unity in diversity" of natural and social worlds. In the form of an expanding subjectivity and consciousness, he contends, not merely the Hegelian spirit but natural life in its totality becomes increasingly equipped with the capacity to determine its own destiny—as distinct from the blind destiny of fate, *moira*. Simultaneously—and herein lies the dialectical corrective—this capacity of increasing self-determination, the gift of a Fichtean "nature rendered self-conscious," must be seen as a tendency latent in the natural world as a whole—not merely a product of humanity taken as *sui generis*, of *Dike*.

In this sense the progress of natural evolution is to be judged not in the form a positivistic dualism that, under the dubious pretext of "value-neutrality," segregates nature from its underlying symbiotic, and, as Bookchin would have it, richly communitarian potentialities. Bookchin insists that these concepts are not merely human determinations but are readily observable within the often-unconscious mutual aid and usufruct of eco-communities that, as Kropotkin illustrated, are an underlying feature of Darwinian natural selection. Accordingly, such values must be placed within a "richly mediated continuum" of social and ecological development in order to comprehend their historical outcomes.[51]

For such reasons does Bookchin lament "the overarching teleology" of Aristotle and Hegel, which "tends to subordinate the contingency, spontaneity, and creativity that mark natural phenomena."[52] Dialectic is, to be sure, "a philosophy of progress in which there is a growing elaboration and self-consciousness, insofar as the world is rational," but its "rational 'end in view' [is] not one that is pre-ordained, to state this point from an ecological viewpoint rather than a theological one, but one that actualizes what is implicit in the potential."[53] The "adequate end" of nature must be seen, for him, as what is immanent in the material conditions of natural history, not something predetermined from above in the traditional manner of teleology. Indeed, he impugns the traditional conception of philosophical teleology as an outgrowth of the hierarchical mentality that germinated under conditions of a dominatory human second nature. The central defect in the stance of such philosophical teleology is that it "could not trust nature to develop on its own spontaneous grounds, any more than ruling social and political strata trust the body politic to manage its own affairs."⁵⁴ This is but one example of the care that Bookchin takes to historicize his own concepts.

In Bookchin's estimation such cosmological dualisms, rooted in the hierarchical reifications of earlier philosophical teleologies,

> . . . tainted the works of Aristotle and Hegel as surely as they mesmerized the medieval Schoolmen. Classical nature philosophy erred not in its project of trying to elicit an ethics from nature, but in the spirit of domination that poisoned it from the start with an often authoritarian, supernatural arbiter who weighed and corrected the imbalances or "injustices" that erupted in nature.⁵⁵

What Bookchin seems to carry out here, though by no means in a systematic form, is a continuation of what Lukács began in his *History and Class Consciousness*. Images of nature are presented immanently, within conditions of their historical becoming, as a series of reifications that must be exposed through an intricate criticism of their hierarchical foundations.

Juxtaposed against these traditions, a genuinely dialectical reason explores, following out the premises of Bookchin's philosophy of nature, how ethical codes and structures in relation to the natural world have formed, dissolved, and reformed as a result of the overall trajectory of human history. In exploring the natural basis of society and its complementarity within history, Bookchin contends that the imperative of ecological thought is to "ecologize" the dialectic by imparting it with a naturalistic sensitivity that, through the history of dialectical philosophy up to this point, has been largely lacking:

> The continuum that dialectical reason investigates is a highly graded, richly entelechial, logically educative, and self-directive process of unfolding toward ever-greater differentiation, wholeness, and adequacy, insofar as each potentiality is fully actualized given a specific range of development . . . there is a "logic" in the development of phenomena, a *general* directiveness that accounts for the fact that the inorganic did become organic, as a result of its *implicit capacity* for organicity . . .⁵⁶

Bookchin is prudent enough, however, to ground this potentially contentious statement in some of the most far-reaching hypotheses of the always contain the immanent possibility of distorting the in-itselfness of nature through the mediation of the cover concept, which displaces consciousness of its mediated character by appearing, falsely, as what is immediate, commonsensical, already present.

Rather than reducing it into an anthropomorphic or theological "purposiveness," then, Bookchin tries to accommodate that which falls outside the reigning bourgeois images of nature by rejecting the imputation of hierarchical values onto the natural world. In this way, he argues, by way of the logic of differentiation applied to the transitional zone between prehuman and human history, that communitarian and symbiotic values are potentially concomitant in the natural world itself. However, in contrast to a teleology or a form of mythopoeic naturalism, what distinguishes this perspective is that these values are considered nascent, rather than transcendental.[63] It is worth noting here that, like his logic of differentiation, Bookchin's attribution of these "germinal" values appear somewhat hollow in the absence of a more prolonged analysis of the history of natural evolution itself, including the embedding of such values in scientifically verifiable processes of Darwinian natural selection. Bookchin wrote neither an extended philosophy of nature nor a philosophy of science, and the structure of his essays on nature, such as "Society and Ecology"[64] and "Towards a Philosophy of Nature,"[65] is too discursive to have allowed for a more rigorous substantiation of his theses on natural history. The neglect of natural history in his work is unfortunate, given that Bookchin's *Ecology of Freedom* thoroughly develops its complement: the anthropological and social dimension of history.

Regardless of these gaps in the concepts, Bookchin stresses the significance of values of differentiation and complementarity as desperate antidotes to the modern ecological crisis:

> The terrible tragedy of the present social era is not only that it is polluting the environment; it is also simplifying natural ecocommunities, social relations, *and even the human psyche*. The pulverization of the natural world is being accompanied by the pulverization of the social and psychological worlds. In this sense, the conversion of soil into sand in agriculture can be said, in a metaphorical sense, to apply to society and the human spirit. The greatest danger we face—apart from nuclear immolation—is the homogenization of the world by

a market society and its objectification of all human relationships and experiences into commodities.[66]

If this late bourgeois "conventional image of nature"[67] that a dialectical naturalism revolts against, then, is the product of the hierarchical values of domination imposed upon nature, this raises the question of the origins of the historical forces that have woven, and continue to weave, its ideological aura, as well as the historical context for more hopeful and ethical alternatives. It is to this question that Bookchin's probative work of anthropological analysis and speculation, *The Ecology of Freedom* (1982), is directed.

The Nature-Concept and the Anthropology of Hierarchy

Bookchin's anthropology of hierarchy, elaborated most comprehensively in *The Ecology of Freedom*, evokes the negative-dialectical undertaking at the core of a dialectical naturalism: to reveal the historical basis of nature's distortion by forces of social ideology into the form of an ultimately false absolute. This illumination establishes the wayward trajectory of official history as well as its concealed notion of an ecological society of freedom and equality that could potentially go beyond it. The work is characterized by an anthropological search for a "legacy of freedom" that would prove capable of transcending the historical processes of reification that have continually placed themselves between social conditions and the immanent possibilities of their rational becoming.[68] In seeking to liberate humanity's image of nature from systems of hierarchy, Bookchin therefore follows out the premises of dialectical naturalism toward the crystallization of a politics oriented toward the liberation of the dialectic of natural and social history. Nature, he illustrates, can only be comprehended in truly ethical terms outside of the domineering mentality of hierarchical social structures. In order to do this, the anthropological origins of the latter must be thoroughly elucidated.

Bookchin begins his *Ecology of Freedom* with the observation that the insular ethical life of "organic society" (the preliterate, tribal community) is nevertheless marked by a redeeming feature that readily distinguishes it from bourgeois society: the absence of communal inequality and of systemic hierarchy.[69] It is precisely the absence of such factors, it is contended, that is characteristic of the early tribe, and one that also explains much about organic society's nonhierarchical and often distinctly cooperative understanding of the natural world. This basic thesis is stated concisely in one of Bookchin's later works:

> However much these [organic] communities may have differed from each other in many social respects, we hear in their language, and detect in their behavioural traits, attitudes that go back to a shared body of beliefs, values, and basic lifeways. As Paul Radin, one of America's most gifted anthropologists, observed, there was a basic sense of respect between individuals and a concern over their material needs that Radin called the principle of the "irreducible minimum." Everyone was entitled to the means of life, irrespective of his or her productive contribution. The right to live went unquestioned so that concepts like "equality" had no meaning if only because the "inequalities" that afflict us all—from the burdens of age to the incapacities of ill health—had to be compensated for by the community.[70]

Drawing on Radin's anthropological concept of the "irreducible minimum," Bookchin characterizes the incipient egalitarianism of organic society as an "equality of unequals," to be counterposed with the "inequality of equals" that prevails within bourgeois society. Hence the stark differences between the egalitarian outlook of organic society and the hypocritical and specious "equality" of bourgeois society:

> Early [bourgeois] notions of formal "equality," in which we are all "equally" free to starve or die of neglect, had yet to replace the *substantive* equality in which those less able to be fully productive were nevertheless reasonably well provided for. . . . There was no need in these organic societies to "achieve" equality, for what existed was an absolute respect for man [sic], for all individuals apart from any personal traits.[71]

In their *Dialectic of Enlightenment*, Horkheimer and Adorno had described organic society in a far less complimentary light, drawing largely, it seems, on Marx's disparaging remarks about "savage" life that occur in the *Grundrisse*.[72] Bookchin on the contrary draws attention to the lack of hierarchy or inequality in the outlook of organic (tribal) society. "Dances seemed to resemble simulations of nature, particularly animals," he notes, "rather than human attempts to coerce nature, be it game or forces like rainfall."[73] Nature rituals, he suggests,

> ... were not coercive, but rather *persuasive*. ... The attempt of organic society to place human beings in the same community of a part with each other, to see in each an interactive partner with others, yielded a highly egalitarian notion of difference as such.[74]

This does not preclude his admission that tribal life was often remarkably parochial and insular, and its hostility and violence toward outsiders was perhaps its greatest defect.[75] This defect of tribalism, he asserts, was probably one of the primary causes that aided the growth of militaristic societies and what many anthropologists have identified as the cult of the "big man": one of the earliest latent forms of patriarchal domination.[76] Along with the initially benign prestige of the elders (early gerontocracy), he identifies the growth of a distinctly male civil society, bound up within the immanent material conditions of militarism and chiefdoms, as one of the germinating factors of hierarchy. Out of the material contradictions of warrior societies emerged a social structure of "command and obedience" that can be traced from late tribal forms right up into their more advanced forms in recent history.[77]

Hierarchy thereby begins to emerge as the most significant historical concept for Bookchin's social ecology. What is illuminated through a speculative analysis of anthropological origins is that, common to both the "primitive" and the bourgeois period alike, prevailing images of "nature" arise out of cultural reifications. Their social function emerges as the legitimation of a prevailing power structure: of the reinforcement of elite rule and as a rationalization for dominant social groups to continue to exploit enslaved or allegedly "inferior" social groups unabated. This notion was raised previously in *History and Class Consciousness*, according to which the reified, bourgeois concept of nature must be traced back to its ultimately social origins in systems of domination. Bookchin, far more expansively than Lukács, ties the genesis of the bourgeois nature-concept to historically entrenched systems of hierarchy.[78]

One might point out the reductive aspects of Bookchin's characterization of the complex history of social domination under the cover concept of hierarchy. After all, does this not risk precisely losing the concrete, the particular, and the nonconceptual beneath an abstraction that simply cannot do justice to the historical nuances of social domination systems? However, it is clearly not Bookchin's intention to subsume the complexities of history under an overarching abstraction; hierarchy must be taken as a conceptual placeholder for concrete relations of domination based upon command and obedience. Accordingly, notwithstanding to whatever extent the concept of "hierarchy" may be inadequate to certain historical intricacies, one risks losing Bookchin at the outset if one ignores the dialectical rejoinder that the cover concept points to the abiding problems of systems of domination, rather than their merely abstract conceptual form. As Bookchin expresses this: "one does not have to explain 'everything' in 'foundational' terms to recognize the existence of *abiding* problems such as scarcity, exploitation, class rule, domination and hierarchy that have agonized oppressed peoples for thousands of years."[79] History, he says, "is precisely what is rational in human development."[80]

In asserting this, social ecology turns the Freudo-Marxian image of the "savage's" domination of nature on its head. It holds fast to the notion that "the domination of nature" has its origins not in an abstract, supposedly ontological "struggle" with nature but rather in the concrete forms human domination has assumed: the historical origins and continuations of hierarchical power structures. In projecting its own values onto nature as such, hierarchical civilization produces a reified concept of the natural world that is but a mirror of its own antagonistic, ultimately exploitative power structure. Just as a history written by the victors remains inadequate to the potentialities of that history and attempts to rationalize the suffering of the vanquished, so a nature-concept congealed in the form of hierarchical social relations cannot be considered adequate to the potentialities of the natural world.

The implications of this are radical, not least because of their overturning of the classical Marxian thesis of an ontological struggle with nature. By locating the genesis of domination in conditions of early humanity rather than an alleged material necessity, as Price observes, "Bookchin opens up a whole new realm of early human experience that has to be taken account of in the formulating of the emergence of hierarchy."[81] Emphatically, for Bookchin it is not the merely material reality of an increasing surplus with the discoveries of agriculture that introduced hierarchy into the historical scene, as it was for Marx. Relations of production must be seen to encompass not merely production, but an extra-economic dimension of social activity. Specifically, the genesis of domination first occurs in the antagonism between the young and old in tribal societies, particularly the latter's dependence on the hard-won gains from nature in a world of scarcity:

> [The elders'] need for social power, and for hierarchical social power at that, is a function of their loss of biological power. The social sphere is the only realm in which this power can be created and, concomitantly, the only sphere that can cushion their vulnerability to natural forces. Thus, they are the architects *par excellence* of social life, of social power, and of its institutionalization along hierarchical lines.[82]

From the nascent hierarchy of gerontocracy to shamanism, warrior societies and patriarchal civil society, Bookchin illustrates how a *consistent* "historical materialism" is nothing less than a dialectical naturalism, because it must take account of these *social* and *cultural* elements of a given mode of production, and its concrete potentialities shape relations of domination and their shifting images of nature. As Price notes, "by stressing the subjective side of the emergence and concretisation of hierarchy, Bookchin moves our conception of dealing with these problems further away from the notion of them as strictly economic factors, as strictly the by-product of the necessary project to control the natural world and render it productive in the move through human history."[83] This counter-Marxian corrective is significant, for it is nothing less than a riposte to the determinism that characterized Marx's (almost certainly illusory) belief in a "progressive" history, a history that seemingly justifies the domination of nature under the pretext that it will lead to human liberation. By contrast, Bookchin emphasizes not the inevitability of capitalist decline but rather its increasing stabilization, and he places his rational faith in the creation of turning points of history that may have allowed for radical, nonbourgeois alternatives to capitalism.

Thus we arrive at the point at which Bookchin's own formulation of dialectical naturalism begins to pass over into a concrete politics. Such a politics, founded on the idea of negating hierarchical systems in the pursuit of human social freedom, understands such a liberation as the process that alone could free nature from its reifying subsumption beneath hierarchical morality. In Bookchin's later works, in contrast to the fledgling anarchist themes that characterized some of his earlier work, hierarchy is fully grasped as a distinct historical trend: a twisted meta-history that countermands the very ability of a democratic body to manage its own affairs on an egalitarian basis and establish a genuinely public life premised on the competence of popular rule. Such a system of rule would be that in which "popular consent" becomes the living substance of political reality, rather than the empty talk of ideological fiction. The reader might perhaps recall that Kropotkin, in his highly evocative description of the contest between the nascent states and the "free communes" of the late Middle Ages, had already indicated as much. Kropotkin had, nevertheless, not fully formulated hierarchical relations as a distinct system or pattern of social history. He had not quite grasped, furthermore, the social significance of the idea of dominating nature—rooted in hierarchical history, as Bookchin attempts to illustrate—that was to culminate in such abhorrent repercussions for the biosphere at the hands of the subsequent, more advanced period of capitalism.

Yet how exactly could Bookchin's formulation of dialectical naturalism, qua social ecology, conceive the present historical context as one of social transformation from a hierarchical history into a profoundly nonhierarchical one? On what basis does it advance the concrete potentialities of a nature-society relation in a form that avoids the historical tarnish of hierarchical rule and social domination? His attempt to respond to such questions was one of hope in the pressing realities of the ecological crisis coupled with popular consciousness of the potentialities of "post-scarcity" technology. If his political visions have thus far failed to germinate in the West, perhaps the fault may not lie with him alone, but rather more with the manipulated popular consciousness and dire cultural conditions met with in the twenty-first century. In confronting history's potentialities, Bookchin's social ecology thereby confronts the discontents of the World-Spirit in the form of a negative dialectics, the revolutionary context of history's "turning points" that could have led to radical alternatives to the present and still offer important principles of hope for us today.

Turning Points as Negative Dialectics

An analysis of the later Bookchin's preoccupation with historical "turning points" would be incomplete without some mention of his scathing assessment of the leading ideologues of recent history, such as Hobbes,

Freud, and even Marx, for their repressive depictions of the natural world. This was probably only made possible because of Bookchin's exposure to the most wide-ranging critiques of the Neo-Marxists (in particular the Frankfurt School), which readily employed concepts such as reification to explain the underlying distortion of consciousness and were generally more concerned with psychological factors than the nineteenth-century anarchists or the pre-Marxian utopians, most of which exhibited (from the perspective of hindsight) a rather one-dimensional view of social consciousness. Kropotkin, for instance, had largely criticized Hobbes on "scientific" grounds, and Élisée Reclus's positivism had led him to largely emphasize the empirical aspects of social geography.

What comes under the most severe criticism in Bookchin's evaluation of socialist history is the tendency of much of what came to be known as "historical materialism" to do away with ethical criticism, indeed with the very notion of a "utopian" element to revolutionary change. What this amounted to in Bookchin's assessment was, ironically, precisely what bourgeois society sought to accomplish: the dissolution of the precapitalist lifeways of community, mutual aid, popular control, and usufruct and its subsumption beneath the bourgeois world of centralized factories, nation-states, and the split between "workers" and "bosses."[84] Marx had often, to his lasting infamy, tended to advance this bourgeois colonization of precapitalist lifeways as "progressive"—an assertion redolent in his famous speech on "free trade."[85]

Although *The Manifesto of the Communist Party* was to celebrate this dissolution of the precapitalist world as historically "progressive," subsequent history has hardly been kind to such a verdict. There is little doubt from the body of his writings that Bookchin regarded it as a little more than a deluded dogma of the nineteenth century—a dogma that was to completely ignore the arguably revolutionary potentialities of the peripheral peoples that had not yet been seamlessly assimilated into the commodity-driven world. Over time, as Bookchin accounts for it, capitalism was to do precisely the opposite of what Marx and Engels predicted: rather than revolutionize the workers, it was to placate and pacify them through bureaucratic unions, top-down control, and corporatist-type solutions to industrial disputes, ultimately leading to the decline of the proletariat as a genuinely revolutionary social stratum.[86]

Bookchin's critique of the historical premises of Marxism takes place within what are probably his two most searching and eloquent essays on the historicity of revolutionary transformation—"Turning Points in

History" and "Ideals of Freedom." Both essays are remarkable not only for their wide range of historical scope but especially in the way that they connect dialectical naturalism's notion of participatory evolution with a passionate condemnation of the sweeping historical determinism that was a hallmark of "scientific" socialism. Here it becomes possible to glimpse just how sincere Bookchin was in his attempt to do away with the dichotomy between "idealism" and "materialism," illustrating that both oversimplify the harrowing complexities of revolutionary transformation in history. In contrast to the materialist assertion that being determines consciousness, for example, Bookchin elucidates how it cannot but end up with an enclosed tautology that utterly fails to glimpse the concrete cultural and social milieu in which capitalism, rooted in an economic rationalism largely alien to previous history, could emerge:

> It would have been impossible to understand why capitalism did not become a dominant social order at various times in the ancient world if inherited cultural traditions had not restrained and ultimately undermined the capitalistic drives that were very much at work in the past ages. One could go on with endless examples of the extent to which "consciousness" seemed to determine "being" (if one wants to use such "deterministic" language) by turning our eyes to the histories of Asia, Africa, and Indian America, not to mention many European countries early in modern times. On the broad level of the relationship of consciousness to being—which still carries considerable weight with Marxist academics even as all else in the theory lies in debris—Marxism begs its own questions. Looking back from its entrenched economistic and bourgeois viewpoint, it defines in bourgeois terms a host of problems that have distinctly nonbourgeois and surprisingly noneconomic bases. Even the failure of precapitalist societies to move into capitalism, for example, is explained by a "lack" of technological development, the poverty of science and, as often happens to be the case in many of Marx's less rigorous works like the *Grundrisse*, by the very cultural factors that are supposed to be contingent on economic factors.[87]

The libertarian-socialist utopians, alternatively, sustained a critique of bourgeois society not simply on its own terms of "political economy" but in the form of a far more holistic, ethically mediated critique of social "evil." For all their failures, what was significant about the anarchists and libertarian utopists for Bookchin was that they sought to transcend the amoralism and repressiveness of the bourgeois order with a far-reaching vision fired in the crucible of human potentiality.[88] In so doing they foreshadowed a vital notion of his articulation of dialectical naturalism, namely, that of participatory evolution. Their appeal to individual freedom, for all of its excesses and ultimately bourgeois orientation, nevertheless once retained a more redeeming moment.[89]

On the other hand, this abandoning of historical determinism also meant, paradoxically, a sense of desperation about capitalism's wide-ranging results in producing a reified consciousness of "embourgeoisement" in the working class. Although social history may have yielded moments of genuine social choice, these needed to be juxtaposed against the darkening pallor of capitalism and the nation-state, which were gradually eroding the very prebourgeois social institutions—such as the commune—that had proven capable of exercising any meaningful influence in history.[90]

Anarchist politics may have ultimately dissolved into an incoherent array of individual insurrections, anti-organizational dogmas, self-congratulatory spontaneity, and reified nature worship. However even anarchism, in light of its most rational potentialities, could have evolved into a more coherent historical movement that would direct the form and content of an ecologically reconciled society. This insight is basic to Bookchin's formulation of dialectical naturalism. By penetrating beneath history's ideological shell and delving into its discontents, its "turning points," Bookchin stresses the double mediation of being and consciousness and the significance of the agency of revolutionary social movements against a purely deterministic model of historical structuration. Indeed, if reality is not adequate to the notion of itself as Hegel maintained, this is nowhere more obvious than the context of social ecology's concern with revolutionary turning points. For these were, liberated from the biases of hindsight, moments wherein the future was uncertain, seemingly susceptible to revolutionary transformation. Taken within the conditions of their immanence, which are neither in good faith reflected in reified historiographies nor in their identity with hegemonic nature concepts, the elucidation of history's turning points is simultaneously an illumination of the historical possibility of remaking society along truly ethical and ecological lines.

Two prominent examples of the exposition of such turning points suggest themselves in Bookchin's works. The first is his dialectical account of the historical flourishing and ultimate negation of the city under the conditions of late bourgeois society; the second is his analysis of technology in *The Ecology of Freedom*, in which Greek notions of *techne* are presented in juxtaposition with the prevailing images of technology under late capitalism. While both of these subjects do not directly concern the context of revolutionary transformation, they nevertheless furnish concise examples for how dialectical naturalism's elucidation of historical turning points is to be carried out in a form that develops Bookchin's politics.

Urbanism, Ecology, and the Historical Mediation of Nature's Image

One of Bookchin's earliest and most neglected writings—*The Limits of the City* (1974)—presents an immanent analysis of the ecological and social potentialities of various turning points in the historical development of the city. This includes considerations that range from the economy to social geography, anthropology, and political institutions. Yet in the final analysis the exposition of the book ends in an unequivocal statement: that with the vast urban transformations ushered in by capitalism and the centralized nation-state, the city has reached its terminal point, its historical "negation" of what were its more humane potentialities. At the stage of late capitalism, the city has become a twisted aberration, a barbarous mockery of the very haven of civilization that it once offered to a humanity still steeped in the blood kin and in various other forms of civic parochialism. In the form of gigantic urban belts that break the boundaries of human comprehension, scale, or popular management, the "city" as such has ceased to be; bourgeois society, with its "law" of infinite growth, has exploded the city beyond the point of all rational and democratic control. We are left with what Bookchin calls "urbanism": the high-density concentration of populations into polluted, congested, and crime-ridden metropolises driven by the purely bourgeois considerations of employment, taxation, and economic growth. It is within a close examination of the city forms of past and present, therefore, that Bookchin presents the reader with a desperate exploration of "the internal connections between different periods of urban history," culminating in the recognition "that urbanism must be viewed as a development that places us in a unique position to go beyond the city as such and produce a new type of community, one that combines the best features of urban and rural life in a harmonized future society."[91]

Bookchin tries to illustrate how urban metropolises have exhausted their once vibrant potentialities and have erected a social geography completely alien to the substance of an ecological and humanly scaled society.[92] The solution presents itself in the form of a reassertion of rational limits to urban growth, and the careful restructuring of urban geography along contours that are comprehensible and manageable in direct-democratic forms. This insight, evidently drawn from Aristotle's *Politics*, is reconnoitered as a plausible potentiality that has developed in the lifeways of the precapitalist world. The possibility of reviving, strengthening, and expanding such "dual power" is the point at which social ecology's dialectical naturalism also becomes a distinctly *political* naturalism.

Bookchin invites us to recall the dialectical contradictions of the city's historical development in order to better appreciate the rapid changes ushered in by market society. He begins the work with the medieval adage that "city air makes people free," an assured point of contrast to the present era that provides the reader with a sense of the stark juxtaposition between its past and present social significance. To this end, he observes that "only in a rational urban situation can the human spirit advance its most vital cultural and social traditions."[93] Bookchin views the emergence of the city in historical terms as a decisive break with the kinship or clan form of social organization.[94] In purely social terms, the city represents a "humanity [that] is exiled from a harmonized universe to the realm of social contradiction, where the problems of material want are felt as harsh antagonisms between one stratum and another."[95] Like much else in history, however, this break was not a clean succession; the earliest forms of the city, particularly in Mesoamerica, constitute a prehistory of "tribal federation" along "increasingly hierarchical lines," but nevertheless one that still regarded the land as inalienable.[96] His discussion of the Hellenic concept of *autarchia* is an excellent example of dialectical naturalism's clarification of this shifting image, premised on a "balance" between individual and society.[97]

Consequently, in Bookchin's words, "in sharp contrast to the modern metropolitan impulse to unlimited growth—an impulse that Hegel would call a "bad infinity"—the Hellenic impulse always emphasized limit, and the *polis* was always limited by what the Greek could take in "at a single view."[98] The medieval commune was to elaborate an even more distinct image of nature, an outgrowth of the communitarian solidarity of its guild system. This solidarity was founded upon "the concrete nature of the labor process, the directness, indeed, familiar character, of nearly all social relations, and the human scale of civic life which fostered a high degree of personal participation in urban affairs."[99] What is characteristic of the social "matrix" of technology in the medieval world is, according to Bookchin, this "natural core."[100] Arising out of contradictions of its own historical making, the medieval guild system retains a social landscape of human scale, intelligibility, and sensual immersion within its natural environment. At this crucial juncture, it is once again apparent that Bookchin holds fast to a conception of nature that is dynamic—conceived within the turning points of a concrete social history. Accordingly, the medieval conception of technology and nature, in which its own reifications are bound up, presents a striking difference to the bourgeois reification of nature:

> Even the prevailing technology retains this natural or organic character: tools are adapted to the proficiency of the craftsman, to his skills, talents, and physiology. The notion that a man is merely an adjunct of an impersonal machine that determines the tempo and nature of his work would have surely horrified members of a medieval guild.[101]

These differences in the prevailing nature-concept pass over into differences in cultural and social outlook that divide the medieval commune from the bourgeois city. The bourgeois city, for Bookchin, is one in which "natural life shrinks from the community to the individual; the city becomes a mere aggregate of isolated human monads—a gray featureless mass, the raw materials of bureaucratic mobilization and manipulation."[102]

We need not follow Bookchin into his concluding exposition of the "Limits of the Bourgeois City," which takes place through an engaging critique of the social geography of Los Angeles and an elaborate analysis of suburban and exurban life, the denuding of the urban landscape through skyscrapers and ghettoization, the burden that urban sprawl places on the natural environment, the psychosocial disconnection between ecology and urbanity, the impotence of the ideology of "city planning," and, in general, the multifaceted depletion of the humane values that once sustained the prebourgeois city.[103] Most noteworthy for our reconstruction of Bookchin's philosophy is how, through the immanent critique of dialectical naturalism, nature may finally appear not as that which is fixed or given as absolute, but as an image founded in particular contradictions of social development:

> The megalopolis, in effect, atavistically travels the full circle of urban history back to the primitive community's dread of the stranger—but now, without the solidarity that the primitive community afforded to its own kind. The freedom which urban territoriality increasingly provided for the outsider, the individuality which the city eventually generated in all who inhabited its environs, the right of the urban dweller to be taken on her or his own merits apart from kinship ties and blood lineages, and perhaps more fundamentally, the solidarity the city forged among its citizens *qua* individuals into a purely social community unified by propinquity and an urbanely rational heritage—all of this is dissolved by the megalopolis into an alienating, crassly utilitarian, externalized mode of sociation in which everyone now reverts to the status of the outsider, to the primal stranger as real or potential foe. The barbarism of the past returns to settle over the forest of skyscrapers and high-rise dwellings like a sickening miasma. If the medieval town celebrated the fact that city air is "free air," the bourgeois megalopolis chokes on a polluted air that is poisoned not only by the toxicants of its industries, motor vehicles, and energy installations, but by a darkening cloud of hostility and fear. By virtue of a dialectical irony unique to itself, the city at its "height" in the most urbanized of urban worlds regenerates the mythic traditions of a humanity that has barely advanced beyond animality, yet without the redeeming innocence that marked this primal age.[104]

Therefore, in Bookchin's terms, the bourgeois metropolis has reached its logical point of negation. The city no longer develops those rational potentialities that had once accrued to it in post-Roman history; late capitalism has dissolved the social and ecological context in which the city, as a functioning political body and at least potentially a forum for democratic and communitarian reason, may have once reconciled itself to the biosphere. Such developments pass over into the most troubling ecological implications that lie at the heart of the contemporary global crisis.

From Techne to Technology

Bookchin's contrast of the Hellenic city-states with the bourgeois metropolis is mirrored in his critique of the "social matrix" of technology. What is most characteristic about the approach of dialectical naturalism to this subject is that it holds technology must not be reified in terms of moral absolutes but within particular conditions of historical immanence.[105] For Bookchin's purposes it is significant that "*[t]echne* includes living an ethical life according to an originative and ordering principle . . ."[106] This is harshly differentiated from capitalist production, wherein the very notion of ethical life is denuded into mere private property relations and "'Living Well' is conceived more or less as limitless consumption within the framework of a totally unethical, privatized level of self-interest."[107]

Much like its context of the city, a dialectical naturalism proceeds here through illuminating the determinate social context of technology. In a famous essay from the 1960s—*Towards a Liberatory Technology*—Bookchin had already drawn attention to the potentialities of a "post-scarcity" society in the wake of the revolutionary potentialities of the New Left, potentialities that seemed to presage a new form of society that would replace late capitalism with humanly scaled, decentralized, and ecological forms of technology.[108] Bookchin's articulations from this period radiate with the utopian promise of a renewal of the Hellenic belief in rational limit, ethical moderation, and qualitative ends. However, under conditions of late bourgeois society post-scarcity remains a concrete potentiality only in ethically denuded, purely technological terms. In a more sophisticated, mechanized, and highly bureaucratic capitalist society, technology is not only employed as a means to diminish the wages and the "input" of workers, as Proudhon presciently warned back in the nineteenth century. As a result of the corrective measures of the state to stem unemployment and stabilize the system, it tends to take on a purely instrumental, authoritarian trajectory of its own. As a means of reinforcing systems of domination, work is redirected from what Marx called "socially necessary labor" to that which serves no necessary or appreciable social function in the creation of use values—except to keep the working class obedient to elite power, and to fuel the burgeoning megaliths of the nation-state's bureaucracy and military-industrial complex. What the bourgeois image of technology has obscured are the fundamental human needs and desires that once beat in the heart of technology, a notion redolent in Fourier and Bloch. In the alienated, distorted, and untrue form of the commodity it is technology that dominates human needs and, in turn, undermines the freedom of their claim over the conditions of life.

Recognition of this important nuance of late capitalist development probably accounts for the dramatic shift in emphasis that distinguishes Bookchin's earlier writings on technology, which were written in the midst of the highly anarchistic and decadent counterculture in the 1960s, from those of the 1980s and 1990s. Later, in *The Ecology of Freedom*, he designates the development and advancement of technology as of secondary importance to the "social matrix," which acculturates the particular form in which technology takes shape, the very "end" to which it is employed.[109] However, as Bookchin repeatedly observes at several key points throughout *The Ecology of Freedom*, in many parts of the premodern world the peasant remained in a largely segregated and distinct cultural stratum, particularly under the decentralized political regimes that were seemingly content to collect taxes and leave them be. In fact, the peasants often retained a rebellious and dignified social attitude, nourished by a close-knit communal solidarity and mutual aid. The joyous "working songs" of the communal peasantry so celebrated in Tolstoy's novels, we are reminded, are relics of a social matrix of technology that was richly communal rather than grasping and predatory.[110]

Preliterate or "organic" society had a functional understanding of the nature-society relation that was completely alien to the bourgeois outlook: these peoples "absorbed technically unique devices into [a] broad biosocial matrix and brought them into the service of their locality."[111] And yet the precapitalist world, due to a unique historical dialectic of its own, was also encumbered, except perhaps in the highly fertile geographic areas, with the recurring burdens of scarcity and monotonous toil. With the technological advances ushered in by capitalism, despite their largely destructive and debased function at the hands of the bourgeoisie, the potentiality of a post-scarcity technology is nevertheless elevated from an abstract to a concrete one. Thereby, by a strange dialectic of its own making, it is capitalism, as Marx had sublimely emphasized, that ushers onto the stage of history the possibility of sublating the limits of a prebourgeois "social matrix" of technology into something that would eventually transcend the dehumanization of capitalist production. But this is to establish only the material preconditions for its realization—preconditions that ironically have in turn been buried beneath the sophisticated and totally administered "superstructure" of technologically advanced capitalist development.

Bookchin shrewdly articulates this dialectical nuance in terms of "sufficient conditions" for revolutionary change, which "are more than strictly economic and involve issues such as organization, politics, democratic institutions, ethics, and yes, traditions, intellectual expression, hopes and aspirations for a better life."[112] The dialectical whole of technology, contextualized within its social matrix, thus encapsulates the relative unity between necessary and sufficient preconditions for a rational and free society. This also involves facing up to the inevitability of human intervention in nature—albeit one that could take on a more benign form in a rational society. Accordingly, Bookchin remarks, Marx's "prescriptive approach toward the humanity-nature relationship has now become a merely descriptive one: *humanity's control over the forces of nature describes an existing situation*."[113] Given the immense ecological damage wreaked by capitalism, a prudent utilization of advanced technology is all but inevitable if humanity is to arrive at a renewed ecological "metabolism" with the natural world. This raises the question of the revolutionary politics that would make it so. Such a politics, given the continual advance of the global ecological crisis, "would have to engage in widespread ecological restoration, and this cannot be done without the use of science, technics, and our active intervention in the biosphere."[114] "Ironic as it may seem," he remarks in a keenly dialectical insight, "in a rational society we would have to exercise control over natural forces *precisely in order to restore first nature*."[115]

This seems to strike a somewhat discomforting chord. For it enticingly straddles the ambiguous historical dialectic between utopia and dystopia, realized by advanced technology, whose surrealism and magic have only been explored by the most probing authors of science fiction. But Bookchin would have been the last philosopher of socialism to retreat into the seeming security and safety of a mythic past for fear of the unsettling technological potentialities of the future. If there is one overriding theme to *The Ecology of Freedom* it is that the potentialities of eco-technology, coupled with a renewed liberatory outlook, have become conditionally necessary if the present pathway of human history is to escape the stagnant power of its "prehistory," a prehistory that could plausibly culminate in its self-annihilation.

Bookchin's dialectical naturalism thereby passes over considerations of a practical politics. It must enquire, if it is to do justice to history's turning points, what "forms of freedom" might be actuated within the conditions of the ever-unfolding present. Bookchin attempted to provide practical answers in the form of what he termed "libertarian municipalism," or alternately "communalism." It is with this subject that a critical reconstruction of his formulation of dialectical naturalism may conclude.

COMMUNALISM AND THE CIVIC DIMENSION OF REVOLUTIONARY ACTIVITY

If a philosophy of dialectical naturalism is distinguished from a mythopoeic naturalism by its interest in the "turning points" of history and the potentialities they awaken, this discloses a renewed emphasis upon the possibilities of a revolutionary movement to "remake" society anew. Hence the core leitmotif of urban and technological transformation that radiates through Bookchin's late texts from the 1990s and early 2000s. Notwithstanding this, if a politics of "communalism" was devised as his final word on the concrete potentialities of the present period, then its formulation in Bookchin's final years—succinct and often understated as it was—remains incomplete. In his own words, indeed, communalism is "a distinct ideology with a revolutionary tradition that has yet to be explored."[116] Nevertheless, Bookchin's late writings do follow out the basic principles of a dialectical naturalism and affirm his conviction that an ecological society could only emerge through the difficult revolutionary transformation of social institutions to embody the production of a democratically formulated ethics.

Communalism was formulated by Bookchin in the 1990s as a form of communitarian political theory that is both anti-statist and founded on principles of neighborhood democracy, multiple layers of confederation, and recallable delegation. In articulating this model, he drew on a wealth of recent revolutionary experience—particularly the French revolutionaries' call for a "commune of communes." Communalism's ultimate aim is to bring about a society that is nonhierarchical and richly permeated by an ethical orientation. It does not aim for the abolition of "authority" (as the parlance of anarchism would have it) but rather the *radical democratization* of all forms of authority, subjecting them to the determinations of democratic reason. This involves, unlike the fiction of representative "democracy," a social power that resides not in a professional or elite class, but the amateurism of a municipal community's collective judgment and administration of public institutions.

To build a plausible case for the practice of communalism, Bookchin draws upon the people's history of the "age of great revolutions"—from the peasant revolts of the late feudal era in Europe to the ultimately abortive twentieth-century revolutions in Russia, Germany, and Spain. This is nowhere more evident than in the major preoccupation of his last decade—the voluminous *The Third Revolution*, which was by far the most protracted work of his life. However, it remains also one of the most obscure, to the point of an almost total neglect of reception. The work itself, completed only in 2006, already seems to be out of print. Its marginal status is perhaps a clue to the fragmented political climate in which it was received. In an era in which the Left has become increasingly fractured, reformist, and liberal in its cultural outlook, Bookchin's efforts to appeal to the values of its more unified and revolutionary past were all but doomed to obscurity. The strange dialectical admixture of historical anxiety and hope that comprises Bookchin's formulation of communalism may be attributed to the observation that it appears in hindsight not as forward-looking (despite how much Bookchin desires to actually project this) as much as an effort to preserve the nonbourgeois legacy of the past against an uncertain, potentially barbarous future for the West. As proof of this we need merely observe that, as early as 1979, Bookchin had reluctantly declared his belief that "the revolutionary era is over."[117]

Yet if the revolutionary era is over, this raises all the more questions about the concrete genesis of a politics founded on the revival of communal direct democracy. This would involve, minimally, a conscious break with the forms of statecraft to which the Marxist-Leninist Left has traditionally gravitated:

> Politics is *not* statecraft, and citizens are *not* constituents or taxpayers. Statecraft consists of operations that engage the state: the exercise of the monopoly of violence, its control of the entire regulative apparatus of society in the form of legal and ordinance-making bodies, and its governance of society by means of professional legislators, armies, police forces, and bureaucracies. . . . Politics, by contrast, is an organic phenomenon. It is organic in the very real sense that it is the activity of a public body—a community, if you will—just as the process of flowering is an organic activity of a plant. Politics, conceived as an activity, involves rational discourse, public empowerment, the exercise of practical reason, and its realization in a shared, indeed participatory, activity. It is the sphere of societal life beyond the family and the personal needs

of the individual that still retains the intimacy, involvement, and sense of responsibility enjoyed in private arenas of life.[118]

It is to the revivification of this "organic" totality of life, desiccated under conditions of bourgeois "democracy," that communalism speaks. To transcend prevailing ideology across the broader class divisions of society would surely require, however, precisely that well-developed and prepared-for moment of revolutionary transformation that seems so distant now in the West and was declared to be over.

This contradiction remains at the core of the communalist project of building neighborhood associations, particularly if they were to ever become a movement that could exert an influence over society at large. Even Bookchin's depiction of the "immediate goal," rising out of the actions of actually existing neighborhood communities, has only a vaguely immanent context:

> The immediate goal of libertarian municipalism [or "communalism"] . . . is to reopen a public sphere in flat opposition to statism, one that allows for maximum democracy in the literal sense of the term, and to in embryonic form the institutions that can give power to a people generally.[119]

Yet for all of the emphasis on the immediacy of the goal, Bookchin is drawing less on what has gone before—in particular the deep divisions of class conflict—and more upon a speculative view of future possibilities.

Despite its seeming marginalization of the issue of class conflict—a dilemma that is by no means abolished merely because of the ecological crisis—communalism calls for nothing less than the restatement of majoritarian democracy in terms that echo the most penetrating analyses of Lenin, Luxemburg, and Benjamin concerning the demassification of the proletariat. It is within the direct experience of recovering a vibrant, egalitarian, and genuinely democratic public sphere that Bookchin envisions "the masses" ceasing to be a mass or a class and becoming the public personalities of a redeemed humanity. This coincides with the elderly Bookchin's conclusive break with anarchist politics, which was to be his definitive statement on a political theory that, in his more youthful years, he had loosely aligned himself with.[120] Communalism would emphatically reject anarchistic concerns with a "lowest common denominator" consensus, in which "the least controversial or even the most mediocre decision that a sizeable assembly of people can attain is the one that is adopted."[121] Contrariwise, a majoritarian model of democracy, all liberal fears of a "tyranny of the majority" aside, promotes dissensus—a factor integral to what he regards as the "dialectic of ideas" thriving on "confrontation" and "opposition," an important means to prevent a rational future society from becoming an "ideological cemetery."[122]

This seems to be a negative reflection of his observation that "many promising movements for basic social change in the recent past were plagued by a pluralism in which totally contradictory views were never worked or followed to their logical conclusions, a problem that has grown even worse today due the cultural illiteracy that plagues contemporary society . . ."[123] Notwithstanding the internal coherence and rigor of communalist political theory, however, its future prospects remain ambiguous. Both *The Third Revolution* and *The Rise of Urbanization and Decline of Citizenship*, the only works to deal with the historical basis of communalism at length, provide few suggestions for dispelling the most pressing obstacles, such as conflicting class interests, patriarchy, and racial divisions, that must be confronted by any revolutionary movement regardless of the strength of their resources or organization. What seems unavoidable however is that revolutionary mediation, if it is not to perish but to endure, must have a strong material "base." Bookchin insists that the "true civicism" of communalism has at least one material precondition: the formation of a coherent network of citizens' militias that could plausibly resist the encroachments of the bourgeois nation-state. To this end, he remarks, communalism "would be a vulnerable project indeed if it failed to replace the police and the professional army with a popular militia—more specifically, a civic guard, composed of rotating patrols for police purposes and well-trained citizen military contingents . . ."[124] Indeed, "Greek democracy would never have survived the repeated assaults of the Greek aristocracy without its militia of citizen hoplites, those foot soldiers who could answer the call to arms with their own weapons and elected commanders."[125]

How the communalist movement would even begin to proceed in the twenty-first-century reformation of citizens' militias—or, more accurately, at what stage of its future political architecture it would undertake this goal, and where and how—is evidently beyond the historical vantage point from which Bookchin could have theorized prior to his passing in 2006. Nonetheless, he insists that for any serious movement for social transformation to become successful, it must achieve the subjugation of the bourgeois economy beneath robust ethical postulates governed by the public institutions of a genuinely democratic community. "The difficulty in tying economics to morality," he observes, "stems from the nature of economic life as we know it today."[126] It is also rendered opaque

> ... because we tend to assume that the economic status quo is a given, a 'natural state of affairs,' that is assumed to be part of a fictitious "human nature." So deeply rooted is the market economy in our minds that its grubby language has replaced our most hallowed moral and spiritual expressions. We now "invest" in our children, marriages, and personal relationships, a term that is equated with words like "love" and "care." We live in a world of "trade-offs" and we ask for the "bottom line" of any emotional "transaction." We use the terminology of contracts rather than that of loyalties and spiritual affinities. This kind of business babble, garnished with electronic terms like "input," "output," and "feedback," could easily fill a dictionary for our times and those that lie ahead.[127]

Yet if communalism is to recover an authentic public sphere, founded on the intense solidarity of village, neighborhood, and city life, it must seek to reorient itself around the nonbourgeois values of a social ecology. Bookchin's sketch of the potentialities of such a "moral economy" is inimitable. A moral economy would

> ... dissolve the antagonism between "buyer" and "seller," to show that in practice both "buyer" and "seller" form a *community* based on a rich sense of mutuality, not on the opposition of "scarce resources" to "unlimited needs." The object exchanged is secondary to the ethical values that are explicitly shared by the participants of a moral economy. For "buyer" and "seller" to care for each other's well-being, for them to feel deeply responsible to each other, and for them to be cemented by a deep sense of obligation for their mutual welfare is to replace a strictly economic nexus with an ethical one—that is, *to turn economics into culture* rather than to visualise it as the "circulation" of things. Where distribution becomes a form of complementarity, it ceases in fact to be economic in the usual meaning of the word and the terms "buyer" and "seller" become meaningless.[128]

The extent to which communalism actually develops the concrete potentialities attached to the late capitalist period remains, nevertheless, obscure. Its assumption that the ecological crisis constitutes a "transclass" phenomenon[129] has by no means been vindicated in recent history; the economic foundations of the global warming denial industry might even suggest that the ecological crisis has heightened class conflict rather than diminished it. Moreover, in the current upheaval of the political climate in Europe, where a resurgent fascism is once again fueled by popular immiseration, and with the increasing threats in the West to supposedly sacrosanct liberal institutions such as the rule of law, the separation of powers, freedom of speech, and the protection of citizen privacy, the Euro-American sphere may be about to plunge into the era of prolonged civilizational unrest, if not the sort of decline that right-wing historian Oswald Spengler prophesized almost a century ago. The ever-present search for new sources of exploitation in the midst of declining rates of profit continues unabated, and with it large geographic areas of former "civilization" are being reared into ecologically barren landscapes.

Yet late capitalism has also illustrated a dynamism and perseverance that would have surely shocked Marx, Lenin, or Rosa Luxemburg had they lived to see it. Whether communalism speaks to the material and social contradictions of the twenty-first century remains to be seen in the future. Nevertheless, by holding fast to what Price refers to as the direct neighborhood action of a Bookchin "minimum programme"—modest community efforts to create and sustain institutions of dual power, such as occupations, participation in municipal elections, and organization of neighborhood groups on the basis of municipal issues—the politics of communalism is founded on a principle of hope that future turning points in history can be opened up on a local and decentralized level.[130]

In all these respects, insightful comparisons can be made between Bookchin's communalism and the autonomous Marxist John Holloway's recent theses on a radical praxis of "cracking" capitalism.[131] A comparison here is illuminating, for it shows, on the one hand, the apparent limits of Bookchin's overlooking of patterns of "continuity" beyond the municipality, as well as, on the other, its significant advantages in attempting to build more sustained turning points than the often carnivalesque spontaneity that Holloway seeks to render into a legitimately radical praxis.

Bookchin's communalism is definitively organized around the presupposition that the only authentic form of praxis is a revolutionary one, addressing directly "the ecological, civic, and subjective forces or the efficient causes that could impel humanity into a movement for revolutionary social change."¹³² By contrast, Holloway's thesis of cracking capitalism is founded on the disparate, "interstitial," collective uprooting of the forms of activity under capitalism that Marx referred to in the form of "abstract labor." In contrast to the abstract labor of the workplace and its traditional union representatives, Holloway looks to patterns of actually existing interstitial "other-doing" beyond the performance principle of abstract labor creation and the social hierarchies upon which late capitalism is founded.¹³³ Communalism too shares this concern, by radically redefining the landscape of social activity to revolve around the creation of new municipal movements and "moral" rather than market economies. The seeming weakness of Bookchin's program here is the lack of any tangible connection to what Price calls the "maximum programme" of dual power—contesting the legitimacy of the state and creating citizens' militias to run a completely democratized and federated landscape of communes.¹³⁴ Founded on a distant hope that citizens' initiatives will eventually culminate in such a "maximum," Bookchin nevertheless provides little concrete insight into the real future prospects of such initiatives coalescing into a revolutionary movement in the West. In this sense, the often impalpable connection between the minimum and maximum is a major uncertainty in his attempt to elaborate the politics of communalism.

Holloway, on the other hand, does not need to confront this problem in the same way because his theses for "cracking" capitalism are based upon the pivotal rejection of revolution as a viable form of anticapitalist praxis. Holloway invites us to imagine how hegemonic images of nature-society relations are, far from permanent and reified, undermined daily by the often invisible "other-doings" of the excluded, marginalized, and self-determined struggles of the oppressed for a more rational and ecological society:

> The revolutionary replacement of one system by another is both impossible and undesirable. The only way to think of changing the world radically is as a multiplicity of interstitial movements running from the particular. . . .
>   . . . Social change is not produced by activists, however important activism may (or may not) be in the process. Social change is rather the outcome of the barely visible transformation of the daily activities of millions of people. We must

look beyond activism, then, to the millions and millions of refusals and other-doings, the millions and millions of cracks that constitute the material base of possible radical change.[135]

Through the other-doing and "negation-and-creation" of nonbourgeois life activity, freed from the discipline of abstract labor, human beings thus already possess an actually existing praxis for recovering a less dominatory relationship with the natural world and with one another.[136] Whether it be in the form of community gardening, neighborhood democracy, indigenous self-determination, or communal or tribal occupations of land for self-sufficient agriculture and industry, Holloway suggests that we must not neglect the negative dialectics of "misfitting" peoples and the lines of continuity that their varied and sometimes subconscious principles of hope sustain. "There is no model to be applied," he remarks, "but there is a fundamental principle of asymmetry in relation to capitalist social relations."[137]

In the context of Holloway's more open-ended autonomism, Bookchin's strict model of municipal politics may appear somewhat rigid, premised upon a perhaps inflexible notion of cause and effect inhospitable to the lines of continuity that extend across diverse constellations of human activity incongruous with, or opposed to, capitalist and hierarchical social structures. By seeking to determine a municipal blueprint for revolutionary change, communalism might risk ignoring the forms of human activity that confront hierarchical social relations immanently and may lead to more sustained dual-power institutions for democratic governance, despite the lack of a direct identification with municipal governance.

Nevertheless, the understated strength of the Bookchin program remains its commitment to sustainable institution building, in lieu of temporary "happenings" or "peak experiences" of the kind of "lifestyle anarchism" that Bookchin denounced so unreservedly in the mid-1990s. In this regard, Holloway's endorsement of carnivalism and even the lifestyle anarchist Hakim Bey's notion of the "temporary autonomous zone"[138] may be self-defeating, for as Bookchin observes:

> A TAZ, in effect, is not a revolt but precisely a simulation, an insurrection as lived in the imagination of a juvenile brain, a safe retreat into unreality. . . . More precisely, like an Andy Warhol 'happening,' a TAZ is a passing event, a momentary orgasm, a fleeting expression of the 'will to power' that is,

in fact, conspicuously powerless in its capacity to leave any imprint on the individual's personality, subjectivity, and even self-formation, still less on shaping events and reality.[139]

What may have first appeared as a weakness of rigidity in communalism may thus actually bestow its greatest advantage. Rather than risking a degeneration into a purely affirmative heterogeneity of "happenings" that are allegedly directed to the task of cracking capitalism, the Bookchin program clearly delineates spontaneity from organization and real power from illusory or compensatory desires for power. In juxtaposition to the anarchism of Holloway's autonomist praxis, Bookchin insists that a communalist movement

> ... should, in effect, demonstrate a serious commitment to their organization—an organization whose structure is laid out explicitly in a formal *constitution* and appropriate *bylaws*. Without a democratically formulated and approved institutional framework whose members and leaders can be held accountable, clearly articulated standards of responsibility cease to exist. Indeed, it is precisely when a membership is no longer responsible to its constitutional and regulatory provisions that authoritarianism develops and eventually leads to the movement's immolation.[140]

In contradistinction to the logic of spontaneous "other-doing," then, communalism emerges with a clear vision of the civic dimension of revolutionary activity:

> In marked contrast to the various kinds of *communitarian* enterprises favored by many self-designated anarchists, such as "people's" garages, print shops, food co-ops, and backyard gardens, adherents of Communalism mobilize themselves to electorally engage in a potentially important center of power—the municipal council—and try to compel it to create legislatively potent neighborhood assemblies. These assemblies, it should be emphasized, would make every effort to delegitimate and depose the statist organs that currently control their villages, towns, or cities and thereafter act as the real engines in the exercise of power. Once a number of

municipalities are democratized along communalist lines, they would methodically confederate into municipal leagues and challenge the role of the nation-state and, through popular assemblies and confederal councils, try to acquire control over economic and political life.[141]

Thus, as Bookchin rejoins, it is only in this strictly *institutionalized* reinvigoration of civic life that the prevailing image of nature-society relations may really shift from a dominatory to a nondominatory one. An enduring and sustained challenge to the logic of bourgeois society, with its crude logic of domination extended over both nature and humanity alike, cannot sustainably be mounted by a praxis that holds fast to a celebratory temporalism, or decadent "anticapitalist" "peak experiences," or a carnival atmosphere that trivializes the actually existing potentialities of meaningful social and economic change into an officially designated window of time.

The accelerating global ecological crisis of the twenty-first century is beginning to reveal the often concealed ecological damage of a planet that has been colonized by the international pathologies of a predatory and grasping market society. To redeem this society, Bookchin's communalism asserts that nothing less is required than consciousness of those turning points of history that could have facilitated a far more complementary reconciliation between humanity and the ecology of the planet it inhabits. Only armed with the knowledge of its errant past and with a program for diligent and well-organized institution building could a future society hope to restore the planet's biosphere to the point of future habitation.

Toward a Communalist Image of Nature

Bookchin's contribution to ecological thinking is not only groundbreaking but far outside of the ideological parameters of prevailing trends in Western political ecology. Whatever the merits of Castree's productivist approach to nature, Latour's concept of human and nonhuman collectives or Holloway's notion of cracking capitalism, what provides Bookchin's dialectical naturalism with a clarity and coherence that is unsurpassed elsewhere is his interest in uncovering the historical and social foundations for an ecological ethics. As we have seen, such a project for an authentic ecological ethics is founded on a model of communalism. The rejuvenation of an ecological ethics within a new society is the thread that connects a dialectical naturalism to the theory of communalism.

There are several key premises underlying this association. Perhaps the most fundamental, as we have explored throughout this book, is the social mediation of images of nature. Through the reification of nature, different societies throughout history have expressed their internal social logic—its morality, rationality, and archetypal journey. But they have also illustrated their flaws and ethical shortcomings in doing so. This is no more true than in the era of capitalism and the nation-state that has followed on the back of the industrial revolution. We have examined only a few of the most decisive moments in this social logic of capitalism, as reflected in some of the foremost social philosophers of the last few centuries. For Bookchin, as we have seen, the dialectic of possibility unleashed by capitalism, particularly in the breathtaking technological advances it has made, have resulted in several key "turning points" that could have produced a more ecological society and a more naturalistic sensibility permeated by a social ethics. This potential for a naturalistic sensibility produced by a rational social structure epitomizes the concept of a dialectical naturalism: a society capable of acting upon itself and its relationship with the biosphere in ethical ways, or in Fichte's famous turn of phrase, a nature rendered self-conscious.

Yet far from a preordained teleology, this is but one nascent potentiality in all the violent meanderings that constitute an often barbaric human history. The older Hegel seems, at least on some readings, to have resigned himself to the blind hope that history would be progressively rational, and one day might become something more than a slaughter bench. An increasingly precarious biosphere, relentlessly besieged by capitalist industry and the military-industrial complexes of the nation-state, would seem to offer us little hope for this. Nevertheless, there was, for Bloch, a potential kindness in technology, something we get a glimpse of in advances in pain reduction, technological support for the disabled, and the ability to connect to loved ones across vast distances. The principle of hope that we witness in technological advances illuminates for us the promise of an ethically guided science and technology. For Bookchin, liberating humanity from hierarchical systems and instituting authentic forms of direct democracy becomes one with this goal: the progress of humanity into true adulthood.

The development of a genuine ecological ethics is antithetical, for Bookchin, to a reifying traditionalism. Just as the young Hegel railed against the positivity (traditionalism) of the Christian religion, and counterposed tradition to the concept of ethical life, for Bookchin there is no promise of redemption in the positivity of capitalist markets and their destructive attempts to transform the biosphere into cost and benefit flowcharts and wasteful and needless commodities. While reification may be unavoidable, what is most necessary to the development of an ecological social sensibility is the spirit of critical self-reflection, deliberation, and debate that only a direct democracy could provide. These crucial foundations to an ecological ethics are lacking in formal bourgeois democracy, as we have explored through Bookchin's fascinating analysis of the social geography of the bourgeois metropolis. The harshness of commodity forms and the disciplining of human life according to the prerogatives of capital accumulation are reflected in the concentration of power that defines the bourgeois era. This concentration of power is anathema to the goal of an ecological ethics: for an ecological ethics is a product not merely of democratic deliberation, which after all can be innocuously practiced even under oligarchies, but of a direct democratic network of institutions backed by sufficient force to protect its values and ethical framework and bring them into actuality.

The psychology underlying communalism is important too, in connecting it to the goal of an ecological ethics. Increased time and scope for sensuality, play, reverence for life and aliveness was perceived by Fourier as important for the mental health of a society. A communalist society would be defined by less repetitive and less frequent forms of work, aided by technology, and a vastly renewed public sphere, with much more free time for participation in communal and private life. Helping the lives of others would cease to become something marginal, to be squeezed in between work hours or degraded by the concept of charity, and would become the rejuvenating bedrock of psychological life. By contrast, bourgeois society remains a society deeply riddled with various forms of abnormal psychology, particularly by depression, anxiety, phobias, obsessive-compulsive disorder, and outright psychopathy. A world increasingly denaturalized and ecologically simplified is, perhaps above all, a world losing its beauty, its sanctuaries and its soothing qualities, absent of noise and pollution. Communalism would seek to restore these interfaces of natural and social life and beautify barren landscapes by the recovery of a vibrant public sphere.

It is by no means guaranteed that communalism, as imagined by Bookchin, would always produce ethical or even ecological outcomes.

Democratic majorities, as for any human collective, are sometimes the victim of prejudices and superstitions and could act in ways that very much undermined the goal of an ecological ethics. And yet, unlike the concentration of power in political and economic elites characteristic of bourgeois society, communalism would expansively open the *possibility* of building more ethically informed institutions and sensibilities through the mechanisms of debate, argumentation, and social reasoning platforms. Human action upon nature would increasingly become the subject of democratic reason, and parties, factions, and groups most interested in protecting nonhuman nature would no longer meet with the same kind of paralyzing resistance as that offered by the intense concentrations of capital that define the political party machinery of the modern nation-state.

With the attainment of a communalist society, the prevailing image of nature would dramatically shift. Reifications of nature as a series of commodities would gradually be dissolved, and nature might well, as for the presocratics over two thousand years ago, come to be seen through more moral reifications of justice, equality, and sensuality. The democratic participation of the "rights" of nonhuman life might also gain far more traction than such concerns do presently, and nonconsensual forms of control over animal life might be seen as increasingly repulsive in the future development of an ethically sophisticated human temperament. In a sense, nature could be allowed to develop its own potentialities alongside the ethical stewardship of a redeemed humanity ethically awoken by its own democratic rationality, rather than the ever-subjugated and violated victim of a hierarchical mentality.

Epilogue

This book has attempted to defend the rigor of a dialectical naturalism at a time when resurgent, reactionary forces are striving to dissolve the consciousness of society back into a mythopoeic understanding of the humanity-nature relationship. This, as the author has attempted to demonstrate, has potent political consequences; much is at stake in the question of how this relationship is conceived into the future. For the first time in history, the survival of human civilization depends on the development of its own ethical sensibility through a revolutionary rethinking of its institutions.

A dialectical naturalism emerges as a fitting sublation of both the bourgeois myth of dominating nature and the romanticist or anarchist myth of natural law. In this lies the most terminal criticism of system building, of fixed concepts that refuse to be adequately historicized. For a dialectical naturalism, nothing is less permissible than an idea of nature that is fixed as a system. The concept of appearance, which as Hegel appertained always contains its measure of truth, forms the point of negation for a dialectical naturalism: it is to show that however much nature may be steeped in the ordinary language of common sense, it nevertheless always comes into being through a process of social mediation. But in this is also established the impossibility of a fixed, intransient "idea" of itself, let alone what is called in Neo-Kantian jargon a "typology." A dialectical naturalism cannot treat concepts abstractly, on the pure level of thought; it is by definition always immersed in the real moment of their formation.

This extends to its own concept. This is especially evident in the context of Bookchin's politics of "communalism." The task left to a dialectical naturalism of the future would be to critically explore precisely what "turning points" are left open to the remaining decades of the twenty-first century and beyond. While the path to utopia must certainly be illumined with much envisioned by Bookchin in his own exploration of the revolutionary past—minimally through a social totality of government and law that has managed to remove itself from the pathos of social domination that makes up so much of the history of civilization—we must expect future history to take unanticipated turns. Such turns could hardly be accommodated in the midst of a political model if it were presented as the last word on history. Rather than a fixed system, therefore, a politics of communalism could only be interpreted, consistent with the premises of dialectical naturalism itself, as a museum of experience to be visited, appraised, and distilled into the most promising revolutionary moments of the future.

Bookchin's formulation of "communalism" remains, nonetheless, relatively silent on the prospects of the future. This, it would seem, is the task that Bookchin would have wanted future generations to pursue: to diligently illuminate those principles of hope that expand before the horizon of possibility. What seems most compelling to note is that such principles must, if they are to succeed, hold fast to the Enlightenment notions of intelligibility, rationality, and coherence. Such principles are precisely those for whom a nihilistic and idolatrous culture industry, anchored firmly on bourgeois ground, is emphatically cheering the demise. Yet without making the dialectic of the past intelligible and coherent to us, the future is all but destined to remain blind, unconscious, and beyond the influence of the ethical. Without such coherence a social revolution would remain at best the product of circumstances, rather than the master of them.

Bookchin's emphatic affirmation of ethical life and intellectual coherence as the cornerstone of social ecology is, in this respect, a crucial reminder to the twenty-first century that it rejects the best achievements of the Enlightenment at its own peril:

> Ethics is based on reason: its distinguishing feature is that prescriptions of right and wrong have to be *justified* by rational activity, not simply by tradition or blind and fearful acceptance. In an ecological society it is ethics that would guide human behavior, elaborated through rational discourse, logic, and the evaluations of experience.[1]

Fascism, authoritarianism, and all other forms of irrational mythopoesis breed in the absence of such justification. A society that has abandoned reason is a society that has abandoned any rational premise that might hold in check fascistic or religious appeals to authority, tradition, or hatred for the "other"—appeals that are all too often smokescreens for the maneuverings of elite power. Like the silent cries of Kafka's sirens, it is only the struggles of the martyrs of reason against the evils of our world that are beautiful. To speak of an ethically rejuvenated humanity, guided by reason, is to begin to redeem their suffering.

Appendix

Theses on Communalism

I. The equivocation of hierarchy with the absence of democracy is false. One cannot describe dialectically even a direct democracy without acknowledging the prominence of factions, the elevated prestige of particular individuals, or the unspoken deference to demagogues or charismatic speakers that may win the floor on a given day. By the same measure, the institutions of a democratic judiciary constitute a binding authority, whose command must be obeyed under threat of violence. So too in the end, despite her elevated social status, rare perfume, and finery, does a courtesan remain a harlot. All inflated ideology aside, a democracy may have its injustices and its hierarchies too; but these nonetheless are redeemed as the necessary foundations for the determinate negation of injustice and of hierarchy. Socrates was not made to drink the hemlock any more ethically simply because his executioner was acting at the behest of a democratic majority. But his death, a crime against humanity, condemns only the democratic majority that murdered him; it does not condemn the *institution* of democracy as such, as the glorifiers of allegedly beautiful aristocracies would like people to believe. For much the same reason, radical social theory is mistaken when it critiques the principle of hierarchy abstractly, rather than its concrete historical application. The achievement of a direct democracy would not signal the abolition of hierarchy as is often supposed, but rather the establishment of a less malicious hierarchy that could make the future dissolution of hierarchy, the outcome of a greater social sensitivity to human needs and philosophical study of the *polis*, one day possible. Likewise, a courtesan's education, aesthetic refinement, and study of philosophy may not have freed her from sexual slavery, but it made possible the conditions of woman's liberation—consciousness and knowledge of her condition.

II. The appeal to the values of democracy and to the values of socialism is not necessarily synonymous. Bookchin's call for the municipalization of the economy is well intentioned, but it is vulnerable to becoming an ideology for demagogues who would seek to perpetuate economic inequality precisely through its legitimation by democratic mandate. All the more unequivocally, and with growing confidence in its realization, one champions the cause of democracy, the more one risks losing sight of the one goal that should take the utmost priority. This is, however, a goal that is not reducible to an unqualified endorsement of democratic reason. It is highly questionable whether a democracy such as Athens, which left a good portion of its population enslaved, malnourished, and in a state of material precariousness, would be more ethical than a benevolent monarchy that ensured that the material needs of all of its subjects were met. As Adorno observes, "there is tenderness only in the coarsest demand: that no-one shall go hungry anymore. Every other seeks to apply to a condition that ought to be determined by human needs, a mode of human conduct adapted to production as an end in itself."[1] Is this any less true for the demand that economic decisions be made by a local municipality?

III. Bookchin's early formulation of a post-scarcity society neglects one decisive factor: the extent to which bourgeois society actively *hinders* unprofitable technological development—in Bloch's words, all except the "military kind." All of the urban myths about cancer researchers with cures lying dormant in their basement freezers for lack of scientific funding may be exaggerated or fabricated; few would deny, however, that they are plausible within the twisted rationality of capitalist development. The internet, as is well known, was originally developed by the United States military. The inhumane and disingenuous smiles of the start-up venture capitalists from Silicon Valley bear some resemblance to these origins. Technological innovation today has been irrevocably alienated from its only justifiable grounding: human needs.

IV. To date, communalism has only been taken up successfully in perhaps the most unassuming of places—on the roughly hewn, stubborn nobility of Kurdish soil. In short: it has been taken up by a people that remain "innocent," largely unblemished by capitalist mediation, still bearing, even, some traces of an earlier tribality. Can we still maintain that communalism is a theory about capitalism?

V. Communalism is not the end goal; at best, it is a *ladder*, a *stepping-stone* to something greater. It is socialism's first step into the glade of *political* wisdom, a socialism shorn of all mystical moralizing about the workers—the determinate negation of that "materialist" idealism that has long made a fetish of the "class struggle" and "commune" without bothering to address the concrete dynamics of the "thing-in-itself"!

VI. Bookchin's idea of communalism addresses the problems of history, of politics, of institution building; but somehow it neglects the most important problem of all: *the collective psychology of the masses that will bring a democratic socialism into actuality.* Bookchin's interest in psychology would appear, from his published works at least, to be marginal; the movement of his thought scarcely ever penetrates the subject. He takes little account of the irrational, unconscious, manipulable element of the masses, shows no consideration for how their behavior is subtly shaped by culture industries, and provides no reckoning of the fascist dimension of populism. These factors could only be ignored at the peril of any revolutionary movement.

VII. Communalism studies the revolutionary past, in order to furnish insights for a revolutionary future. But nothing is more abstract than the word "revolution"—especially if not furnished *itself* by the concrete nexus of potentialities pertaining to a particular culture, a particular historical moment, a particular gravitational force that seizes humanity just as inexplicably as the magic of aesthetic inspiration. Bookchin believes that this moment can occur through local electioneering, coherent leadership, consciousness of history, and so on—in short, all within the temporal sequence of late capitalism, all within the bounds of decadent Anglophone culture, all despite the vulgarities that tarnish "populist politics." But does not Camus's character Dr. Rieux finally grasp the significance of life only when in the depths of a plague-ridden city? Did Rome not require its Attila the Hun, need its disease of feudal Christendom, in order to experience its Renaissance? It is beyond frightening to ponder that a return to fascism or world war may be necessary, dialectically speaking, in order to shake an opiated humanity violently awake, to restore to it an awareness of the preciousness of life, freedom, and reason. *Nemo saltat sobrius.*

VIII. Bookchin's simple depiction of Nietzsche's philosophy as reactionary belittles the sublimity of Bookchin's own triumph over it. For the great limitation of Nietzsche's philosophy is not its "amoralism"—taking root, as it did, in an age that pompously celebrated the various hypocrisies of its repressive morality as if they were pure and virginal. Nietzsche, rather, teeters on the precipice of a future that he cannot foresee—intoxicated by a Dionysian spirit whose appetite he can only sate by turning, almost necrophilously as it were, back into the past. He grasps at phantoms—the Superman, the aristocratic man, the master morality, the glory of Hellas—because he sees in them a life-affirming principle. And yet the demonic spite that he felt for the fruits of Christian civilization, which lends itself to the form of polemic, extended even to the distortion of his subject matter, which can know only the mood of suspicion and recognize only that which deceives. He was keenly aware of this fate, as *Ecce Homo* reveals. Nietzsche's malice, directed toward Christian morality, exposed the radical falsity of its truths; but like a double-edged blade, his malicious distrust of the dialectic constrained him, imprisoned him, tortured him—he built his philosophical house not as a garden but as a prison. Bookchin, like the original members of the Frankfurt School before him, ameliorates this malice in moments of what Nietzsche would doubtless have derided: through *compassion* for the suffering of the oppressed, through *sympathy* for the victims of the World-Spirit. And here Bookchin triumphs magnificently, not least because he refuses to enter the Nietzschean asylum: he alone is courageous enough, unlike Adorno and his Nietzschean demons, to speak of morality and ethics in redeeming tones and to carefully distinguish the latter from the former. He alone has enough modernity to grasp the revolutionary implications of a *democratically reasoned* morality without that excessiveness of modernity that has long since transformed the self-styled disciples of Nietzsche into purveyors of the very decadence that his philosophy railed against.

IX. Communalism is, as Bookchin formulates it, in support of majoritarian decision making. But this should not be taken to mean *mob rule*. This distinction is commonly overlooked by advocates of unrestrained democracy for good reason. For an honest appraisal of democratic reason could not render its operation into an implacably positive event. Democratic reason, in accord with its ethically ambivalent nature, is not to be conflated with reason as such. Its concepts become inevitably distorting when they seek to render a value judgment on its process as an absolute—in other words, to falsely make democratic reason appear identical with reason. The conscious grasp of objective reason by virtuous leaders and philosophers does not mean that, on a given day, a democratic majority will comprehend and sensibly implement its imperatives. Indeed, democratic reason combines two contrary developments into a tenuous unity: mob rule, as represented by the various demagogues in

Thucydides's history of Athens, and judicious government that aims at the collective welfare. One should also add a third, disruptive element to this dialectic: the influence of individual cunning and egoistic advantage, as exemplified by Alcibiades and his mercenary orientation. Would we be so hubristic as to imagine that a communalist utopia could abolish this tension? The more one penetrates through to the historical substance of democratic reason, to wit, the more one becomes reluctant to place a value judgment upon it at all. In the *Philosophy of Right* Hegel expresses the belief that public opinion is to be both respected and despised. A maxim less dialectical than this could only be dishonest.

X. Communalism is a vision for the achievement of democratic civilization, but it is not a theory of late capitalism.

XI. The neglect of social psychology on Bookchin's part is the last and most enduring residue of his youthful *Trotskyism*, of the *mechanistic communism* that could develop no viable psychoanalytic understanding of why the working classes sided with fascism in the 1930s and why the lower economic strata of the West today seem to be moving in the same direction. Communalism will remain an incomplete theory so long as it resists augmentation into a *critical social psychology of late capitalism*.

XII. The fate of *woman* under patriarchal civilization, which has been preserved and not abolished through capitalism, is one of the most decisive phenomena underlying the transformation of an irrational and repressive society into a rational and nonrepressive one; yet Bookchin scarcely addresses woman or her historical fate beyond a handful of passages in his *Ecology of Freedom*. Öcalan's theory of *democratic confederalism*, which places the emancipation of woman at its epicenter, is therefore the *continuation* of communalism, even the *completion* of it, for it has properly recognized in the struggle of woman against patriarchy the seeds of the most important struggle of all.

XIII. The slow ecological death of the planet can be arrested only by the actions of those who *love and affirm what is alive*. It is, therefore, among the highest of intellectual crimes to disparage aesthetics, literature, and music as distractions or as needless indulgences. The love of *creation* reinforces psychologically, at least according to Erich Fromm's psychoanalytic theory, a reverence for all that is alive in nature, and therefore in humanity.

XIV. That the world would appear differently from the standpoint of its redemption is precisely why revolutionary struggle needs more artists, more philosophers, more poets, more literary authors, more community-involved volunteers, and could perhaps make do with a few less "activists." Such strata form the bedrock of civil society out of which any vibrant communalist movement must emerge; properly speaking, they form the self-consciousness of civil society. Therefore, freedom is not the sole property of activists; it is the spirit of those humble visionaries who, in a world that makes an ideology out of despair, dare to make of life something pleasant and worth living, dare to embody in their actions the principles of a better world.

Notes

Preface

1. The classic study of the social process of reification in capitalist society, including the reification of work and of "natural laws" in bourgeois jurisprudence, remains Lukács's groundbreaking work *History and Class Consciousness*, trans. R. Livingstone (Cambridge: MIT Press, 1971 [1921]), specifically the chapter entitled "Reification and the Consciousness of the Proletariat."

2. For a sense of how far the influence of Bookchin's philosophy has begun to reach globally, see, for example, Joris Leverink, "Murray Bookchin and the Kurdish Resistance," *Roar Magazine*, 9 August 2015, available at https://roarmag.org/essays/bookchin-kurdish-struggle-ocalan-rojava/ (accessed November 2017).

3. The two principal scholarly works that explore the parameters of these flashpoints in great detail are Andy Price's *Recovering Bookchin* (2012) and Damian White's *Bookchin: A Critical Appraisal* (2008).

4. I am aware that I advance this claim despite several passages of Bookchin's pre-1990s works, which emphatically condemn Marx's Victorian sensibilities and his sometimes exaggerated anti-naturalism. It is often overlooked that this critique was considerably softened by Bookchin's works in the 1990s—in particular in *Marxism, Anarchism and the Future of the Left* (1996)—and it is in the sense of Bookchin's later, and far more positive, engagement with Marx that this book develops its ultimate conclusions about this complicated theoretical relationship.

5. See, for instance, Murray Bookchin, *Towards an Ecological Society* (Edinburgh: AK Press, 1982).

6. Noel Castree, "Capitalism and the Marxist Critique of Political Ecology," in *The Routledge Handbook of Political Ecology*, ed. T. Perreault, G. Bridge, and J. McCarthy, 279–292 (Abingdon: Routledge, 2015); see also Neil Smith, *Uneven Development* (Oxford: Blackwell, 1984).

7. See Castree, "Capitalism and the Marxist Critique of Political Ecology," 4.

8. See particularly the essays contained in Bookchin's *Towards an Ecological Society* (1982), which develop his critique of productivism in Eco-Marxist literature.

9. Max Horkheimer, "Traditional and Critical Theory," in *Critical Theory: Selected Essays* (New York: Continuum, 2002 [1972]), 188–243.

10. Herbert Marcuse, "1970s Interventions," in *The New Left and the 1960s* (Routledge: London, 2005), 174.

11. See footnote to pp. 373 and 374 of Murray Bookchin, *The Ecology of Freedom: The Emergence and Dissolution of Hierarchy* (Palo Alto: Cheshire Books, 2005 [1982]).

12. See generally Murray Bookchin, *The Modern Crisis* (Sydney: Black Rose Books, 1986), for Bookchin's most succinct critique of "green" capitalist movements and thought.

13. Marcuse, "1970s Interventions," 175.

Introduction

1. Rosa Luxemburg, *The Accumulation of Capital* (London: Routledge, 2003 [1918]).

2. See generally Bruno Latour, *Politics of Nature: How to Bring the Sciences into* Democracy, trans. C. Porter (Cambridge: Harvard University Press, 2004).

3. Ibid.

4. See generally Bruno Latour, *Reassembling the Social: An Introduction to Actor-Network Theory* (London: Oxford University Press, 2005).

5. William E. Connolly, *Facing the Planetary: Entangled Humanism and the Politics of Swarming* (Durham: Duke University Press, 2017).

6. Timothy Morton, *Ecology Without Nature: Rethinking Environmental Aesthetics* (Cambridge: Harvard University Press, 2009).

7. Timothy Morton, *The Ecological Thought* (Cambridge: Harvard University Press, 2012).

8. Félix Guattari, *The Three Ecologies* (New York: Continuum, 2008 [1989]), 14.

9. Ibid., 28.

10. Ibid., 49–50.

11. See, for instance, Robyn Eckersley, *The Green State: Rethinking Democracy and Sovereignty* (Cambridge: MIT Press, 2004).

12. Where, in this introduction, a full source for a fragment of a primary source of presocratic philosophy is not provided, the reference is to Richard McKirahan's 1994 sourcebook *Philosophy Before Socrates* (Indianapolis: Hackett, first ed.).

13. See generally Gregory Vlastos, *Studies in Greek Philosophy*, vol. 1 (Princeton: Princeton University Press, 1996).

14. A concise account of the historical and political-theoretical dimensions of Athenian democracy is given in chaps. 3, 4, and 13 of Hansen's work on

this subject. See Mogens Herman Hansen, "The Athenian Constitution Down to 403 BC: A Historical Sketch," "Athens as City-State and as Democracy," and "The Character of Athenian Democracy," in *The Athenian Democracy in the Age of Demosthenes: Structure, Principles and Ideology*, trans. J. A. Crook (Norman: University of Oklahoma Press, 1991).

15. This insight is suggested by Murray Bookchin in the first essay of *The Philosophy of Social Ecology* (Montreal: Black Rose Books, 1995).

16. See generally fragments 39DK 2. 1–9, 3, taken from the testimonia of Sextus Empiricus, *Against the Mathematicians* VII, 123–125, for Empedocles's views on the relation between human reason and the senses.

17. Frag. 31DK 17, taken from Simplicius, *Commentary on the Physics* 157.25–159.10. The relationship between Empedocles and Parmenides is furnished with a good discussion in John Burnet's account: "Empedokles," in *Greek Philosophy: Thales to Plato* (London: MacMillan and Co., 1950), 71–75.

18. Frag. 39DK 38, taken from Clement, *Miscellanies* V viii 48.3; see also 39DK 37, 51.

19. See in particular the surviving fragment of *On Nature* from Strasbourg Papyrus d, p. 144 of John Burnet, *Early Greek Philosophy* (London: A. & C. Black, 1920 [1896]).

20. Vlastos, *Studies in Greek Philosophy*, 61. See also the discussion of Empedocles's terminology on p. 64.

21. None of this is to deny the outbursts of collective idiocy and arrogance that sometimes seized the democratic body, particularly in Athens and Syracuse. Plutarch's biographies *Dion* and *Timoleon* offer much illumination of the latter.

22. Vlastos, *Studies in Greek Philosophy*, 123.

23. Vlastos, *Studies in Greek Philosophy*, 84 (original emphasis).

24. Ibid., 85.

25. Ibid., 87.

26. For further analysis of these historical tendencies, including of Luther, Calvin, and Robespierre, see Max Horkheimer, "Egoism and Freedom Movements: On the Anthropology of the Bourgeois Era," in *Between Philosophy and Social Science: Selected Early Writings*, trans. G. F. Hunter, M. S. Kramer, and J. Torpey (Cambridge: MIT Press, 1995 [1936]), 49–110.

27. Janet Biehl, *Rethinking Ecofeminist Politics* (Montreal: Black Rose Books, 1991), 67.

28. Leo Löwenthal, *An Unmastered Past: The Autobiographical Reflections of Leo Löwenthal*, ed. M. Jay (Berkeley: University of California Press, 1987), 242–243.

29. See generally Herbert Marcuse, *A Study on Authority* (London: Verso Books, 2007 [1936]).

30. A brief, yet important note is necessary here, in order to explain a seeming gap in the analysis of Hegel developed in chapter 1. At no point in

the later analysis of Hegel is his *Philosophy of Nature*, which forms the second part of the *Encyclopedia of the Philosophical Sciences*, discussed. This is not due to accident or neglect on the author's part. In fact, I have read thoroughly the first of the three volumes that comprise this work and consulted many passages of the remaining two. As a result, I have been dissuaded from even discussing it at all, so underwhelming and unoriginal is the foundation of the system of Hegel's *Philosophy of Nature*. Its lack of originality emerges not so much from its antiquated scientific principles but rather from its turgid reiteration of Christian metaphysics woven into a crude patchwork of entirely derivative Neo-Fichteanisms. The work's overall character is so derivative, in fact, that were an analysis to be provided here, it would quickly bore the reader with a needless repetition of the same themes developed in the analysis of Fichte. To illustrate this, I need merely quote from one paragraph of the first volume:

> Nature is *implicitly* divine in that it is in the Idea; but in *reality* its being does not correspond to its Notion, and it is rather the unresolved contradiction. Its distinctive characteristic is its positedness, its negativity. The ancients grasped *matter* in general as non-ens, and nature has also been regarded as the Idea's *falling short* of itself, for in this external shape the Idea is inadequate to itself. It is only to the external and immediate stage of sensuous consciousness that nature appears as that which is primary, immediate, as mere being. Even in such an element of externality, nature is, nevertheless, the representation of *the Idea*, and consequently one may and should admire the wisdom of God within it. (*Hegel's Philosophy of Nature*, 1: 209)

According to Hegel, therefore, the nature philosophy of "the ancients" begins with Plato and Aristotle and their dismissal of the organicism of the presocratics—a most dubious appeal to authority if there ever was one. Indeed, for Hegel nature is merely an offense to the identity of spirit, an eternal negative, "an alienation in which spirit does not find itself" (1: 204). Its "distinctive characteristic" is its positedness by the idealistic consciousness, a positedness in fact itself a form of severing alienation; such alienating consciousness could never penetrate one inch farther than the *formalism* of apprehending nature as a state of abstract negativity counterposed to itself. As a result of this disguised origin of the alienating and alienated, the abstract opposition of nature and spirit is held fast as an ontology beyond all criticism; Hegel stubbornly refuses to come down from the Fichtean podium to the humble concrete in which spirit is also a "natural" spirit pervaded by biological and relational necessities. As he writes toward the close of the final volume, "The transition to the existent genus takes place implicitly, in the Idea, in the Notion, that is to say, in the sphere of eternal creation. There however, the sphere of nature is closed" (3: 176).

But it is not as closed as the ideology of the Christian World-Spirit would have us believe: for we are, at every moment, immersed in the continuum of the earth's biosphere.

31. Theodor W. Adorno, *Hegel: Three Studies*, trans. S.W. Nicholsen (Cambridge: MIT Press, 1993 [1963]), 59.

32. Plato, *Theaetetus*, trans. R. H. Waterfield (London: Penguin Books, 1987), 13–132.

33. Hegel, *Phänomenologie des Geistes*, cited and translated in Gillian Rose, *Hegel contra Sociology* (London: Verso Books, 2009 [1995]), p. 76.

34. Herbert Marcuse, *Reason and Revolution: Hegel and the Rise of Social Theory* (London: Routledge and Kegan Paul, 1968 [1941]), 5–6.

35. Bookchin, *The Philosophy of Social Ecology*, 123.

36. Lenin's passage on Pissarev's theory of the dream remains a magnanimous example of the process of dialectical philosophy:

> "One gulf is different to another," wrote Pissarev concerning the gulf between dream and reality. "My dreams can overtake the natural course of events, or they can go off at complete tangents, down paths that the natural course of events can never tread. In the first case dreaming is totally harmless; it can even encourage and strengthen the working man's power to act. . . . There is nothing about such dreams which impairs or cripples creativity. In fact, quite the contrary. If a person were completely devoid of all capability of dreaming in this way, if he were not able to hasten ahead now and again to view in his imagination as a unified and completed picture the work which is only now beginning to take shape in his hands, then I find it absolutely impossible to imagine what would motivate the person to tackle and to complete extensive and strenuous pieces of work in the fields of art, science, and practical life. . . . The gulf between dream and reality is not harmful if only the dreamer seriously believes in his dream, if he observes life attentively, compares his observations with his castles in the air and generally works towards the realization of his dream-construct conscientiously. There only has to be some point of contact between dream and life for everything to be in the best order."

In our movement there are unfortunately precious few dreams of this kind. And those people are chiefly responsible for this who boast how sober they are and how "close" they stand to the "concrete," and those are the representatives of legitimate criticism and the illegitimate politics of trotting behind. (Lenin, *What Is to Be Done?* cited in Bloch, *The Principle of Hope*, 1: 10).

37. See Ludwig Feuerbach, "Towards a Critique of Hegel's Philosophy," in *The Fiery Brook: Selected Writings*, trans. Z. Hanfi (London: Verso Books, 2013).

38. Theodor W. Adorno, Introduction to *Negative Dialectics* (2001), trans. D. Redmond, available at http://members.efn.org/~dredmond/NDIntro.txt (accessed January 2014).

39. It is worthy of note that in Raya Dunayevskaya's writings this is enunciated too, when she draws on the moments in which Hegel, in the spirit of negative dialectics, defined the absolute as that which provoked a "new beginning" and was not comprehensible outside of a state of contradiction.

40. Adorno, Introduction to *Negative Dialectics*, available at http://members.efn.org/~dredmond/NDIntro.txt (accessed June 2014).

41. Ibid.

42. Ibid.

43. Ernst Bloch, *The Principle of Hope*, vol. 1, trans. N. Plaice, S. Plaice, and P. Knight (Oxford: Oxford University Press, 1986 [1959]), 4.

44. Marcuse, *Reason and Revolution*, 5–6.

45. The analysis of social ecology provided here, however, does not primarily concern itself with any doctrinaire programs that Bookchin himself may or may not have supported. What is discussed in relation to praxis is only the barest outlines of communalism's notion of a revived civicism, in addition to an evaluation of its differences with John Holloway's recent program of interstitial change and some succinct criticisms of communalism's programmatic narrowness. Even so, it is not the author's intention to be tied down in ephemeral debates on praxis; rather, these criticisms are offered only for the purposes of stimulating further thought on alternative possibilities to which future political organizations may be fruitfully directed. A quotation attributed to Goethe in the preface to the works of François Rabelais runs as follows: "the fashion of this world passeth away and I would fain occupy myself with the things that are abiding." In our counterrevolutionary era, this conviction provides the correct viewpoint for evaluating the worth of praxis relative to theory.

46. This general line of criticism, originally adopted by Robyn Eckersley, is also adhered to by Peter Hay, whom while providing a reasonably cohesive account of social ecology does not sufficiently interrogate the premises of Eckersley's critique. See generally Peter Hay, *Main Currents in Western Environmental Thought* (Bloomington: Indiana University Press, 2002), 288–302.

47. Bookchin, *The Philosophy of Social Ecology*, 21–22.

Chapter One

1. For further analysis, see Marcuse, *A Study on Authority*.

2. See John Dewey, *Leibniz's New Essays Concerning the Human Understanding: A Critical Exposition* (Chicago: Scott, Foresman and Co., 1902), 59–63.

3. See generally Theodor W. Adorno, *Kant's Critique of Pure Reason*, trans. E. Jephcott and R. Tiedeman (Palo Alto: Stanford University Press, 2001).

4. This anti-naturalism did not succumb to the dialectical sensitivity of Hegel, although he did occasionally undermine it. In fact, in significant passages of Hegel's philosophy it was reaffirmed, particularly in the *Philosophy of History* lectures. By contrast, in Hegel's earlier works one can sense an underlying frustration at the division between humanity and nature construed by Fichte, as if the veil that stood between them was apparently ontological, apparently the "preconditioned" that forms the very fabric of the conditioned. Whereas what divides nature from social relations is in truth something far more concrete and, for that reason, something less immediate, as Hegel intuitively grasped. Yet its secret is discernable only within the discontents that official history, Hegel's included, would dismiss as inessential.

5. Theodor W. Adorno, *Subject and Object*, s. 2, available at http://platypus1917.org/wp-content/uploads/2011/12/adorno_onsubjectandobject.pdf (accessed August 2014).

6. Immanuel Kant, *Critique of Pure Reason*, trans. J. M. D. Meiklejohn (Mineola: Dover, 1900 [1855]), 279–280 (original emphasis).

7. See Bookchin, *The Philosophy of Social Ecology*, 47–50.

8. Kant, *Critique of Pure Reason*, 279–280 (original emphasis).

9. G. W. F. Hegel, *Science of Logic*, trans. W. H. Johnston and L. G. Struthers, vol. 2 (New York: MacMillan Books, 1929 [1816]), 227. Earlier, Hegel writes of Kant's presentation of the nature of reason:

> The notions of Reason, in which a higher force and a deeper content were of necessity divined, are less constitutive than even the categories; they are mere ideas. Their use may certainly be permissible, but these unintelligible essences, which should wholly unlock the truth, are to signify no more than hypotheses; and it would be completely arbitrary and reckless to ascribe any truth to them in and for themselves, since they *can occur in no kind of experience.*—Could it ever have been thought that philosophy would gainsay the validity of the intelligible essences because they are without the spatial and temporal material of sensuousness? (2: 224)

10. Adorno, *Kant's Critique of Pure Reason*, 174.

11. Ibid., 173.

12. Adorno, *Subject and Object*, s. 2.

13. Bookchin, *The Philosophy of Social Ecology*, 48 (original emphasis).

14. Ibid.

15. Immanuel Kant, *Critique of Judgement*, trans. J. H. Bernard (Amherst: Prometheus Books, 2000), 28.

16. Ibid., 174 (original emphasis).

17. Friedrich Schiller, *On the Aesthetic Education of Man*, trans. R. Snell (Mineola: Dover Books, 2004 [1795]), third letter.

18. Ibid., fourth letter.

19. Ibid., seventh letter.

20. Max Horkheimer, *Eclipse of Reason* (New York: Oxford University Press, 1947), 97.

21. Günter Zöller, *Fichte's Transcendental Philosophy: The Original Duplicity of Intelligence and Will* (Cambridge: Cambridge University Press, 2002), 104.

22. J. G. Fichte, "Annals of Philosophical Tone [excerpt]," in *Fichte: Early Philosophical Writings*, trans. and ed. D. Breazeale (Cambridge: Cambridge University Press, 1988), emphasis added.

23. Feuerbach, "Principles of the Philosophy of the Future," in *The Fiery Brook: Selected Writings*, s. 22 (original emphasis).

24. J. G. Fichte, *System of Ethics*, trans. D. Breazeale and G. Zöller (Cambridge: Cambridge University Press, 2006), 261.

25. Ibid., 342.

26. On this subject see especially Fichte, *System of Ethics*, 278–279.

27. Ibid., 261.

28. Horkheimer, *Eclipse of Reason*, 107–108.

29. This contention is developed more fully in Murray Bookchin's essay "A Philosophical Naturalism" in his 1995 work *The Philosophy of Social Ecology*.

30. Fichte, "Lectures Concerning the Scholars' Vocation," in *Fichte: Early Philosophical Writings*.

31. See, for instance, Fichte's endorsement of Alexander as the living spirit of "civilisation" in *Characteristics of the Present Age* (London: Dodo Press, 2009), 34–36.

32. For the context see generally Adorno's *Hegel: Three Studies*.

33. J. G. Fichte, *The Science of Knowledge*, trans. A. E. Kroezer (London: Trübner & Co., 2013 [1889]), 348.

34. G. W. F. Hegel, *The Difference Between Fichte's and Schelling's System of Philosophy*, trans. H. S. Harris and W. Cerf (Albany: State University of New York Press, 1977 [1801]), 128.

35. Rose, *Hegel contra Sociology*, 67.

36. Ibid., 72.

37. Ibid. (original emphasis).

38. G. W. F. Hegel, *Hegel's System of Ethical Life and His First Philosophy of Spirit*, trans. H. S. Harris and T. M. Knox (Albany: State University of New York Press, 1967), 142–143.

39. Ibid., 147.

40. For the context of this analysis, see Walter Benjamin's study *The Origin of German Tragic Drama*, trans. J. Osborne (London: Verso Books, 2006).

41. Hegel's use of the term "Romantic" requires qualification. For Hegel, Romanticism is a far more expansive term than common usage nowadays would suggest. Although it roughly correlates with the art of the Romantic movement

produced within Hegel's lifetime, Rose reminds us that for Hegel, "The 'romantic form of art' refers to the place of art in the cosmopolitan Christian religion and includes the feudal religion" (*Hegel contra Sociology*, 145).

42. G. W. F. Hegel, *Aesthetics: Lectures on Fine Art*, vol. 1, trans. T. M. Knox (Oxford: Oxford University Press, 1975), 436–437.

43. Ibid.

44. For a good explication of Hegel's theory of the landscape painting, see Katerina Deligiorgi, *Hegel: New Directions* (London: Routledge, 2014), 166–168.

45. Hegel, *Aesthetics: Lectures on Fine Art*, 1: 518.

46. Ibid., 525 (original emphasis).

47. Georg Lukács, *The Theory of the Novel*, trans. A. Bostock (London: The Merlin Press, 1978), 113.

48. Ibid.

49. Marcuse, *Reason and Revolution*, 48.

50. Ibid., 113.

51. Hegel (1977 [1807]), *Phenomenology of Spirit*, s. 70 (preface).

52. See Marcuse (1968), *Reason and Revolution*, pp. 124–125.

53. G. W. F. Hegel, *Phenomenology of Spirit*, trans. A. V. Miller (Melbourne: Oxford University Press, 1977 [1807]), s. 109.

54. Marcuse, *Reason and Revolution*, 107 (emphasis added).

55. Ibid., 113.

56. Ibid.

57. G. W. F. Hegel, *Science of Logic*, trans. A. V. Miller (New York: Humanity Books, 1969 [1816]), 543 (original emphasis).

58. Ibid.

59. Ibid., 547 (original emphasis).

60. Ibid.

61. Ibid., 549 (original emphasis).

62. Ibid., 552 (original emphasis).

63. Ibid., 157.

64. Marcuse, *Reason and Revolution*, 156 (original emphasis).

65. Aristotle, "Physics," in *The Basic Works of Aristotle*, ed. R. McKeon (New York: Modern Library, 2001), 194a 32–33.

66. Hegel, *Science of Logic* (Johnson and Struthers translation), vol. 2: 211.

67. G. W. F. Hegel, *The Philosophy of History*, trans. J. Sibree (Mineola: Dover, 1956 [1899]), 25.

68. Ibid., 41.

69. Ibid., 93.

70. Ibid., 99.

71. Ibid., 218.

72. Ibid., 221.

73. Ibid., 244–245.

74. Karl Marx, *The Economic and Philosophic Manuscripts of 1844 and the Communist Manifesto* (Amherst: Prometheus Books, 1990 [1844]), 167 (original emphasis).

75. It may be remarked with some justice that while for Feuerbach ontology was a purely philosophical category, for the young Marx it was essentially a historical one. Engels, in writing his pamphlet *Feuerbach: The Roots of the Socialist Philosophy*, was doubtless correct to chastise Feuerbach for failing to extend his critique of idealism into the historicization of philosophy, a shortcoming exemplified in Feuerbach's dubious assertion that changes in the structure of the social totality coincide with religious changes. On the other hand, Feuerbach's insistence on the *natural* dimension of social relations, and steadfast refusal to subsume nature under a concept of spirit, is more favorable to the development of a dialectical naturalism than the later Marx's identitarian ontology of natural-human antagonism, as discussed later in this work.

76. Ludwig Feuerbach, *The Essence of Christianity*, trans. G. Eliot (Amherst: Prometheus Books, 1989), 91.

77. Ibid., 276–277.

78. Ludwig Feuerbach, *The Essence of Religion*, trans. A. Loos (Amherst: Prometheus Books, 2004), 70.

79. M. W. Wartofsky, *Feuerbach* (Cambridge: Cambridge University Press, 1977), ix.

Chapter Two

1. Karl Marx and Friedrich Engels, *The German Ideology* (Amherst: Prometheus Books, 1998), 46.

2. Ibid., 69.

3. Andre Gorz, *Capitalism, Socialism, and Ecology*, cited in John Bellamy Foster, "Paul Burkett's Marx and Nature 15 Years After," in Monthly Review 66, 7 (2014): available at http://monthlyreview.org/2014/12/01/paul-burketts-marx-and-nature-fifteen-years-after/#en6 *(accessed October 2015).*

4. Bookchin, "Marxism as Bourgeois Sociology," in *Towards an Ecological Society*, 201–206. It is important to note that Bookchin's views were later qualified, seemingly in a more favorable direction, and that this negative appraisal does not necessarily constitute Bookchin's definitive view on Marx's concept of nature. In a later interview, he remarks: "Considering the historical circumstances a hundred and fifty years ago, when he did his most important political writing, I would say that it's at least understandable that Marx was not imbued with an ecological outlook" (*Marxism, Anarchism and the Future of the Left*, 266).

5. Alfred Schmidt, *The Concept of Nature in Marx*, trans. B. Fowkes (London: New Left Books, 1971).

6. Giovanni Pizza, "Second Nature: On Gramsci's Anthropology," *Anthropology and Medicine* 19, 1 (2012): 95–106.

7. Antonio Gramsci, cited in ibid., 97.

8. The interpolation that, for Marx, humankind must "conquer" or "dominate" nature, and in doing so becomes irretrievably bound up with the apparatuses of social domination—what might be called the "domination thesis"—has its origins in the Frankfurt School, especially Theodor Adorno and Max Horkheimer's *Dialectic of Enlightenment* and Herbert Marcuse's *One-Dimensional Man*. Yet this thesis is deeply at odds with Marx's belief (however unfounded) that capitalism would give impetus to the forces of human liberation through the creation and collectivization of the proletariat and, in doing so, produce the potentialities for a qualitatively new social ethics and qualitatively new reconfiguration of nature. Marx's various comments about the struggle of humankind with nature, read with due emphasis upon its place within his theory of gestational communism, are thus arguably not those of an "anti-ecologist," insofar as they raise the possibility of a more ecological society arising out of the material forces and contradictions of capitalism.

9. Neil Smith and Phil O'Keefe, "Geography, Marx and the Concept of Nature," *Antipode* 12, 2 (2006): 30–39.

10. See, for an example of this, Paul Burkett's *Marx and Nature: A Red and Green Perspective* (Chicago: Haymarket Books, 1999). While Burkett's work is highly meritorious for its vigorous reconstruction of the centrality of capitalist mediation in Marx's account of the society-nature metabolism, it also becomes, in a way characteristic of much of the broader "eco-Marxist" literature, highly anachronistic when it attempts to render Marx into a late-twentieth-century ecologist, armed with a vocabulary and outlook that would have been utterly alien to his time. Worse, nature tends to take on a distinctly instrumental image in Burkett's account of Marx, which tends to reduce it to a lifeless matter, by way of a reified reproduction of the jargon of political economy. In support of this assertion it is merely necessary to point to the frequency with which economistic concepts like "natural wealth" are employed judiciously by Burkett. By subtly redefining nature in such reductionist terms, Burkett ends up with something closer to a tautological defense of the jargon of classical political economy than an investigation into the historical context that underpins Marx's idea of nature.

11. Schmidt, *The Concept of Nature in Marx*, 76.

12. Marx, *The Economic and Philosophic Manuscripts of 1844 and the Communist Manifesto*, 65–66.

13. Ibid., 77 (original emphasis).

14. Ibid., 107.

15. Ibid., 108.

16. Ibid.

17. Ibid., 107, 109.

18. Schmidt, *The Concept of Nature in Marx*, 63 (original emphasis).

19. See Bookchin, "Marxism as Bourgeois Sociology," in *Towards an Ecological Society*, 193–210.

20. Karl Marx and Friedrich Engels, "The Manifesto of the Communist Party," in *The Portable Karl Marx*, ed. E. Kamenka (London: Penguin Books, 1983), 208.

21. Herbert Marcuse, in "The Struggle Against Liberalism in the Totalitarian View of the State," in *Negations: Essays on Critical Theory* (London: MayFly Books, 2009 [1968]), gives a spirited defense of such alleged "anti-ecologism" in Marx in a critical essay touching on the subject of fascist eco-politics:

> The interpretation of the historical and social process as a natural organic process goes behind the real (economic and social) motive forces of history into the sphere of eternal and immutable nature. Nature is interpreted as a dimension of mythical originality (well characterized in the phrase 'blood and soil'), present in all things as a prehistorical dimension. Human history truly begins only when this dimension is overcome by being transformed. In the new *weltanschauung*, mythical, prehistorical nature has the function of serving as the real adversary of responsible, autonomous, rational practice. As something justified through its mere existence, this nature stands opposed to that which requires rational justification; as what must be absolutely acknowledged, against all that is first to be known critically; as the essentially dark, against all that derives its substance from the clarity of light; as the indestructible, against everything subject to historical change. (6)

22. See Bookchin, "Reflections on Marx and Marxism," in *Anarchism, Marxism and the Future of the Left*.

23. Bookchin, "Marxism as Bourgeois Sociology," in *Towards an Ecological Society*, 200.

24. Ibid., p. 200.

25. Marx cited in ibid., 201.

26. Gillian Rose, *The Melancholy Science: An Introduction to the Thought of Theodor W. Adorno* (London: The Macmillan Press, 1978), 39–40.

27. Marx and Engels, "The Communist Manifesto," in *Economic and Philosophic Manuscripts of 1844 and the Communist Manifesto*, 216–222.

28. This is a literal rendering of a passage in Marx and Engels's *The German Ideology*, cited in Bookchin, "Marxism as Bourgeois Sociology," in *Towards an Ecological Society*, 204.

29. See generally ibid., 193–210.

30. Karl Marx, "The British Rule in India," in *Dispatches for the New York Tribune: Selected Journalism of Karl Marx* (London: Penguin Books, 2007 [1853]), 217–218.

31. Burkett's *Marx and Nature: A Red and Green Perspective* is a case in point.

32. Schmidt, *The Concept of Nature in Marx*, 63.

33. Ibid., 9. This more reductive account of human activity is given a degree of support in a certain passage of Marx and Engels's *The German Ideology*: "Man can be distinguished from animals by consciousness, by religion or anything else you like. They themselves begin to distinguish themselves from animals as soon as they begin to *produce* their means of subsistence, a step which conditioned by their physical organisation" (37). Nevertheless, the extremely broad sweep of social relations captured by Marx's concept of "production" indicates that he is not necessarily championing the idea of "dominating" nature, inasmuch as nature's mediation through human social activity.

34. See generally the concluding chapter to Rose's *Hegel contra Sociology*.

35. John Locke, *Second Treatise of Civil Government*, chap. 5, available from http://www.constitution.org/jl/2ndtr05.htm (accessed March 2014).

36. Karl Marx, *The Grundrisse: Foundations of the Critique of Political Economy*, trans. M. Nicolaus (London: Penguin Books, 1993), 491 (original emphasis).

37. Ibid., 492.

38. Karl Marx, *Capital*, trans. B. Fowkes and D. Fernbach (London: Penguin Books), 3: 959.

39. Goethe cited in Marx, "The British Rule in India," in *Dispatches for the New York Tribune*, 219.

40. See the second chapter of Bookchin's *The Ecology of Freedom* for the context.

41. See chapter 3 of Bookchin's *The Ecology of Freedom* for further clarification of these points. For a critical analysis of Bookchin's engagement with twentieth-century anthropology, the best source (to my knowledge) is chapter 5, "Reassessing Bookchin's Social History," of Andy Price's *Recovering Bookchin: Social Ecology and the Crises of Our Time* (Porsgrunn: New Compass Press, 2012).

42. See generally Peter Marshall, *Demanding the Impossible: A History of Anarchism* (London: Harper-Perennial Books, 2008).

43. An important qualification must be made here. In speaking of the structure of the anarchist nature-concept, the author refers to a recurring tendency, rather than a homogeneous and undifferentiated concept that spans the entire canon of anarchist thought. Nevertheless, aside from anarcho-syndicalism and certain writings of Pierre-Joseph Proudhon, there are few exceptions to the anarchist tendency to appeal to a vague "revolutionary spontaneity" and an often mystifying and incoherent concept of "natural law" in lieu of the theorization

of *social* laws, relations, and forms of organization that would take the place of hierarchical society and its irrational mores. A mythopoeic naturalism is remarkably persistent throughout the writings of Bakunin and Kropotkin, to cite the two canonical thinkers examined in this study.

44. Alex Pritchard, *The International Political Theory of Pierre-Joseph Proudhon*, 7, available at http://www.anarchist-studies-network.org.uk/documents/Proudhon.doc.

45. Ibid., 20.

46. Cited in K. Steven Vincent, *Pierre-Joseph Proudhon and the Rise of French Republican Socialism* (Oxford: Oxford University Press, 1984), 218.

47. The author has deliberately avoided associating Murray Bookchin with anarchism here, despite the fact that he was almost single-handedly responsible for its renewal in a number of his works from the 1960s, 1970s, and 1980s. As will become clearer in the third chapter of this study, it can be seen that in its most mature form social ecology emerges as a determinate negation of the mythopoeic naturalism at the ideological core of post-Proudhonian anarchism, as well as—perhaps even more emphatically—a rejection of anarchist politics. One should not be surprised that as a result of his mature formulation of "dialectical naturalism," Bookchin felt compelled in the late 1990s to publicly break with anarchist politics in favor of a politics of "communalism," which emphasized the formation of confederal neighborhood institutions as opposed to an anarchic stress on spontaneity, instinct, and "natural law."

48. Lukács's immanent critique of the Romantic nature-concept is discussed in chapter 3.

49. See generally Jean-Jacques Rousseau, "Discourse on the Origins of Inequality," in *The Basic Political Writings* (2nd edition), trans. and ed. D. A. Cress (Indianapolis: Hackett, 2011).

50. Theodor W. Adorno, *The Jargon of Authenticity*, trans. K. Tarnowski and F. Will (London: Routledge, 2003), 5.

51. One might locate the recurring seductiveness of a mythopoeic naturalism within the conditions of early capitalist society in the lingering images of feudal social harmony—in particular the guild system, the free communes and townships of Europe, and the sometimes ethical and mutualistic forms of conduct that grew up around various precapitalist social constellations. Additionally, as Freudian theory reminds us, we should not be too quick to dismiss the significance of a lingering and collective guilt complex as a result of the genocidal displacement of various civilizations in the new world, at the hands of a predatory colonial and mercantilist order. Out of such guilt may easily arise an exaggerated cultural belief in the innocence and purity of precolonial political constellations. In reality, one must always question to what extent the feudal, aboriginal, and Mesoamerican world had in their possession a genuinely nonhierarchical and cosmopolitan moral order—particularly with the persistence of patriarchy, slav-

ery, and various religious hierarchies. But whatever is lacking in the outlines of historical reality can be readily filled in by forms of the speculative imagination, and especially by the various wish fulfillments that the utopian imagination has at its disposal. This may help us to understand the power of the "noble savage" myth for both Diderot and Rousseau, not to mention countless others in their wider intellectual circle at the pinnacle of the French Enlightenment. It may also help to explain the emergence of ideologies such as post-Proudhonian anarchism in the nineteenth century, which had sought to imbue mere instinct with an ethical orientation and thereby weave moral and even revolutionary theories out of a theory of "nature." Because of its holding fast to a moralistic naturalism, anarchist political philosophy could only terminate with the playing off of nature against culture: with the poetic evocation of "natural human society," "mutual aid," or "natural morality." One might easily riposte such mythopoeic naturalism by observing that the state, capitalism, and other pathologies of civilization are themselves just as much a product of "nature" as the morality and instinctual "laws" anarchist theory posits. And yet, because anarchism is often revived today by various irresponsible elements of a self-styled "revolutionary" youth, its historic defects must be carefully laid bare in greater detail, in order for us to grasp its theoretical incoherence, and therefore the incoherence of its praxis.

52. Few of Bakunin's surviving writings are in print, and those that are, are often of questionable integrity, sometimes lacking basic standards of referencing and historical details. Accordingly, the following immanent critique of Bakunin cites primary text passages from the most reputable and scholarly source the author could find: Brian Morris's *Bakunin: The Philosophy of Freedom* (Montreal: Black Rose Books, 1993).

53. Ibid., 81.

54. Ibid., 80.

55. Ibid.

56. See Murray Bookchin, "Introduction to the Third Edition,' in *Post-Scarcity Anarchism* (Edinburgh: AK Press, 2004).

57. Cited in Morris, *Bakunin: The Philosophy of Freedom*, 90.

58. Ibid., 91.

59. Ibid., 140.

60. Ibid., 88.

61. Ibid., 87.

62. Ibid., 81.

63. Ibid.

64. Theodor W. Adorno, "Freudian Theory and the Pattern of Fascist Propaganda," in *The Culture Industry*, ed. J. M. Bernstein (London: Routledge, 1991), 140–141.

65. Horkheimer, "Rise and Decline of the Individual," in *Eclipse of Reason*, 148.

66. Étienne de La Boétie, *Discourse on Voluntary Servitude*, available at http://www.constitution.org/la_boetie/serv_vol.htm (accessed November 2015).

67. Morris, *Bakunin: The Philosophy of Freedom*, 80.

68. See Frederick C. Beiser, "Herder's Philosophy of Mind," in *The Fate of Reason: German Philosophy from Kant to Fichte* (Cambridge: Harvard University Press, 1993), 133.

69. Peter Kropotkin, *Mutual Aid: A Factor of Evolution* (New York: Cosimo Books, 2009 [1902]), ix.

70. See generally Dawkins's 1986 documentary *Nice Guys Finish First* (Produced by J. Taylor), BBC Horizon, aired 14 April, season 22, episode 14. Also see generally the second edition of Richard Dawkins, *The Selfish Gene* (London: Oxford University Press, 1989), chap. 12.

71. See Stephen Jay Gould's essay "Kropotkin Was No Crackpot," *Natural History* 106 (1997): 12–21, available at http://www.marxists.org/subject/science/essays/kropotkin.htm (accessed December 2013).

72. Kropotkin, *Mutual Aid*, xiii–xiv.

73. Ibid., 76–77.

74. See Rousseau, *Discourse on the Origins of Inequality*, in *The Basic Political Writings*, part 1.

75. Kropotkin, *Mutual Aid*, 111 (emphasis added).

76. Ibid., 151.

77. The author refers here specifically to Kropotkin's statement, in chapter 1 of the *Ethics* that "mutual aid is the predominant fact of nature." It is worth noting, however, that in the following paragraph he also says: "If mutual support is so general in Nature, it is because it offers such immense advantages to all those animals which practice it, that it entirely upsets the balance of power to the disadvantage of the *predatory* creatures. It represents the best weapon in the great struggle for life which continually has to be carried on in Nature against climate, inundations, storms, frost, and the like, and continually requires new adaptations to the ever-changing conditions of existence." See Peter Kropotkin, *Ethics: Origin and Development* (Honolulu: University Press of the Pacific, 2002 [1910]).

78. Kropotkin, *Mutual Aid*, 298–299.

79. Ibid., p. 299.

80. Kropotkin, *Ethics*, 26.

81. Ibid., 201–202.

82. See Catherine Mackinnon, *Towards a Feminist Theory of the State* (Cambridge: Harvard University Press, 1989).

83. Kropotkin, *Ethics*, 193.

84. See generally the two middle chapters of *Mutual Aid*.

85. Kropotkin, *Mutual Aid*, 199–200.

86. Ibid., 216.

87. Ibid., 217.

88. See, for example, Bookchin's discussion of the difficulty of this distinction in *The Spanish Anarchists* (Edinburgh: AK Press, 1998), 10.

89. Reference could certainly be made here to the most prominent of contemporary academic anarchists: David Graeber and Noam Chomsky. Both have produced works delving into the historical and philosophical basis of anarchism without questioning its underlying naturalism.

90. See, for example, James C. Scott, *The Art of Not Being Governed: An Anarchist History of Upland Southeast Asia* (New Haven: Yale University Press, 2009); Mikhail Bakunin, *Stateless Socialism: Anarchism*, trans. G. P. Maximoff, available at http://dwardmac.pitzer.edu/Anarchist_Archives/bakunin/stateless.html (accessed August 2014).

91. See Mikhail Bakunin, "The State and Marxism," in *Marxism, Freedom and the State*, trans. K. J. Kenafick (Ithaca: Freedom Press, 1984).

92. Pëtr Kropotkin, *The State: Its Historic Role*, available at http://theanarchistlibrary.org/library/petr-kropotkin-the-state-its-historic-role (accessed September 2014).

93. Ibid.

94. Peter Kropotkin, "Law and Authority," in *Anarchism: A Collection of Revolutionary Writings* (New York: Dover, 2003), 206.

95. See generally Kropotkin's essays collected in *Anarchism*, for the context.

96. Peter Kropotkin, *The Conquest of Bread* (Charleston: Bibliobazaar), 146–147.

97. See Sam Dolgoff, *The Cuban Revolution: A Critical Perspective* (Montreal: Black Rose Books, 1976).

98. Bookchin, "Introduction to the Third Edition," in *Post-Scarcity Anarchism*, xxxix.

99. This is discussed in chapter 3.

100. Marshall, *Demanding the Impossible*, 337.

101. Murray Bookchin, "The Communalist Project," *Harbinger: A Journal of Social Ecology* (2002): available at http://www.social-ecology.org/2002/09/harbinger-vol-3-no-1-the-communalist-project/ (accessed February 2015).

102. Hans Jonas, *Das Prinzip Verantwortung* (Frankfurt am Main: Insel, 1979).

Chapter Three

1. The two most comprehensive texts to date to have undertaken such an explication have only appeared in print quite recently. These are Damian White's (2008) *Bookchin: A Critical Appraisal* and Andy Price's (2012) *Recovering Bookchin: Social Ecology and the Crises of Our Time*.

2. Charles Fourier, "The Vices of Commerce," in *The Utopian Vision of Charles Fourier*, trans. and ed. J. Beecher and R. Bienvenu (Boston: Houghton Mifflin, 1972), available online at http://www.marxists.org/reference/archive/fourier/works/ch12.htm (accessed December 2013).

3. Fourier, "On Economic Liberalism," in *The Utopian Vision of Charles Fourier*.

4. Fourier, "The Rise of Commerce and the Birth of Political Economy," in *The Utopian Vision of Charles Fourier*.

5. Charles Fourier, "On the Role of the Passions,' in *Charles Fourier, 1772–1837: Selections from His Writings*, published online by The History Guide. Available at http://www.historyguide.org/intellect/fourier.html (accessed May 2013).

6. Ibid.

7. Ibid.

8. Ibid.

9. Ibid.

10. Ibid.

11. Walter Benjamin, "Paris, Capital of the 19th Century (Exposé of 1939)," in *The Arcades Project*, trans. H. Eiland and K. McLaughlin (London: The Belknap Press of Harvard University Press, 1999 [1982]), 17.

12. Lukács, *History and Class Consciousness*, 135–136.

13. Ibid., 136.

14. Ibid.

15. Ibid., original emphasis.

16. Ibid.

17. Ibid.

18. Ibid., 136–137.

19. Ibid., 137.

20. Bloch, *The Principle of Hope*, 2: 688–689.

21. Ibid., 658–659.

22. Ibid., 666–667.

23. Ibid., 699.

24. In his *Recovering Bookchin*, Price observes of this: "It can be argued that Bookchin's dialectical methodology falls down more fundamentally in its claims to objectivity, of its elevation of *his* version of the way natural evolution unfolds above any other version" (103, original emphasis). Price adds, significantly, that the validity of this critique must be balanced against Bookchin's Hegelian stress on latent potentiality, and Bookchin's admission that counter tendencies to complexity, directiveness, and ethical choice/agency in natural evolution certainly *do* exist (104–106).

25. Bookchin, *The Philosophy of Social Ecology*, 47.

26. Ibid., 56.

27. Ibid. (original emphasis).
28. Ibid.
29. Bookchin, *The Philosophy of Social Ecology*, 173.
30. Ibid., 65 (original emphasis).
31. Murray Bookchin, *Re-Enchanting Humanity: A Defense of the Human Spirit Against Anti-Humanism, Misanthropy, Mysticism and Primitivism* (London: Cassell, 1995), 86 (original emphasis).
32. For an in-depth analysis of these themes in relation to Bookchin's part in the "deep ecology" debate of the late 1980s, see chapter 2 of Price, "The Ecology of Bookchin: The Philosophical Objection to Deep Ecology," in *Recovering Bookchin*.
33. Ibid., 97 (original emphasis).
34. Ibid.
35. Here, the dissonance between Adorno's negative dialectics and Bookchin's conception of "dialectical naturalism" may seem quite potent. After all, where Adorno maintains in his *Minima Moralia* that "the whole is the false," Bookchin simply reverses the order of the Hegelian formulation to insist "the true is the whole." But is this not really to say the same thing from an apparently opposite proposition? For if the true is alone the whole, this would seem to side with the critical suspicion of Adorno's negative dialectic, which detects precisely the untruth of the *illusory* whole in the sheen of the cover concept. The "falsity" of the whole resides in the fact that it is untrue to its potentialities and to its discontents, and hence according to both formulations, its attempt to suppress what is nonidentical with itself.
36. Ibid., 98 (original emphasis).
37. Ibid., 101–102.
38. It is crucial to note here, in all fairness to Eckersley, that her views have evolved considerably since this debate. These views are considered succinctly later in this section.
39. Robyn Eckersley, "Divining Evolution: The Ecological Ethics of Murray Bookchin," *Environmental Ethics* 11 (1989): 115 (original emphasis).
40. See Price, *Recovering Bookchin*, 128–129.
41. Murray Bookchin, *Remaking Society* (Montreal: Black Rose Books, 1989), 35.
42. Murray Bookchin, "Recovering Evolution: A Reply to Eckersley and Fox," *Environmental Ethics* 12 (1990): fn. 9.
43. Damian White, *Bookchin: A Critical Appraisal* (London: Pluto Press, 2008), 118.
44. Bookchin, *Remaking Society*, 36 (original emphasis).
45. Robyn Eckersley, "Ecological Interventions: Prospects and Limits," in *Ethics and International Affairs* 21, 3 (2007): 295–296.
46. Ibid., 301.

47. Ibid., 304–307.

48. Robyn Eckersley, "Geopolitan Democracy in the Anthropocene," *Political Studies* 65, 4 (2017): 996.

49. Jessica Dempsey, 'The Tragedy of Liberal Environmentalism' in *Canadian Dimension* 51, 2 (2017): available at https://canadiandimension.com/articles/view/the-tragedy-of-liberal-environmentalism (accessed January 2018); more expansively, see Jessica Dempsey, *Enterprising Nature: Economics, Markets, and Finance in Global Biodiversity Politics* (Hoboken: Wiley, 2016).

50. White, *Bookchin: A Critical Appraisal*, 118.

51. Bookchin, *The Philosophy of Social Ecology*, 124.

52. Ibid.

53. Ibid., 125–126.

54. Ibid., 63.

55. Ibid.

56. Bookchin, *The Philosophy of Social Ecology*, 28.

57. Ibid., 59–61.

58. See generally Adorno's *Hegel: Three Studies* for the context.

59. See Peter Kropotkin, *Evolution and Environment*, ed. G. Woodcock (Montreal: Black Rose Books, 1995), 117–159.

60. Ibid.

61. Ibid.

62. Bookchin, *The Philosophy of Social Ecology*, 76 (original emphasis).

63. Ibid., 65–66.

64. This essay is contained in Bookchin, *Remaking Society*.

65. This essay is contained in Bookchin, *The Philosophy of Social Ecology*.

66. Ibid., 85 (original emphasis).

67. Ibid.

68. As Price has noted in his discussion of White's (2009) commentary on Bookchin's anthropology, the *Ecology of Freedom* remains a speculative work; it is not to be noted as an outstanding example of anthropological rigor. Nevertheless, Bookchin's conclusions about early human history do remain plausible. See Price, *Recovering Bookchin*, 164–171.

69. See generally the introduction to *The Ecology of Freedom*.

70. Bookchin, *Remaking Society*, 47.

71. Ibid., 47–48.

72. See Max Horkheimer and Theodor W. Adorno, *Dialectic of Enlightenment* (London: Verso Books, 1997 [1945]), 21.

73. Bookchin, *Remaking Society*, 49.

74. Ibid.

75. Ibid., 50.

76. See generally the early chapters of Bookchin's *The Ecology of Freedom* for the context.

77. See generally *The Ecology of Freedom* and *Remaking Society*.
78. Bookchin, *Remaking Society*, 32–33.
79. Bookchin, *The Philosophy of Social Ecology*, 163.
80. Ibid., 157–158.
81. Price, *Recovering Bookchin*, 149.
82. Bookchin cited in ibid., 155.
83. Ibid., 156.
84. Bookchin observes, "Many French, and especially Spanish workers [up to the 1930s] were recruited from villages and small towns, when they were not simply craftspeople in large cities like Paris. The same is true of the working classes that made the 1917 revolution in Russia. Marx, it is worth noting, to his lasting confusion, generally viewed these highly volatile strata as *der alte scheisse* (literally, 'the old shit') and in no way counted on them to make the revolutions that his followers were to celebrate after his death" (*Remaking Society*, 131).
85. It is highly noteworthy that Rosa Luxemburg, while strongly influenced by Marx, had strikingly more sympathetic views of precapitalist lifeways than Marx seems to have held—a fact that becomes particularly clear in contrasting her assessment of India under English colonialism in chapter 27 of her 1918 work *The Accumulation of Capital* with Marx's assessment of the same subject in his journalistic writings.
86. In Herbert Marcuse's writings from the 1960s, particularly *One-Dimensional Man*, this theme was to be reiterated trenchantly. Like Bookchin, Marcuse had initially turned to the New Left for inspiration in the absence of a revolutionary proletariat—and emerged disillusioned (as is well documented via his later *Essay on Liberation*).
87. Bookchin, *Remaking Society*, 130.
88. Ibid., 125.
89. Ibid., 120.
90. Ibid., 125.
91. Murray Bookchin, *The Limits of the City* (Montreal: Black Rose Books, 1974), xi.
92. Bookchin laments that "there seems to be little widespread understanding that the quantitative changes to which [the book has] alluded have decisively worsened the quality of urban life, supplying modern cities with characteristics that are radically different from the best traits and traditions of urbanism" (*The Limits of the City*, 2).
93. It is important to note here that by the phrase "urban environment," Bookchin probably has in mind the human scale of cities that number as few as ten thousand people; in a lecture tour of the early 1990s, for instance, this is clearly his point of reference with regard to the social geography of early New York, which was geographically divided into many distinct towns and a very small, by contemporary standards, urban area.

94. See generally Bookchin, *The Limits of the City*, 5–35.
95. Ibid., 12.
96. Ibid., 10–11.
97. Ibid., 141.
98. Bookchin, "The Myth of City Planning," in *Towards an Ecological Society*, 143–144.
99. Bookchin, *The Limits of the City*, 49.
100. Ibid.
101. Ibid., 50.
102. Ibid., 50–51.
103. See generally the chapters entitled "The Limits of the Bourgeois City" and "Community and City Planning," in *The Limits of the City*, 57–139.
104. Bookchin, "The Myth of City Planning," in *Towards an Ecological Society*, 147–148.
105. Bookchin, *The Ecology of Freedom*, 304.
106. Ibid., 305.
107. Ibid.
108. This essay is collected in Bookchin, *Post-Scarcity Anarchism*.
109. Bookchin, *The Ecology of Freedom*, 335.
110. See ibid., 342–343.
111. Ibid., 347.
112. Ibid., 276.
113. Ibid. (emphasis added).
114. Ibid.
115. Ibid. (original emphasis).
116. Cited in Janet Biehl, *Bookchin Breaks with Anarchism*, available at http://theanarchistlibrary.org/library/janet-biehl-bookchin-breaks-with-anarchism (accessed April 2014).
117. Cited in ibid.
118. Bookchin, *Marxism, Anarchism and the Future of the Left*, 173–174. See also Bookchin's essay *The Communalist Project* (2002), published online at http://www.social-ecology.org/2002/09/harbinger-vol-3-no-1-the-communalist-project/ (accessed July 2014).
119. Bookchin, *Marxism, Anarchism and the Future of the Left*, 175.
120. See Biehl, *Bookchin Breaks with Anarchism*.
121. Bookchin, "Communalism: The Democratic Dimension of Anarchism," in *Marxism, Anarchism and the Future of the Left*, 148.
122. Ibid., 149.
123. Janet Biehl, *The Murray Bookchin Reader* (Montreal: Black Rose Books, 1997), 190.
124. Ibid., 194.
125. Ibid., 194.

126. Bookchin, *The Modern Crisis*, 78.
127. Ibid., 79–80.
128. Ibid., 90.
129. Bookchin's notion of a transclass interest must be understood within a particular context, in order for it not to be misconstrued. He writes in *Marxism, Anarchism and the Future of the Left* that "ecological problems, while clearly produced by capitalist growth, have existed for a long time and cannot be anchored simply in a specific class society" (273). This is the full extent of what is meant by a "transclass" interest. Moreover, his emphasis on hierarchy must be considered with reference to his statement: ". . . I must say absolutely and categorically . . . that I do not and never did intend the concept of hierarchy to replace the concept of class in social analysis and theory" (271). His emphasis on a transclass interest is not intended to displace the immanent reality of class conflict, nor its relationship with the ecological crisis. Rather, it stresses "that the oppressed are not exclusively class beings, important as this is, but also neighborhood beings, and that class consciousness always has a civic dimension, a geographic and residential as well as an industrial locus it requires for its existence (316).
130. Price, *Recovering Bookchin*, 218–223.
131. John Holloway, *Crack Capitalism* (London: Pluto Press, 2010).
132. Bookchin, "The Communalist Project."
133. See generally Holloway, *Crack Capitalism*, chap. 1–7.
134. Price, *Recovering Bookchin*, 223–227.
135. Holloway, *Crack Capitalism*, 11–12.
136. Ibid., 17–19.
137. Ibid., 39.
138. Ibid., 32–33.
139. Murray Bookchin, *Social Anarchism or Lifestyle Anarchism: An Unbridgeable Chasm* (Montreal: Black Rose Books, 1995), 24.
140. Bookchin, "The Communalist Project" (original emphasis).
141. Ibid.

Epilogue

1. Bookchin, "Reflections on Marx and Marxism," in *Marxism, Anarchism and the Future of the Left*, 289.

Appendix

1. Theodor W. Adorno, *Minima Moralia*, trans. E. Jephcott (London: Verso, 2005 [1974]), 156.

Bibliography

Adorno, Theodor W. *The Culture Industry*. Ed. J. M. Bernstein. London: Routledge, 1991.

———. *Hegel: Three Studies*. Trans. S. W. Nicholsen. Cambridge: MIT Press, 1993 (1963).

———. *The Adorno Reader*. Ed. B. O'Connor. Carlton: Blackwell, 2000.

———. *Kant's Critique of Pure Reason*. Trans. E. Jephcott and R. Tiedemann. Palo Alto: Stanford University Press, 2001.

———. *Negative Dialectics*, trans. D. Redmond, 2001 (1970). Available online at http://members.efn.org/~dredmond/ndtrans.html (accessed January 2014).

———. *The Jargon of Authenticity*. Trans. K. Tarnowski and F. Will. London: Routledge, 2003.

———. *Minima Moralia*. Trans. E. Jephcott. London: Verso, 2005 (1974).

———. *The Stars Down to Earth and Other Essays on the Irrational in Culture*. London: Routledge, 2007 (1994).

———. *Subject and Object*. Available at http://platypus1917.org/wp-content/uploads/2011/12/adorno_onsubjectandobject.pdf (accessed August 2014).

Adorno, Theodor W., and Max Horkheimer. *Dialectic of Enlightenment*. London: Verso, 1997 (1972).

Alexander, Samuel. "Hegel's Conception of Nature." *Mind* 11, 44 (1886): 495–523.

Aristotle. *The Basic Works of Aristotle*. Ed. R. McKeon. New York: Modern Library, 2001.

Bakunin, Mikhail. *Stateless Socialism: Anarchism*, trans. G.P. Maximoff, 1953. Available at http://dwardmac.pitzer.edu/Anarchist_Archives/bakunin/stateless.html (accessed August 2014).

———. *Marxism, Freedom and the State*. Trans. K. J. Kenafick. Ithaca: Freedom Press, 1984.

Benjamin, Walter. *Illuminations*. Trans. H. Zohn. New York: Schocken Books, 1968.

———. "Goethe: The Reluctant Bourgeois." Trans R. Livingstone. *New Left Review* 1, 133 (1982).

———. *The Arcades Project*. Trans. H. Eiland and K. McLaughlin. London: The Belknap Press of Harvard University Press, 1999 (1982).

———. *The Origin of German Tragic Drama*. Trans. J. Osborne. London: Verso Books, 2006.

Beiser, Frederick C. *The Fate of Reason: German Philosophy from Kant to Fichte*. Cambridge: Harvard University Press, 1993.

Biehl, Janet. *Rethinking Ecofeminist Politics*. Montreal: Black Rose Books, 1991.

———. *The Murray Bookchin Reader*. Montreal: Black Rose Books, 1997.

———. *The Politics of Social Ecology: Libertarian Municipalism*. Montreal: Black Rose Books, 1997.

———. *Bookchin Breaks with Anarchism*, 2007. Available online at http://theanarchistlibrary.org/library/janet-biehl-bookchin-breaks-with-anarchism (accessed June 2014).

Bloch, Ernst. *The Principle of Hope*, 3 vols. Trans. N. Plaice, S. Plaice, and P. Knight. Oxford: Oxford University Press, 1986 (1959).

Bookchin, Murray. *The Limits of the City*. Montreal: Black Rose Books, 1974.

———. *Towards an Ecological Society*. Edinburgh: AK Press, 1982.

———. *The Modern Crisis*. Sydney: Black Rose Books, 1986.

———. *Remaking Society* (Montreal: Black Rose Books, 1989).

———. "Recovering Evolution: A Reply to Eckersley and Fox." *Environmental Ethics* 12 (1990). Available at http://dwardmac.pitzer.edu/Anarchist_Archives/bookchin/recover.html#8 (accessed January 2015).

———. *Which Way for the Ecology Movement? Essays by Murray Bookchin*. Edinburgh: AK Press, 1994.

———. *The Philosophy of Social Ecology*. Sydney: Black Rose Books, 1995.

———. *Re-Enchanting Humanity: A Defense of the Human Spirit Against Anti-Humanism, Misanthropy, Mysticism and Primitivism*. London: Cassell, 1995.

———. *Social Anarchism or Lifestyle Anarchism: An Unbridgeable Chasm*. Edinburgh: AK Press, 1995.

———. *From Urbanization to Cities: Toward a New Politics of Citizenship*. London: Cassell, 1996.

———. *Marxism, Anarchism and the Future of the Left*. Edinburgh: AK Press, 1996.

———. *The Third Revolution*, 4 vols. London: Cassell, 1996–2006.

———. *The Spanish Anarchists*. Edinburgh: AK Press, 1998.

———. "The Communalist Project." *Communalism* 2 (2002). Available at http://new-compass.net/articles/anarchism-and-power-spanish-revolution (accessed April 2014).

———. *Social Ecology and Communalism*. Porsgrunn: New Compass Press, 2002.

———. *Post-Scarcity Anarchism*. Edinburgh: AK Press, 2004 (1971).

———. *The Ecology of Freedom: The Emergence and Dissolution of Hierarchy*. Palo Alto: Cheshire Books, 2005 (1982).

Buck-Morss, Susan. *The Origin of Negative Dialectics: Theodor W. Adorno, Walter Benjamin and the Frankfurt Institute*. New York: The Free Press, 1979.

Burkett, Paul. *Marx and Nature: A Red and Green Perspective.* Chicago: Haymarket Books, 2009.
Burnet, John. *Greek Philosophy: Thales to Plato.* London: MacMillan and Co., 1950.
———. *Early Greek Philosophy* London: A. & C. Black, 1920 (1896).
Castree, Noel. "Capitalism and the Marxist Critique of Political Ecology." In *The Routledge Handbook of Political Ecology,* ed. T. Perreault, G. Bridge, and J. McCarthy, 279–292. Abingdon: Routledge, 2015.
Clarke, John. *A Social Ecology,* 2000. Available at http://theanarchistlibrary.org/library/john-clark-a-social-ecology (accessed June 2014).
Connolly, William E. *Facing the Planetary: Entangled Humanism and the Politics of Swarming.* Durham: Duke University Press, 2017.
Dawkins, Richard. *Nice Guys Finish First.* Documentary film produced by J. Taylor. BBC Horizon, aired April 14, 1986, season 22, episode 14.
———. *The Selfish Gene.* London: Oxford University Press, 1989.
Deligiorgi, Katerina. *Hegel: New Directions.* London: Routledge, 2014.
Dempsey, Jessica. *Enterprising Nature: Economics, Markets, and Finance in Global Biodiversity Politics.* Hoboken: Wiley, 2016.
———. "The Tragedy of Liberal Environmentalism." *Canadian Dimension* 51, 2 (2017). Available at https://canadiandimension.com/articles/view/the-tragedy-of-liberal-environmentalism (accessed January 2018).
Dewey, John. *Leibniz's New Essays Concerning the Human Understanding: A Critical Exposition.* Chicago: Scott, Foresman and Co., 1902.
Dolgoff, Sam. *The Cuban Revolution: A Critical Perspective.* Montreal: Black Rose Books, 1976.
Eckersley, Robyn. "Divining Evolution: The Ecological Ethics of Murray Bookchin." *Environmental Ethics* 11 (1989): 99–116.
———. *The Green State: Rethinking Democracy and Sovereignty.* Cambridge: MIT Press, 2004.
———. "Ecological Interventions: Prospects and Limits." *Ethics and International Affairs* 21, 3 (2007): 295–296.
———. "Geopolitan Democracy in the Anthropocene." *Political Studies* 65, 4 (2017): 996.
Engels, Friedrich. *The Condition of the Working Class in England.* London: Penguin Books, 1987 (1845).
———. *Feuerbach: The Roots of the Socialist Philosophy.* Trans. A. Lewis. New York: Cosimo Publications, 2008 (1903).
Feuerbach, Ludwig *Principles of the Philosophy of the Future.* Trans. M. Vogel. Indianapolis: Hackett, 1986 (1843).
———. *The Essence of Christianity.* Trans. G. Eliot. Amherst: Prometheus Books, 1989.
———. *The Essence of Religion.* Trans. A. Loos. Amherst: Prometheus Books, 2004.
———. *The Fiery Brook: Selected Writings,* trans. Z. Hanfi. London: Verso Books, 2013.

Fichte, J. G. *The Science of Knowledge.* Trans. A. E. Kroeger. London: Trübner & Co., 1889.

———. *Attempt at a Critique of All Revelation.* Trans. G. Green. Melbourne: Cambridge University Press, 1978 (1793).

———. Fichte*: Early Philosophical Writings.* Trans. and ed. D. Breazeale. Ithaca: Cornell University Press, 1988.

———. *System of Ethics.* Trans. D. Breazeale and G. Zöller. Cambridge: Cambridge University Press, 2006.

———. *Characteristics of the Present Age.* London: Dodo Press, 2009.

———. *The Science of Knowledge.* Trans. A. E. Kroeger. Forgotten Books, electronic republication, 2013. Available at http://www.forgottenbooks.com/readbook/ The_Science_of_Knowledge_v3_1000096752#1 (accessed July 2015).

Fleming, Marie. *The Geography of Freedom: The Odyssey of Élisée Reclus.* Montreal: Black Rose Books, 1988.

Foster, John Bellamy. "Paul Burkett's Marx and Nature 15 Years After." *Monthly Review 66, 7 (2014). Available at* http://monthlyreview.org/2014/12/01/paul-burketts-marx-and-nature-fifteen-years-after/#en6 *(accessed October 2015).*

Fourier, Charles. "Attractive Labor," 1802. In *Charles Fourier, 1772–1837: Selections from His Writings.* Published online by The History Guide. Available at https://www.marxists.org/reference/archive/fourier/works/ch26.htm (accessed May 2013).

———. "On the Role of the Passions." In *Charles Fourier, 1772–1837: Selections from His Writings.* Published online by The History Guide. Available at http://www.historyguide.org/intellect/fourier.html (accessed May 2013).

———. *The Utopian Vision of Charles Fourier.* Trans. and ed. J. Beecher and R. Bienvenu, published by J. Cape. Available online at http://www.marxists.org/reference/archive/fourier/works/ch12.htm (accessed December 2013).

Fromm, Erich. *The Anatomy of Human Destructiveness.* London: Penguin Books, 1974.

Goldman, Emma *The Individual, Society and the State*, 1940. Available online at http://theanarchistlibrary.org/library/Emma_Goldman__The_Individual__Society_and_the_State.html (accessed February 2014).

Gould, Stephen Jay. "Kropotkin Was No Crackpot." *Natural History* 106 (1997): 12–21. Available at http://www.marxists.org/subject/science/essays/kropotkin.htm (accessed December 2013).

Grant, Iain Hamilton. *Philosophies of Nature After Schelling.* New York: Continuum, 2008.

Guattari, Félix. *The Three Ecologies.* New York: Continuum, 2008 (1989).

Hansen, Mogens Herman. *Athenian Democracy in the Age of Demosthenes: Structure, Principles and Ideology.* Trans. J. A. Crook. Norman: University of Oklahoma Press, 1991.

Hay, Peter. *Main Currents in Western Environmental Thought.* Bloomington: Indiana University Press, 2002.
Hegel, G. W. F. *The Philosophy of History.* Trans. J. Sibree. Mineola: Dover, 1956 (1899).
———. *Hegel's System of Ethical Life and his First Philosophy of Spirit.* Trans. H. S. Harris and T. M. Knox. Albany: State University of New York Press, 1967.
———. *Science of Logic.* Trans. W. H. Johnston and L. G. Struthers (New York: Macmillan Books, 1929 (1816).
———. *Science of Logic.* Trans. A. V. Miller. New York: Humanity Books, 1969 (1816).
———. *Hegel's Philosophy of Nature*, vols. 1–3. Trans. M. J. Petry. London: Allen and Unwin, 1970.
———. *Aesthetics: Lectures on Fine Art*, vol. 1. Trans. T. M. Knox. Oxford: Oxford University Press, 1975.
———. *The Difference Between Fichte's and Schelling's System of Philosophy.* Trans. H. S. Harris and W. Cerf. Albany: State University of New York Press, 1977 (1801).
———. *Phenomenology of Spirit.* Trans. A. V. Miller. Melbourne: Oxford University Press, 1977 (1807).
———. *Philosophy of Right.* Trans. S. W. Dyde. New York: Dover, 2005 (1896).
Holloway, John. *Crack Capitalism.* London: Pluto Press, 2010.
Horkheimer, Max. *Eclipse of Reason.* New York: Oxford University Press, 1947.
———. "The End of Reason." In *The Essential Frankfurt School Reader*, ed. A. Arato and E. Gebhardt. New York: Urizen Books, 1978 (1941).
———. "Reason Against Itself: Some Remarks on Enlightenment." *Theory, Culture & Society* 10, 79 (1993): 79–88.
———. *Between Philosophy and Social Science: Selected Writings.* Trans. G. F. Hunter, M. S. Kramer, and J. Torpey. Cambridge: MIT Press, 1995 (1936).
———. "Traditional and Critical Theory." In *Critical Theory: Selected Essays*, trans. Matthew J. O'Connell and others, 188–243. New York: Continuum, 2002 (1972).
Horkheimer, Max, and Theodor W. Adorno. *Dialectic of Enlightenment.* London: Verso Books, 1997 (1945).
Jonas, Hans. *Das Prinzip Verantwortung.* Frankfurt am Main: Insel, 1979.
Kant, Immanuel. *Critique of Pure Reason.* Trans. J. M. D. Meiklejohn. Mineola: Dover, 1900 (1855).
———. *Logic.* Trans. R. S. Hartman and W. Schwarz. New York: Dover, 1988 (1800).
———. *Critique of Judgement.* Trans. J. H. Bernard. Amherst: Prometheus Books, 2000.
———. *Critique of Practical Reason.* Trans. T. K. Abbott. New York: Dover, 2004 (1909).

Kropotkin, Pëtr. *The State: Its Historic Role*, 1896. Available at http://theanarchist library.org/library/petr-kropotkin-the-state-its-historic-role (accessed September 2014).

———. *The Great French Revolution: 1789–1793*, 1909. Trans. N. F. Dryhurst. Available at http://theanarchistlibrary.org/library/petr-kropotkin-the-great-french-revolution-1789-1793 (accessed September 2014).

———. *Evolution and Environment*. Ed. G. Woodcock. Montreal: Black Rose Books, 1995.

———. *Ethics: Origin and Development*. Honolulu: University Press of the Pacific, 2002 (1910).

———. *Anarchism: A Collection of Revolutionary Writings*. New York: Dover, 2003.

———. *The Conquest of Bread*. Charleston: Bibliobazaar, 2008.

———. *Mutual Aid: A Factor of Evolution*. New York: Cosimo Books, 2009 (1902).

Latour, Bruno. *Reassembling the Social: An Introduction to Actor-Network Theory*. London: Oxford University Press, 2005.

———. *Politics of Nature: How to Bring the Sciences into Democracy*. Trans. C. Porter. Cambridge: Harvard University Press, 2004.

Leverink, Joris. "Murray Bookchin and the Kurdish Resistance." *Roar Magazine*, August 9, 2015. Available at https://roarmag.org/essays/bookchin-kurdish-struggle-ocalan-rojava/ (accessed November 2017).

Locke, John. *Second Treatise of Civil Government*, 1689. Available from http://www.constitution.org/jl/2ndtr05.htm (accessed March 2014).

Löwenthal, Leo. *On Sociology of Literature* (excerpt), 1948. Trans. A. Blunden. Available at https://www.marxists.org/reference/archive/lowenthal/1948/literature.htm (accessed July 2014).

———. *An Unmastered Past: The Autobiographical Reflections of Leo Löwenthal*. Ed. M. Jay. Berkeley: University of California Press, 1987. Available at http://publishing.cdlib.org/ucpressebooks/view?docId=ft8779p24p&brand=ucpress (accessed July 2014).

Lukács, Georg. *History and Class Consciousness*. Trans. R. Livingstone. Cambridge: MIT Press, 1971 (1921).

———. *The Young Hegel: Studies in the Relations Between Dialectics and Economics*. Trans. R. Livingstone. London: The Merlin Press, 1975.

———. *The Theory of the Novel*. Trans. A. Bostock. London: The Merlin Press, 1978.

Luxemburg, Rosa *The Accumulation of Capital*. London: Routledge, 2003 (1918).

Mackinnon, Catherine. *Towards a Feminist Theory of the State*. Cambridge: Harvard University Press, 1989.

Mannin, Ethel. *Bread and Roses: A Utopian Survey and Blueprint*. London: Macdonald Publishing, 1943.

Marcuse, Herbert. *Reason and Revolution: Hegel and the Rise of Social Theory*. London: Routledge and Kegan Paul, 1968 (1941).

———. *The New Left and the 1960s*. Routledge: London, 2005.
———. *A Study on Authority*. London: Verso Books, 2007 (1963).
———. *Negations: Essays in Critical Theory*. London: MayFly Books, 2009 (1968).
Marshall, Peter. *Demanding the Impossible: A History of Anarchism*. London: Harper-Perennial Books, 2008.
Marx, Karl. *The Economic and Philosophic Manuscripts of 1844 and the Communist Manifesto*. Amherst: Prometheus Books, 1990 (1844).
———. *The Eighteenth Brumaire of Louis Bonaparte*. New York: International Publishers Co., 1963.
———. *The Portable Karl Marx*. Ed. E. Kamenka. London: Penguin, 1983.
———. *Capital*, 3 vols. Trans. B. Fowkes and D. Fernbach. London: Penguin Books, 1990–1993.
———. *The Grundrisse: Foundations of the Critique of Political Economy*. Trans. M. Nicolaus. London: Penguin Books, 1993.
———. *Dispatches for the New York Tribune: Selected Journalism of Karl Marx*. London: Penguin Books, 2007 (1853).
———. *The Poverty of Philosophy*, 2009. Available at http://www.marxists.org/archive/marx/works/1847/poverty-philosophy/ (accessed September 2014).
Marx, Karl, and Friedrich Engels. *The German Ideology*. Amherst: Prometheus Books, 1998.
McKirahan, Richard D. *Philosophy Before Socrates: An Introduction with Texts and Commentary*. Indianapolis: Hackett, 1994.
Morton, Timothy. *Ecology Without Nature: Rethinking Environmental Aesthetics*. Cambridge: Harvard University Press, 2009.
———. *The Ecological Thought*. Cambridge: Harvard University Press, 2012.
Morris, Brian. *Bakunin: The Philosophy of Freedom*. Montreal: Black Rose Books, 1993.
O'Connor, Brian. *Adorno's Negative Dialectic: Philosophy and the Possibility of Critical Rationality*. Cambridge: MIT Press, 2004.
Oppenheimer, Franz. *The State*. Montreal: Black Rose Books, 2007 (1922).
Pippin, Robert. *The Persistence of Subjectivity: On the Kantian Aftermath*. Cambridge: Cambridge University Press, 2005.
Pizza, Giovanni. "Second Nature: On Gramsci's Anthropology." *Anthropology and Medicine* 19, 1 (2012): 95–106.
Plato. *Theaetetus*. Trans. R. H. Waterfield. London: Penguin Books, 1987.
Price, Andy. *Recovering Bookchin: Social Ecology and the Crises of Our Time*. Porsgrunn: New Compass Press, 2012.
Pritchard, Alex. *The International Political Theory of Pierre-Joseph Proudhon*, 2010. Available at http://www.anarchist-studies-network.org.uk/documents/Proudhon.doc (accessed September 2015).
Proudhon, Pierre-Joseph. *The System of Economical Contradictions; or, The Philosophy of Misery*, vol. 1. Gloucester: Dodo Press, 2009 (1846).

Read, Herbert. "The Philosophy of Anarchism." In *Anarchism: A Documentary History of Libertarian Ideas, Vol. 2: The Emergence of the New Anarchism, 1939–1977*, ed. R. Graham, 1–7. Montreal: Black Rose Books, 2009 (1940).
———. *A One-Man Manifesto*. Edinburgh: AK Press, 1994.
Rose, Gillian. *The Melancholy Science: An Introduction to the Thought of Theodor W. Adorno*. London: The Macmillan Press, 1978.
———. *Hegel contra Sociology*. London: Verso Books, 2009.
Rousseau, Jean-Jacques. *The Basic Political Writings*, 2nd edition. Trans. and ed. D. A. Cress. Indianapolis: Hackett, 2011.
Schiller, Friedrich. *On the Aesthetic Education of Man*. Trans. R. Snell. Mineola: Dover Books, 2004 (1795).
Schmidt, Alfred. *The Concept of Nature in Marx*. Trans. B. Fowkes. London: New Left Books, 1971.
Schopenhauer, Arthur. *The World as Will and Representation*. Trans. E. F. J. Payne, 2 vols., third edition. New York: Dover Books, 1958 (1859).
Scott, James C. *The Art of Not Being Governed: An Anarchist History of Upland Southeast Asia*. New Haven: Yale University Press, 2009.
Smith, Neil. *Uneven Development*. Oxford: Blackwell, 1984.
Smith, Neil, and Phil O'Keefe. "Geography, Marx and the Concept of Nature." *Antipode* 12, 2 (2006): 30–39.
Stanley, John L. "Marx's Critique of Hegel's Philosophy of Nature." *Science & Society* 61, 4 (1997–1998): 449–473.
Vincent, K. Steven. *Pierre-Joseph Proudhon and the Rise of French Republican Socialism*. Oxford: Oxford University Press, 1984.
Vlastos, Gregory. *Studies in Greek Philosophy, Volume 1: The Presocratics*. Ed. D. W. Graham. Princeton: Princeton University Press, 1993.
Vogel, Steven. *Against Nature: The Concept of Nature in Critical Theory*. Albany: State University of New York Press, 1996.
Wartofsky, Marx William. *Feuerbach*. Cambridge: Cambridge University Press, 1977.
White, Damian. *Bookchin: A Critical Appraisal*. London: Pluto Press, 2008.
Woodcock, George. *Anarchism: A History of Libertarian Ideas and Movements*. London: Penguin Books, 1962.
Zöller, Günter. *Fichte's Transcendental Philosophy: The Original Duplicity of Intelligence and Will*. Cambridge: Cambridge University Press, 2002.

Index

actuality, 61
Adorno, Theodor, xi, xvi, 19–20, 26, 30–31, 33–34, 80, 136 n. 35, 150. *See also* Critical Theory
anarchism, 15, 87–97, 102, 110–118
  Bookchin's relationship with, 91, 115, 118, 157, 167
Anaximander of Miletus, 9
absolute, 39, 98
alienation, 147
anthropology, 68, 81, 149–153
Anti-naturalism, 45, 64, 67, 73, 80, 82, 84, 119
Aristotle, 62, 123, 159
Aufheben / Aufhebung. See Sublation
autarchy, 93

Bakunin, Mikhail, 89–96
Becoming, 37, 44, 104, 145, 149
Benjamin, Walter, 125–126. *See also* Critical Theory
Bloch, Ernest, 20–21, 129–131
Boétie, Étienne De La, 95
Bookchin, Murray, x, x n. 4, xiv, xv, 19–20, 22, 35, 115, 117–120, 131, 132–158, 136 n. 35, 159–177, 179–180

Capitalism
  protestant, 54
categorical imperative, 31

Castree, Noel, x
communalism, 120, 165–171, 173–174, 176, 178–180
Comte, Auguste, 107–108
conditions
  sufficient, 164
conflict
  class, 167
Consciousness
  unhappy, 55
Connolly, William, 5
co-productivity, 130
counter-enlightenment, 71
Critical Theory, x, 7
culture industry, 94

Darwin, Charles, 105
Darwinism
  Benevolent, 96, 98, 104
  Social, 90
Dawkins, Richard, 99
deep ecology, 135–141
Deleuze, Gilles, 6
deme, 9
democracy
  Athenian, 9 n. 14
  bourgeois, 9
  Hellenic reification of, 8, 10, 50
  representative, 9
democratic deliberation, 4
democratization, 165

221

Descartes, René, 32
determinate negation, 3, 18, 38
determinism, 61, 64, 157
   economic, 72
dialectic, 17
   master-slave, 83
Dialectical naturalism, 20, 22–23, 35, 37, 46, 76, 87, 107, 115, 119–120, 125, 132, 136–138, 140, 143, 153, 165, 179
   definition of, ix, xv, 20, 22–23, 35, 37, 46
   logic of, 60, 63
differentiation, 31, 97, 105, 110, 146–148
dissensus, 6
Dolgoff, Sam, 114
domination/hierarchy, 86, 102–103, 111, 114, 148–154
domination thesis, 73 n. 8
dualism, 32, 144–145
duality
   spirit and nature, 65–66
Dunayevskaya, Raya, 19 n. 39

Eckersley, Robyn, 7, 137–139, 141–143
ecocide, 141
eco-centrism, 137–138
economy
   moral, 169, 171
ecosystem, 2
Ego/Non-Ego duality, 38–39, 41, 43, 44
Empedocles, 9, 10
Enlightenment
   bourgeois, 25–26, 30, 35, 45, 48, 50
   the, 136
Epistemology
   anti-naturalist, 27

era
   revolutionary, 166
ethical life, 47–48, 61, 64, 128, 176. *See also* Hegel, Georg Wilhelm Friedrich
ethics, 155
   ecological, 15, 72, 142, 176
equality, 150
externality, 67

fascism, 78 n. 21, 94, 102
Feminism, Radical, 105
feudalism, 108
Feuerbach, Ludwig, 39, 67–70
Fichte, Johann, 38–44
first nature, 136
freedom
   subjective, 51
feudalism, 108–110
Fourier, Charles, 111, 120–126

Goethe, Johann Wolfgang von, 85
Gorze, Andre, 72
Gould, Stephen Jay, 99
Gramsci, Antonio, 72–73
"green" capitalism, xii
Guattari, Félix, 6

Hegel, Georg Wilhelm Friedrich, 14 n. 30, 17, 30 n. 4, 38, 44–67, 49 n. 41, 84, 146, 176
hegemony
   ideological, 2, 21. *See also* Gramsci, Antonio
Heraclitos, 58
Hobbes, Thomas, 98, 100
Holloway, John, 170–173
Horkheimer, Max, xi, 41, 150. *See also* Critical Theory
humanism, 40
human scale, 158

Hume, David, 56

ideology
  critique of, 69
Identity, 47
  thinking, 57, 106
immanent critique, 67
immediacy, 16, 25, 55
individualism
  liberal, 87, 92–93, 117
individuation, 102
institutionalism, 113, 115, 123, 125, 142, 174, 178
institutionalization, 91
intersubjectivity, 42
irrationalism, 135

Jonas, Hans, 118
judgment
  aesthetic, 36

Kant, 133
  Immanuel, 27–35
Kropotkin, 154
  Peter, 96–117, 146–147, 206

labour
  abstract, 30
  association of, 75, 123
  collective, 40
  socially necessary, 78, 79
law
  natural, 45–46, 90, 96–97, 113
Leibniz, Gottfried Wilhelm, 27
liberal environmentalism, xii, xiii, xiv, 3, 15. *See also* individualism, liberal
liberalism, 94, 142. *See also* individualism, liberal *and* liberal environmentalism
Locke, John, 84

logic, dialectical, 58
Lukács, Georg, 126–129
Latour, Bruno, 4
Luxemburg, Rosa, 155 n. 85

Marcuse, Herbert, xi, xii, 17, 18, 21, 41
Marshall, Peter, 116
Marx
  Bookchin's relationship with, x, xvi, 77, 79–81, 86, 155–156
  Karl, 15, 70–87, 106
Marxism
  Eco-Marxism, x
  Neo-Marxism, x
  Western, 7
materialism, historical, 71, 74, 79, 106
mediation, 34, 70, 74, 76, 79, 110, 117, 138, 175
monism, 137
morality, 105, 138
Morton, Timothy, 5
mutual aid, 97–117

nascence, 138–140, 143
Nature
  beautification of, 52
  concept of, 3, 15, 26, 47–50, 73, 77, 83, 88, 105, 109
  concrete, 69
  domination of, 34, 86
  historization of, 71–72
  nonhuman, 22, 101, 139, 141
  reification of, xv, 25–26
  struggle against, 41
nature-as-property, 84
nature-concept. *See* nature, concept of
Naturalism
  developmental, 104

Naturalism *(continued)*
  dialectical, 107
  humanistic, 75
  medieval, 81
  mythopoeic, 16, 67, 89 n. 51, 97, 111, 107, 117, 119
  political, 159
  reified, 118
negation
  determinate, 3, 18, 38. *See also* Sublation
negative dialectics, xvi, 3, 19–20, 136 n. 35, 172
Neo-Kantianism, 132–134
neoliberalism. *See* politics, identity
Notion
  doctrine of, 33, 47, 49, 55, 61–63

paideia, 9
Painting
  landscape, 52
philosophy
  dialectical, 18, 19
  presocratic, 8
pluralism, 168
political economy, 121
politics
  identity, 13
  nature's relationship to, 7
Potentialities/potentiality
  concrete, 45, 55, 60
positivism, 4, 55–58, 97, 106–108, 127, 135
Power
  labour, 40
Price, Andy, 132 n. 24, 153
production
  forces of, 78, 80, 86
  relations of, 80
Productivism, xi, 72, 74, 78
Property
  private, 47–49, 54

Proudhon, Pierre-Joseph, 87–89
Proust, Marcel, 28

reason, 43
  democratic, 142, 177
  dialectical, 18, 68, 145
  instrumental, 34, 41, 77, 82–83, 86, 127
Reciprocal determination, 43
reductionism, 67
regression
  technological, 78
reformism, xii, xiii
reification, ix n. 1, 3, 8, 57, 78, 87, 126–129, 157, 175, 177
Reified thinking, ix, xiii
relation
  subject-object, 84
relativism, 94
Res cogito, 32
Res extensa, 32
Revolution, French, 17, 67, 91, 110
Revolution, Spanish, 110
Romanticism, 37, 53–54, 88, 116
Rose, Gillian, 46–47
Rousseau, Jean Jacques, 100, 127–128

scale, human, 124
Schiller, Friedrich, 29, 35–38
second nature, xi, 100–101, 104, 110, 116, 136, 144, 147
selection, natural, 99
Schmidt, Alfred, 74, 77
Schopenhauer, Arthur, 28
skepticism, 56, 58
sense-certainty, 55–56, 60
Sittlichkeit. *See* ethical life
Smith, Neil, x
social ecology, 22, 113, 119, 13, 22 n. 45, 132
  concept of, xiv, xv

socialism
　authoritarian, 111, 124
　libertarian, 111
　utopian, 124
society
　ecological, 79
　organic, 163
　natural human, 89–92, 114
solipsism, 53
sovereignty, 82–83
species being, 76
statism, 108, 111–112
stoicism, 12
subjectivism, 113
subjectivity, 93
Sublation, 38
symbiosis, 147

techne, 158, 162
technology, 4, 31, 78, 130–131, 158, 160, 162–164, 175
teleology, 63, 144, 175
thing-in-itself, 31. *See also* Kant, Immanuel
transclass, 170, 170 n. 129
turning points, 157–158

urbanism, 158–161
utopia, 120, 180
　concrete, 31

Vlastos, Gregory, 8, 10

Wartofsky, Marx, 69
World-Spirit, 43, 64–66, 102

www.ingramcontent.com/pod-product-compliance
Lightning Source LLC
Chambersburg PA
CBHW030646230426
43665CB00011B/981